Touri

Otherness

TOURISM AND CULTURAL CHANGE

Series Editors: Professor Mike Robinson, *Ironbridge International Institute for Cultural Heritage, University of Birmingham, UK* and Dr Alison Phipps, *University of Glasgow, Scotland, UK*

TCC is a series of books that explores the complex and ever-changing relationship between tourism and culture(s). The series focuses on the ways that places, peoples, pasts, and ways of life are increasingly shaped/transformed/created/packaged for touristic purposes. The series examines the ways tourism utilises/makes and re-makes cultural capital in its various guises (visual and performing arts, crafts, festivals, built heritage, cuisine etc.) and the multifarious political, economic, social and ethical issues that are raised as a consequence.

Understanding tourism's relationships with culture(s), and vice versa, is of ever-increasing significance in a globalising world. This series will critically examine the dynamic inter-relationships between tourism and culture(s). Theoretical explorations, research-informed analyses and detailed historical reviews from a variety of disciplinary perspectives are invited to consider such relationships.

Full details of all the books in this series and of all our other publications can be found on http://www.channelviewpublications.com, or by writing to Channel View Publications, St Nicholas House, 31–34 High Street, Bristol BS1 2AW, UK.

Tourism and the Power of Otherness

Seductions of Difference

Edited by
David Picard and Michael A. Di Giovine

CHANNEL VIEW PUBLICATIONS
Bristol • Buffalo • Toronto

Library of Congress Cataloging in Publication Data
A catalog record for this book is available from the Library of Congress.
Tourism and the Power of Otherness: Seductions of Difference/Edited by David Picard
and Michael A. Di Giovine.
Tourism and Cultural Change: 34
Includes bibliographical references and index.
1. Tourism--Psychological aspects. 2. Culture and tourism. 3. Other (Philosophy)
4. Difference (Psychology) I. Picard, David.
G155.A1T589518 2014
910.01'9–dc23 2013032181

British Library Cataloguing in Publication Data
A catalogue entry for this book is available from the British Library.

ISBN-13: 978-1-84541-416-0 (hbk)
ISBN-13: 978-1-84541-415-3 (pbk)

Channel View Publications
UK: St Nicholas House, 31–34 High Street, Bristol BS1 2AW, UK.
USA: UTP, 2250 Military Road, Tonawanda, NY 14150, USA.
Canada: UTP, 5201 Dufferin Street, North York, Ontario M3H 5T8, Canada.

The policy of Multilingual Matters/Channel View Publications is to use papers that
are natural, renewable and recyclable products, made from wood grown in sustainable
forests. In the manufacturing process of our books, and to further support our policy,
preference is given to printers that have FSC and PEFC Chain of Custody certification.
The FSC and/or PEFC logos will appear on those books where full certification has been
granted to the printer concerned.

Typeset by R.J. Footring Ltd, Derby
Printed and bound in Great Britain by Short Run Press Ltd

For Éma, Vera, Ana Lula, Lucía, Padma, Keila Luna, Eva Yani, Marta, Lucas, Alexander, Sebastian, Zachary and Chalcedony

Contents

Figures

Contributors

Camila del Mármol holds a PhD in anthropology and works as an assistant professor at the University of Barcelona, Spain. She has pursued ethnographic research in the Catalan Pyrenees, focusing on the processes of heritage development. Her areas of interest include the transformation of political and economic structures in rural spaces and the social perceptions of 'territories'.

Christian Ghasarian is professor of anthropology at the University of Neuchâtel, Switzerland. His work focuses on multiculturalism in La Réunion, New Age practice in the USA and Europe, and social relations in French Polynesia. Major publications include: *Des plantes psychotropes. Initiations, thérapies et quête de soi* (2010); *Anthropologies de la Réunion* (2008); *De l'ethnographie à l'anthropologie réflexive* (2002); and *Introduction à l'étude de la parenté* (1996).

Michael A. Di Giovine is assistant professor of anthropology at West Chester University and honorary fellow at the University of Wisconsin-Madison. A former tour operator, his research in Europe and Southeast Asia focuses on tourism/pilgrimage, heritage, food and religion. The author of *The Heritage-scape: UNESCO, World Heritage, and Tourism*, and the book reviews editor for *Journeys*, he also has written on the cult of Padre Pio of Pietrelcina, the focus of his PhD dissertation at the University of Chicago.

Pamila Gupta is a senior researcher based at WISER at the University of the Witwatersrand in Johannesburg, South Africa. She received her PhD in anthropology from Columbia University in 2004. Recent publications include 'Gandhi and the Goa question', *Public Culture* (2011); she was also a co-editor with Isabel Hofmeyr and Michael Pearson of *Eyes Across the Water:*

Navigating the Indian Ocean (UNISA Press, 2010). Her current research looks at Goan migration and Portuguese decolonisation in the Indian Ocean.

Marcela Knapp is a PhD candidate in sociology at the University of Giessen, Germany. She has studied African studies, sociology and Spanish in Berlin. Her main areas of interest are postcolonial theory, alterity studies and cultural sociology. Her current research analyses the role of fiction in socio-political debates.

Paula Mota Santos (PhD anthropology, University College London, 2005) is assistant professor of anthropology at Fernando Pessoa University, Porto, Portugal. She has been a visiting scholar in the Department of Landscape Architecture and Regional Planning, University of California at Berkeley. Her research is centred on the relationship between social identity and space, and visual anthropology. She has published on heritage, tourism, immigration, photography and film/documentary and directed two documentaries.

David Picard is senior researcher at the Centre for Research in Anthropology (CRIA) in Lisbon, Portugal. His publications include *Tourism, Magic and Modernity* (Berghahn Books, 2011) and several co-edited books: *Festivals, Tourism and Social Change* (Channel View, 2006); *The Framed World: Tourism, Tourists and Photography* (Ashgate, 2009); *Emotion in Motion: Tourism, Affect and Transformation* (Ashgate, 2012); and *Couchsurfing Cosmopolitanisms* (Transcript Verlag, 2013). He currently carries out research on modernisation processes in south-west Madagascar and on Antarctic tourism.

Noel B. Salazar is research professor in anthropology at the University of Leuven, Belgium. His research interests include anthropologies of mobility and travel, the local–global nexus, discourses and imaginaries of Otherness, culture contacts, heritage and cosmopolitanism. He is the author of *Envisioning Eden* (Berghahn Books, 2010) and articles in journals such as *Annals of Tourism Research, Journal of Sustainable Tourism, International Journal of Heritage Studies* and *Anthropological Quarterly*.

Clare A. Sammells is assistant professor of anthropology at Bucknell University, Lewisburg, Pennsylvania. She has conducted ethnographic fieldwork in highland Bolivia and among Bolivian migrants living in Spain. Her research and publications focus on tourism (specifically solstice celebrations) and foodways. She co-edited a volume entitled *Adventures in Eating: Anthropological Experiences in Dining from Around the World* (University Press of Colorado, 2010), in which her chapter discusses Bolivian tourist cuisine.

Sanne Scheltena graduated in cultural anthropology from the University of Amsterdam, the Netherlands. She has conducted fieldwork in Turkey. Her main research interests are tourism encounters, embodied experience, sensory anthropology and qualitative research methods.

Mathilde Verschaeve graduated in ethnology and social anthropology at EHESS (School for Advanced Studies in the Social Sciences), Paris, France, in 2011. The research she carried out for her MA dissertation focused on rural tourism development in Romania. She also worked as a French–Romanian translator for the non-governmental organisation Médecins du Monde and now teaches information literacy at a secondary school.

Hannah C. Wadle is a PhD candidate in social anthropology at the University of Manchester, UK. Her current research explores the role of tourism in the transformation processes of the former socialist countries in Eastern Europe, with a specific focus on Poland. She is presently preparing a co-edited book exploring the relationship between tourism and yearning (*Sehnsucht*) in Central and Eastern Europe.

Frauke Wiegand is a PhD candidate at the Department of Visual Culture, University of Copenhagen, Denmark, where she is working on tourist experience and *memoryscapes* in southern Africa and elsewhere. Her main research interests are migratory aesthetics, postcolonial theory and cultural memory. She is a co-editor of *Transvisuality: The Cultural Dimension of Visuality* (Liverpool University Press, 2013), a three-volume anthology in visual culture studies.

1 Introduction: Through Other Worlds

David Picard and Michael A. Di Giovine

Two souls, alas, are housed within my breast
And each will wrestle for the mastery there
The one has passion's craving crude for love
And hugs a world where sweet the senses rage
The other longs for pastures fair above
Leaving the murk for lofty heritage.
Johann Wolfgang Goethe (1856)

Introduction[1]

In this book we explore the paradoxes of Self–Other relations in the social field of tourism. We are particularly interested in the power of different forms of Otherness to seduce and to disrupt, and eventually also to renew, the social and cosmological orders of 'modern' culture and everyday life. Drawing on a series of ethnographic case studies, the contributors to this volume investigate the production, socialisation and encompassment of different Others as a political and also an economic resource to govern social life in the present. Based on their observations, they interrogate the presumed capacity of 'different' people, times and places to reveal, revitalise or renew an ostensibly concealed 'Other in Us' (Pandian & Parman, 2004), and thus to act as a cosmological centre of Self located beyond the immediate realms of the everyday – either as far away in space and time, or as buried deep inside ourselves. What the notion of the 'Other in Us' seems to pull to the surface here is a specific modernist cultural norm to think about and shape Self as a presumably stable entity that is constituted and maintained through relations with Others, presumed to be equally stable. This notion seems to arise from the philosophical and theological grand narratives of modernist thinking. Because of its specific historically and culturally con-textualised inductive quality, it provides a good starting point from which to explore the 'deep structural frames' (Donati, 1992) underlying 'modern' culture in a wider sense.

The different works included in this volume focus on the way alterity is conceptualised and invoked through diverse forms of Western tourism. They demonstrate that, while the Others respectively under consideration are produced and maintained through processes of 'delineation', as suggested by Waldenfels (2007), at the same time they intimately respond to a set of sensual and semiotic desires that structure the order and cosmology of the tourists' everyday lives. In that way, these Others are highly seductive entities that promise encounters with the enchanted worlds of a past golden age, the wonders of an authentic or divine nature, or alternatively futuristic glimpses of worlds to come. As socially dramatised forms of Otherness, places like the idealised countrysides of the Catalan Pyrenees or of Eastern Europe, the eroticised nature of Mediterranean males or the romanticised continent of Africa, or the magical powers of shamans, able to reveal a presumed inner self, seem able to provide both metaphors and a material ground to evoke and satisfy touristic quests for mythical enchantment, transformation and renewal.

Building on earlier anthropological works on the experiential structure of tourism practice (Adler, 1989; Graburn, 1983a; Turner, 1972), the case studies included in the book demonstrate that these and other forms of Otherness, through their seductive power and ability to initiate a temporary disruption of social order, play a crucial role in maintaining tourists' social life back home. They produce what Alma Gottlieb (1982) calls 'ritual inversions' – just as carnivals, feasts and religious ceremonies do in other times and social contexts. In this sense, they constitute ceremonial grounds in which tourists 'play, pray and pay' (Graburn, 1983b) – in other words, situations in which they liberate and activate their body, consume accumulated economic and emotional surplus, and re-enchant and sometimes also fundamentally change the moral and cosmological order of the world.

For most tourists the journey is a success when they return home as transformed beings. In most cases, this means that they feel socially, physically and mentally renewed; they have 'recharged their batteries'. In more marginal cases, the disruption experienced as part of the journey does not end with the return home. Tourism is here able to act as a trigger for deeper social and moral transformations, such as changes of jobs, partners or routines; some people decide to do what they have always dreamt of doing – move to the countryside, come out of the closet, become politically active or start that degree in film studies. Here, the outer journey seems able to lead to a process of inner transformation or even emancipation (Frey, 1998; Chabloz & Morier, 2009; Graburn, 2012; Picard, 2012). Whether the transformation is recharging or renewal, tourism is embedded within a wider cultural framework and broader historicity that suggests how people are to think about, or how to feel about, their relationship to the wider world.

Most of the anthropological research carried out over the past 40 years seems to demonstrate that the Otherness of such symbolically distanced realms is not an inherently ontological or otherwise stable quality, but that it stems from a process of projection and ontological boundary work (Barth, 1969; Csordas, 1994; Waldenfels, 2007; Whittaker, 1992). Particularly in the field of tourism, the realms of the journey are anchored in socially constructed imaginaries and meta-narratives that imbue them with magic and meaning (Bruner, 2004; Salazar & Graburn, 2014). In this sense, the perceived beauty of a landscape, the divine forces observed in nature, the outstanding value of an urban environment or the perceived effervescence of an exotic human life context are not objective qualities inherent to a given site or society, but stem from the socially framed subjective mind-set and culture of the respective tourists. Hence, contrary to what the term suggests, in the context of Western tourism, Otherness and its presumed magic are not *other to*, but always intimately and often uncannily *within* the Self (Picard, 2011, 2012).

The conception and practice of Self–Other relations seem to pertain here to a specific cultural ontology formed upon the highly resilient Judaeo-Christian episteme of the 'Other in Us' (Pandian & Parman, 2004), as well as the neo-Platonic philosophies of Plotinus and Augustine, who saw the purified soul as the vehicle to 'restore' the human to a more perfect state, in union with God (see Chadwick, 1998: 6), fulfilling one's identity (Plotinus 1957: 357). Germane to this discussion, Plotinus's means of achieving this union with God is introspection: 'go into yourself', he exhorted (1957: 63). For both Plotinus and Augustine, an interior journey was necessary to eschew the corruption of the sensory body – in its attraction to the chaos of the created world – and focus on a presumed pure, uncorrupted soul that can be the means of perfecting the created Self (see Chadwick, 1998: xxi–xxii). These philosophies, which saw the individual beset by Otherness – both inside and outside the body – laid the groundwork for subsequent thinking concerning the importance of introspection in the quest to bring fullness, completion or better understanding of the Self.

Anthropologists, for example Nadège Chabloz and Julien Raout (2009), and earlier Edward Bruner (1991) and Marie-Françoise Lanfant (1995), have observed that the contemporary practice of Otherness in Western tourism eventually always exposes a quest for the Self – at least, that part of the Self that presumably remains 'hidden' or concealed in the contexts of the everyday. What these anthropological observations indicate is that the earlier philosophical and theological conceptions of the 'Other in Us' have flowed into the wider common sense of modern culture. They seem to constitute a highly resilient cultural frame to think about personhood in general. This is demonstrated in this volume by Christian Ghasarian (Chapter 10), who, in his chapter on New Age travel practice, argues that recent forms of neo-paganism among mainly Western tourists are driven by a quest for an 'inner journey', an aspiration to 'rediscover' a quality of human existence presumably lost or obscured by the disenchantments brought about by modernity. In a similar vein, many of those participating in Western mass tourism seem to believe, or at least aspire to believe, that contact with specific forms of Otherness encountered as part of the journey can help them to reveal, or to reconnect to, such a presumably hidden or repressed facet of Self. Such revelation or reconnection usually presupposes that the specific forms of Otherness encountered during the journey are ontologically connected to these hidden facets of Self, for example as a result of a forgotten historical kinship or a shared cosmological realm of origin. Touristic immersion in natural environments, for instance, often makes tourists appreciate a common ancestry in nature (they may even candidly state that 'humanity is part of nature'). Marcela Knapp and Frauke Wiegand (Chapter 9) show how tourists (mainly European) travelling to Africa believe their journey will help them to uncover an authentic, yet presumably obscured, quality of Self. A more 'real' and 'more close to nature' fantasy of Africa inscribed in the tourism imaginary constitutes here a kind of mirror, by means of which tourists 'discover' what they conceive of as their 'inner selves'. Similarly, cultural heritage sites often allow tourists to evoke realms of a shared historical past that presumably has continued a hidden social life in the Self and is revealed through the contact with the authentic origin or through evocation by means of a convincing copy.

The different case studies presented in this book suggest that these intimately bound forms of Otherness are always in a mutually constitutive relation with the touristic Self. The process of delineation is interactive and intersubjective; this is an observation that seems to follow earlier, philosophical theorisations, most notably those by Hegel (1807). 'Other' becomes 'Other', for and in connection with – here – the tourist. It constitutes itself as an objectified Other in relation to the tourist or, at a wider scale, in relation to the worlds represented by the tourist. Intersubjective contact thus activates relations at different scales. Both hosts and guests are not only individual persons but, in most cases, mobilise larger social entities of which they are a part. Their interpersonal contact is simultaneously inscribed in a wider contact zone in which social categories such as ethnicity, nationality, gender, age, class and religion are mobilised to make sense of the respective Other and transform it into a symbolically unified moral person.

Camila del Mármol (Chapter 2) illustrates how the mountainous landscape of the Pyrenees is elevated in status as an almost motherly land of origin for the emergent Catalan nation. Through the fabricating work of folklore, the aesthetisation of a bucolic existence and the renovation of architectural infrastructures, people, sites and itineraries in the Pyrenees become touristically accessible ceremonial stages to re-invoke an idealised 'authentic' rural past. Similarly, yet on a much smaller scale, the nationalist theme park in the Portuguese town of Coimbra, studied by Paula Mota Santos (Chapter 3), constitutes a miniature assemblage in which the 'gigantic' pretensions of the fading Portuguese empire of the 1940s is made tangible and experienceable to park visitors.

At the same time, the politically instituted formulations about the quintessence of Portugal in the Coimbra theme park, or of Cataluña in the Pyrenees, create what Fernando Ortiz (1947) has defined as a 'contact zone', within which these formulations are processed by various social actors, often contested, reformulated and reinstated in an auto-ethnographic fashion (see also Bruner, 2005; Pratt, 1992; Picard, 1996). Tourism operates not only on the scale of the societies that generate tourists, but also on a more encompassing, global scale. By integrating Other people, territories and time-spaces to its specific touristic realms, scripts and narratives, tourism purposely creates these Others in the specific terms of its liturgical needs. The chapter authors demonstrate how the tourism contact zone produces frames that challenge the populations in destinations to appropriate and nurture projections of their own Otherness. Pamila Gupta in her work on tourism development in Goa, India (Chapter 5), illustrates the frictions created by the inherent contradictions between what destinations put up as a play for tourists (among others because tourism provides economic income) and what the myriad imaginaries of various actors – international and national tourists, different types of locals, service providers and so on – associate with the place and with tourism as an integral part of the place. Similarly, in their work on touristic heterotopias of two Eastern European locales, Mathilde Verschaeve and Hannah Wadle (Chapter 4) explore the tensions between touristic projections of a technologically and historically 'backward' post-socialist space and the aspirations of local populations to be 'modern'.

They show that being Other in terms of such projections can become a powerful means to formulate and institutionalise new 'local' identities and to develop forms of what has elsewhere been called 'vernacular cosmopolitanism' (Werbner, 2006). For many destinations, providing a liturgical ground for the touristic ceremonial not only becomes a profit-generating economy but, in a wider understanding of world society, gives them specific societal roles, not unlike that of priests, monks or theatre actors in other historical contexts. In many ways, the integration of these destinations into the international tourism economy transforms them into socially and symbolically embodied transfigurations of a globally extended modern mythical universe. From the perspective of destination societies, seducing and disrupting the order of the modernist Self by promising (and also ultimately satisfying) pleasures that are otherwise inhibited in modern society becomes a specific social role they can play in the broader global society.

***

To grasp the complexity of tourism practice as an ethnographic object, it is useful to return tourism research to the very foundations of the anthropological approach. Indeed, it makes little sense to study any singular facet or moment of tourism practice in isolation. Instead, tourism practices are more usefully explored from within the wider social contexts in which they are produced. If the overwhelming majority of today's tourists are citizens of the industrialised countries of Europe, the Americas and Asia, an anthropological study of tourism thus has to be concerned with the 'cultures' of these countries. In other words, it has to investigate the wider social institutions and structures of experience that allow people to think about themselves as social beings, to participate in social life and to maintain and renew the moral frames of being and becoming. Most of the contributors here focus on European forms of tourism and subsequently explore more specifically what kinds of overarching conceptions and knowledge of Otherness have been institutionalised and naturalised in different European societies.

A major concern is to examine anthropologically how different Western religious and lay philosophies have shaped the formation and normalisation of specific everyday cultures of Selfhood and related forms of Otherness consumed in tourism. In much of modern culture, such Self–Other relations seem to be shaped by a disciplining process where various disarticulated parts are bound into, and subsequently interiorised in terms of, the normative ideal of a homogeneous, unified individual or moral person (see Asad, 1993). The doctrine of a unified person that has marked much of the philosophical and theological thinking in the Western world prior to the Enlightenment seems to have instituted here a dominant culture of thinking about the Self.

The normative order underlying this culture has not been uncontested. Since the 19th century, spiritualists and, later, hippies have been resurrecting and romantically reinterpreting Oriental philosophies, stressing in particular the open-endedness and multiplicity of reality (Howes, 1991).[2] If in the 19th century this was manifest as a longing for the immediate and first-hand experience of the 'Other' in the forms of spirits, ether and otherworldly knowledge through concepts that intersected the domains of sensation and intellect (mesmerism, with its imponderable fluids; spiritism, with its invisible actors), this also eventually led to the discovery of an entirely different domain of causality: the imagination, the unconscious, forgotten ancestries, in which the Self was no longer considered to be unified, but rather was as separate, unpredictable and mysterious as the spirits. More recently, these have become manifest through the increase in self-knowledge and self-cultivating practices such as meditation, yoga and, in the tourism context, visits to ashrams in India, shamanist-type tourism tours in the Amazon, middle-class Mexicans' involvement in healing ceremonies with ayahuasca and other hallucinogens, and so on (Heelas, 1996; see Chapter 10). The emerging academic fields of psychoanalysis, social phenomenology and social interactionism, and also avant-garde philosophical and artistic movements like surrealism and, later, postmodernism, equally challenged the idea of a unified Self, claiming instead that Self is formed through a myriad of beings, experiences and identities (for overviews, see Lock, 1993; MacCannell, 2011).

However, our aim in this book is not so much to engage in a general philosophical debate about personhood *per se* – the presumably intrinsic or extrinsic processes or principles that underpin the cultural, psychological or divine construction of personhood. Rather, we are interested in an inductive observation of different forms of the 'modern person' as they appear in the contexts of tourism. In this sense, we are not working *inside* a philosophical debate or 'philosophical anthropology'; rather, we are building on a classical anthropological concern with the cultures of cosmology, philosophy and ethics, and are investigating how these have shaped an often-simplified cosmology of the everyday.

Using 'culture' as the main analytical category is, of course, problematic because it tends to lead to attempts to unify a myriad of ideas, practices and social forms within a single concept. Following Dean MacCannell's (1976) initial proposition, we suggest resolving this problem inductively, by observing the common structures underlying the social practices of tourism and the values and imaginaries they cultivate and make manifest. In this sense, the notions of a 'modernist' Self and culture as we understand and use them in this book emerge from a dialectic between social practices and the collective mind-sets by which these practices are framed, and, at the same time, by which they are allowed to be perpetuated and renewed. The works developed in the volume thus adopt the phenomenological epistemology of historical anthropology (Comaroff, 1982; Jackson, 2012; Sahlins, 1987). Contrary to the earlier Functionalist and Structuralist aspirations to reveal presumed 'elementary forms' of social life or human culture (Durkheim, 2008; Lévi-Strauss, 1974; Malinowski, 1939; Radcliffe-Brown, 1961), we understand 'modernist' culture, cosmology and conceptions of the Self in terms of a social structure of experience that is shaped through the historical institutionalisation of dominant social norms and philosophical world visions.

What we ultimately wish to present in this book is an illustration of how a 'modernist Self' evolves within the broader culture of a 'modernist cosmology'. One of the most resilient meta-narratives shaping modern life and cosmology, and persistently resurfacing in tourism practice, seems to stem here from the philosophical ideas concerning an authentic, yet delineated, 'state of nature' (Hobbes, 1651; Rousseau, 1762). The wider cosmological framework of modern social life seems to be defined by two historically distinct states – that of nature and that of culture – and the 'decision' by humans to give up some of their 'natural rights' in order to pass from the first state to the second, seen as a condition to guarantee peaceful relations among humans (Sahlins, 1972). Much of contemporary tourism practice seems to unfold within the cosmological framework of a presumed 'social contract' leading humanity from an authentic state of nature to the formation of society. In this context, tourism emerges as a specific ritual aimed both at renewing the myth of the presumed original state of nature and at reinstating social order – a traditional 'rite of intensification' (Chapple & Coon, 1942: 426), as Graburn (1983a: 12) pointed out long ago.

The 'modern Self' and the relations to which it pertains with the imagined realms of origin or ancestral nature may best be theorised through another episteme brought about by Western culture: that of sympathetic magic. If we take out the universalising claim made by Frazer to use the notion of magic to theorise relations of proximity and distance in any human society, and, rather, consider magic as an emic concept brought about by modernist theology and philosophy, it actually provides a compelling theoretical framework to think about how modern subjects think about tourism and tourist destinations. The latter often seem to act here as metaphoric grounds able to re-articulate the presumably separate parts of life (and Self) in a wider 'original' whole. In many ways, they are 'magical' by virtue of their supposed sympathy with the allegedly hidden facets of an assumed 'true' or 'inner' Self. In this sense, 'magic', which in Western society has long been considered to be the superstition or the potentially dangerous supernatural power of others (Greenwood, 2009; Meyer & Pels,

2003; Tambiah, 1990; Wygant, 2006), effectively seems to be a constitutive element of modernist thinking and the forms of social life it has shaped. Accessing such 'magic' by means of touristic travel seems crucial to maintain and renew the moral and political order of modern life (Picard, 2011).

The Paradoxes of Modernist Cosmology and Self

To approach social formations of Otherness as part of modern culture and tourism, it makes the most sense to start with an exploration of the social settings that frame the formation of the Self as the constitutive entity of such Otherness. If tourism is a social phenomena brought about by modernity or 'modern culture' in a larger sense, it seems useful to explore the social logics and inherent paradoxes inscribed in the narratives of time and being that form what can be called 'modernist cosmology'.

The phenomenologist Theodor Lessing was one of the first to point out the modernist obsession with 'history',[3] which he suggested had become the single most powerful institution to socialise time. By adding meaning to strategically selected sequences of historical events, social actors use history as a highly flexible allegorical category to legitimate the political orders of the present and near future. In his monograph *Geschichte als Sinngebung des Sinnlosen* (*History as Giving Meaning to the Meaningless*), published in 1919, he argues that time in itself is not imbued with any moral logic or continuity, thus challenging the dominant philosophical narratives of the early 20th century. For the optimists among the European philosophers, he wrote, history is seen as a sequence of necessary challenges, wars and crisis, which eventually lead humanity to an end defined by progress and enlightenment. The pessimists, instead, considered history a process of progressive disenchantment from an original state of nature, marked by the development of social asymmetries, the exploitation of some by others and an eventual downfall. Important is that both philosophical narratives generate a cosmological framework defined by a progressive distanciation of humanity from a presumed *ur*-state found in nature. For the optimists, nature – including the interior human, in the form of animalistic remnants and instincts – is to be 'tamed' through education and the cultivation of refinement. For the pessimists, nature is considered a happy golden age, to which humanity ought to return in a utopian future.

Lessing argues that both perspectives of historical philosophy – and the broader logic of time they postulate – are built upon the mythical and religious cosmologies of earlier theological texts. On the one hand, they refer to biblical images of Eden as a first garden of timeless happiness. On the other hand, they pick up on the crucial turning-point of the biblical narrative when Adam and Eve are cast out of the garden and initiate history, with all its sufferings and the certainty of death (Genesis 3: 14–24). Mircea Eliade calls this the conclusion of the 'sacred myth', or 'sacred time', in which the human is both the central character and the victim, and which the gods finally depart, creating 'historical time'. This in and of itself is a juxtaposition between Self and Other – historical versus sacred, profane time versus sacred time. Yet, Eliade argues, sacred time – and, indeed, the sacred itself – is temporarily attainable, 'irrupting' in place-based hierophanies (the many recreations of the culture's *axis mundi*), when the sacred myth is re-enacted through ritual celebrations (Eliade, 1959: 68–113). Through a re-enactment of the cosmological myth, tourism allows modern subjects to reiterate the 'quest to return to Eden' or a presumed authentic 'state of nature'. The *a priori* secularist cosmology of tourism and the Self–Other relations it operates thus seem far from being devoid of inherent meaning. In this sense, the presumed existentialist humanist and moral recognition among the Moderns that their being in the world has no deeper signification (Taylor, 2007) has simply not taken place in mainstream modern society.

While the two historical narratives that emerge as dominant structural frames of modern, Western cosmology seem inherently contradictory – following, as they do, apparently oppositional logics – they constitute in their complementarity an overall framework to conceptualise time and to supply social actors with meaningful metaphors to think about their acts of being and becoming. It seems that it is this complementarity and inherent conflict between opposing logics (the quest to return to Eden; the quest to get away from Eden and determine one's own destiny so as to reach a higher state of being) that constitutes a more general framework for the formation of what can be called the 'modernist self'. The latter appears always torn between antagonistic forces and desires, on the one hand, to enjoy the pleasures of nature and the senses and, on the other, to discipline the senses as a means to reach a morally higher state (Hollis, 1985). Much of the European and North American romantic movements made the inner struggle inherent in the contradictions of this myth a major theme in itself. In that way, modern everyday culture and the 'modern Self' appear marked by a constant tension between a presumed human 'inner' or 'original' nature and societal efforts to delineate such a nature. (See the Goethe poem on the first page.)

Such a notion was already present, in perhaps an extreme form, in the neo-Platonic theology of Saint Augustine of Hippo, who postulated that the Self is already formed at birth, as a result of inheritance, filiation and even memory. In his notion of 'original sin', Saint Augustine famously claimed that humans are born 'guilty' and therefore have an obligation to spend their lives working towards redemption (Markus, 1989). This redemptive process was conceived of as a pilgrimage on earth (see Walsh *et al.*, 1958: 465), a journey, laden with suffering and temptation, from the earthly city (*civitas terrena*) to the city of God (*civitas Dei*) (Walsh *et al.*, 1958: 191). These are less physical places than they are moral orders, and it is achievable by listening to the soul – the aforementioned 'Other in Us' – who is privy to deciphering God's message, yet is obscured by the human tendency to privilege its human faculties, bodily senses and base impulses. In particular, he argues that the *libido dominandi*, the 'lust to dominate', is a universal human impulse and marks the overriding ethic of the *civitas terrena*, the human social system. It is by overcoming the Self's very human nature – the *libido* – that the faithful can leave profane society and move to the 'sacred' City of God, becoming its citizen. This is considered an interior journey, of course – a disciplined voyage of transformation on which the profane and imperfect Self meets the divine and perfect Other by, paradoxically, shedding the very sensory impulses and attachments that mark the Self. Yet, as on most touristic itineraries, Augustinian pilgrims do not simply interact with one type of Other, waiting for them at the destination. Rather, they join a 'pilgrim band' of others like themselves, who are following the same itinerary. For Saint Augustine, these are literally Others – cultural and terrestrial: 'The City of God invites all people from all nations and races together and unites them into a single pilgrim band ... she takes no issue with customs, laws and traditions' (see Walsh *et al.*, 1958: 465). Thus, in the process of Augustine's journey to redemption through alterity, the pilgrim becomes another Other: a member of the City of God on Earth, the *civitas Dei supra terram*, or the Church. Where the earthly city is marked by the *libido dominandi* – the lust for dominating Others – the Church pointedly is marked by the peaceful assimilation of them (Milbank, 2006: 392–393). It should be noted, furthermore, that St Paul argued that the Church is not merely a social system or a religious institution, but rather the literal (not metaphoric) 'body of Christ', a sort of Durkheimian organism composed of unequal members who, together, are greater than the sum of its parts (1 Corinthians 12: 12–14). For Augustine, therefore, these pilgrims not only have the Other in Us but, as Christians within the Church, are themselves Others in the collective Us, who, together, through the collective consumption of the eucharist, form Jesus Christ's mystical Self. Thus, in this theology, Augustine sketches out a double movement from Self to Other: the first is the long-term pilgrimage in which the individual ultimately peregrinates from a profane, human Self – immersed in human society – to a sacred Other in communion with the deity; the second occurs in the interim process, in which the pilgrim nevertheless becomes something Other than himself or herself – a Christian, a member of a sacred society, the 'pilgrim Church on earth' as the Catholic liturgy calls it today.

It can be argued that Augustine's focus on the imperfection of the Self, and an individual's subsequent journey to seek 'fullness', provided the underlying basis for contemporary notions of the 'modern Self', which, as the chapters in this volume demonstrate, inform secular and religious tourism. Yet the humanistic turn during the Renaissance and the subsequent Enlightenment created a significant shift in the way Western culture perceived the modern Self and the way in which the individual could achieve 'fullness'. According to philosopher Charles Taylor (2007), rather than conceiving fullness as a condition in which man's highest spiritual and moral aspirations pointed towards God – as in the Augustinian model sketched out above – humanism turned to the diversity of outside sources in this world, frequently denying God. This produced a new sense of Self and its place in the cosmos. No longer was the Self necessarily conceptualised as open or even vulnerable to the supernatural world, but it was 'buffered' from it. That is, the Self could be fully realised through the means of this material existence.

By the Enlightenment, the fullness of the Self was believed to be achieved through the sovereign control generated in mankind's own sense of dignity and power. Thus, while Augustine argued that fullness could be achieved only by abandoning one's own material satisfaction and personal power to control the world (the *libido dominandi*), for humanists and Enlightenment thinkers such as the French philosopher René Descartes, fullness of the Self could be achieved only by searching in the sensory world, having sovereign control of the mind over the body (Taylor, 2007: 244–245). That is, while for Augustine the intellect within the soul guides the Self to find truth in the sacred Other beyond the sensory world, Descartes stressed the ability of humans to find truth through their own reflections about the world. By claiming that truth can be found through the act of thinking, Descartes elevated the mind as sole expression of the Self, disconnected and independent from the body and other forms of the external physical world, which, he claimed, were at the mind's disposal (Reiss, 2002). Descartes's philosophy laid a base for the 19th-century ideology of humanity, where notions of the centric Self were extended from the individual person to wider, societal entities. In this sense, a community, a social class, a kinship group, a nation or even humanity itself is variably considered in terms of what Marcel Mauss (1938) later terms a 'moral person', who may consider other moral persons – lower social classes, foreigners and so on – as belonging to an external world that is at their disposal. The Modernist defenders of evolutionary theory asserted that some people were so far from the kind of human civilisation they felt they represented (the white European educated classes) that they were 'doomed' to disappear – like an ill-fated animal that eventually vanishes through natural selection, as suggested by Charles Darwin in his game-changing study, *The Origin of Species* (2005 [1859]).

The political and social consequences of incorporating such a philosophy into mainstream politics were dramatic. Zygmund Bauman (1991) describes the development, by the end of the 19th century and in the early 20th century, of the model of a 'gardening state' that attempted to govern humanity by 'weeding' out those 'human species' who did not fit in the ideal worlds of the human gardener. Bauman argues that it was this notion of gardening that eventually led to the racist excesses and genocides that marked Europe and its empires in the early 20th century, and that culminated in the horrors of the Holocaust.

In the period following the Second World War, ideas of specific national or ethnic character traits innate to the human body, and by extension to the wider moral person of social classes or other groups, moved to the background. Yet they did not disappear. Ideas of an 'inner' or 'true' Self, innate to a person and/or a group of belonging, continued to resurface. Many nationalist, anti-colonial and class-struggle movements, for instance, claimed the existence of a prototypical 'character' defining their respective members and that had 'survived' colonisation, political suppression and forced acculturation. Inspired by the Surrealist movement, which had, in turn, been inspired by psychoanalysis, anti-colonial militants like Mexican artist Frida Kahlo asserted the persistence of an inheritance (in her case pre-Columbian) that was believed to have survived at a deep cultural level and that could be brought back to the surface (Le Clézio, 1993). In a similar vein, the anti-colonial militants of the *négritude* and the later black-power movements in the Americas argued for the survival of African cultural traces in the culture of the descendants of former slaves from Africa (Bastide, 1970).

The argument flowed into the fields of the social sciences, with important new works carried out around the new concept of syncretism. The latter is based on the idea of transformation and resilience of formal aspects, grammar and social practices of African culture in the new forms of social life emerging from the contact with European and other cultures in the colonies (Herskovits, 1958). While supporting the scientific approach to syncretism, authors like Roger Bastide (1970), working in Brazil, criticised what they saw as the *négritude*'s and black power movements' naïve appropriation of representations of a mythical Africa which actually stemmed from European fantasies about that continent (rather than from any presumably surviving 'deep culture'). The initially philosophical idea that a person's Self is inscribed in a history extending beyond its own life and body (i.e. that there is an inherited 'true' or 'inner' self) equally appears in most religious movements, including the Catholic Church, and also the rapidly spreading neo-pagan religions in Europe, frequently alluding to forms of previous lives and reincarnation (Fedele & Blanes, 2011; see Chapter 10).

***

A radically alternative philosophical position that equally entered the worldview of modern everyday culture suggests that a person is essentially a product of socialisation. For thinkers in the tradition of John Locke, a person is a 'conscious thinking thing' that emerges from both experiences and reflections upon those experiences (Locke, 1778). In 1807, Friedrich Hegel suggested that the self becomes conscious about itself only after it encounters another conscious self. By dialectically recognising each other, the two entities become mutually constitutive. To explain this observation, Hegel uses the relation between master and subordinate as a guiding metaphor. Masters will recognise themselves via their relations to a subordinate; and vice versa, subordinates become aware of themselves only in relation to their masters (Hegel, 1807). One would not exist without the other.

In the late 19th and early 20th century, the philosophical debate about Selfhood was carried into the emerging field of social and cultural anthropology, which in turn heavily influenced the formation of the dominant paradigms of 20th-century, 'modern' culture. In one of the first major works on the social formations of Self, George Herbert Mead (1967) argued that notions of personhood and self-consciousness are not inherently given qualities of a presumably 'inner' or 'true' Self, but that they arise in the process of social experience and activity (Mead, 1967: 135). For Mead, the Self is a specific structure of subjective experience that is formed and maintained through a process of objectivation; individuals become conscious of their Selves by internalising the attitudes of others towards them and by experiencing other selves in the intersubjective processes of social interaction (Cronk, 2001). Later, Michel Foucault (1988) equally rejected the idea of ascribing persons with an 'inner' or 'true' essence, but instead suggested an approach to the formation of Selves in terms of discourses about Self that are instituted and become normative knowledge. From that point, the Self emerges as an objectified and interiorised discourse entangled in the power relations that govern the relationships between people in society. Building on Foucault, Talal Asad argues that the separation of 'inner' and 'outer' Selves was an innovation of the modern era, and points out that, in the Middle Ages, monastic rites were designed for moral self-fashioning;

the complete moral individual needed to condition the interior Self through repetitive, ritual discipline of the exterior body. It was those penitential marks of suffering, on the outward body, that were believed to reveal the purity and moral fullness within (Asad, 1993: 105–115).

Locke and his followers' ideas, and their reinterpretations during the 20th century (MacCannell, 2011), imply an epistemic revolution that questions not only the view of an inherent logic to history, but also that of the ontological 'solidity' of social classes and hierarchies *per se*. Hitherto considered naturally or divinely given, notions like history and social orders were to be reconsidered as stemming from historical processes and social constructions.

Challenging the presumed 'nature' of social hierarchies is a dangerous enterprise and many authors writing in this vein have paid a high price. Theodor Lessing was a professor at a German university who, after aggressively challenging Adolf Hitler's fantastical racial ideologies, was sacked and fled to exile, but was eventually assassinated by Nazis. While authors not unfriendly to the Nazi regime, such as, perhaps most famously, Martin Heidegger, made an international career and are today key references in the field of social phenomenology, persecuted authors like Lessing were forgotten. While Lessing's work widely anticipated much of today's key texts on the politics of history, it has never been translated into English. Most of the internationally recognised authors working in this field never even mention his name.

While the academic and philosophical debate about Selfhood has persisted to the present day, its more recent developments seem to have had little connection to, or influence on, the wider common-sense cultures that mark the everyday lives of most people in the Western world. The dominant paradigms surfacing in Western mass tourism, for instance, widely remain those based on the two types of earlier philosophical conceptualisations of Self, that is, either as a divine given, or as an ego creation. The egoic culture of the 'modernist Self' thus appears to parallel the paradox inherent in the modernist cosmological myth of Eden described above. It lies in the co-presence of two, respectively exclusive, *a priori* conceptions of Self – one striving for personal growth and moral elevation, the other searching for an inner truth, or traces of an inner truth presumably lost as a result of modernist disenchantment. The co-presence of these two facets of Self and their respective social logics may well generate what Jarett Zigon (2009; see also Chapter 2) calls a 'moral crisis'. While nurturing a sense of cosmologically framed 'homesickness' expressed through the quest to return to a primordial nature, it does, at the same time, everything to get away from such a nature, in an effort to cultivate a sensible and morally refined person.

Magical Mirrors and Self-Revelation

The socioculturally shaped, inherently divided, modernist Self described above becomes most obvious in the contexts of tourist practice. These are commonly framed, on the one hand, by narratives that suggest a magical reconnection to a 'true self', which is variably achieved through immersion in the otherwise distanced realms of a wild and divine nature, through contact with sexually or emotionally 'more intense' or mystically 'more knowledgeable' people, and also through visits to the remnants of past or 'lost' civilisations. In her work on embodied encounters between tourists and tourism workers in a coastal town in Turkey, Sanne Scheltena (Chapter 8) describes how northern European women are seduced by what they perceive as the more 'sensual' and 'attentive' way in which Turkish men act towards them and thus 'make them feel like women'. The 'Mediterranean' is thus constituted as an idiom defined by a sexually and emotionally heightened intensity, which allows tourists to connect to and inhabit a facet of the Self from which they otherwise feel alienated: their sexual body seems to resurface in these projected relations is the concept of the Cartesian duality between body and mind. The 'Mediterranean' appears to be conceived by a relative lack of sensory control when compared with the 'northern European'. In the eyes of the tourists, and equally in those of the Turkish men, the latter allow the former to 'let go'. Similar to the realms of wild nature, the 'Mediterranean' acts as a kind of mirror or trigger through which tourists 'connect' to what they perceive as a 'lost state', or a repressed state of the (natural) body.

In a similar vein, the American anthropologist Alma Gottlieb (1982) observes that, as part of their touristic ceremonies, many middle-class Americans like to immerse themselves in an imagined realm of 'poverty'. The latter is usually created through metaphors that evoke a simple, yet happy and almost timeless, existence. The most popular stage on which to experience such a 'happy poverty' is probably supplied by the tropical resort hotel. Here, tourists typically engage in a reduced form of social life, based on the absence of work obligations, the abundance of food and drink, the heat, reverberations and nakedness felt by the body, the symbolism of the garden of Eden evoked by the architectural features of hotel gardens, bars, pools and the wider landscape of tourist destinations (Picard, 2011). In her work on the touristic allure of poverty in highland Bolivia, Clare Sammells (Chapter 7) examines how specific materials and performances are mobilised to construct and bring to life to the imaginary realms of such 'happy poverty'. Huts covered with thatch roofs and the performance of bargaining are two of the idioms she explores, arguing that these become tokens, mobilised in the touristic contact zone, which enable communication and mutual participation. The idea of poverty equally appears in other types of tourism, sometimes very explicitly, in forms of 'slum tourism' and volunteer tourism (Frenzel & Koens, 2012). Émilie Crossley (2012) explains that, for many travellers taking part in these forms of tourism, the experience of poverty and total difference is part of a wider quest for moral transformation. It typically takes place at crucial moments in a person's social life: during the passages from youth to adulthood, in situations of mid-life crisis, or upon retirement (see Frey, 1998; Graburn, 2002; Leite & Graburn, 2009).

If the narratives inscribed in the modernist tourism ritual allow tourists to connect to a presumed 'true' or 'inner' Self found in nature, poverty, or any other state of idealised ancestry or origin, they firmly institute processes of social reintegration at the same time. Following Arnold van Gennep's (2004 [1909]) and, later, Victor Turner's (1995 [1969]) work on the ritual process, it has been observed that the first part of the touristic journey is usually marked by a preliminary (or separation) phase of departure (e.g. the separation from home, the travelling to a destination, the arrival at the destination) and a liminal phase marked by the enactment of various tourism practices in the destination (Adler, 1989; Di Giovine, 2009; Graburn, 2002; Lett, 1983; Seliinniemi, 2003). During and especially at the end of the liminal phase of the journey, one can observe the transition to a third phase, of 'reintegration' or 'reaggregation'. Both the separation and reaggregation phases are marked with appropriate transitional rituals, ones that facilitate travellers' moves from their quotidian lives to their liminal touring. For example, 'welcome' and 'farewell' dinners are particularly important elements on a group tour, even on itineraries that do not provide many 'inclusions'. These not only provide a venue for a tour leader to disseminate important preliminary or concluding information, but also serve to transition the group into and out of their liminal state. Unlike more 'authentic' meals consumed in restaurants or private homes, in which more adventuresome food might be offered, the welcome meal in particular often offers either 'fusion' fare or basic stereotypical plates that serve to ease travellers, through their palate, into a new environment, and help cultivate among them a 'taste' for the place (literally and figuratively) (see Di Giovine, 2009: 155–185).

The reaggregation phase already occurs during the journey, mainly at the moments of breaks, dinners and individual or collective recollections. In these moments, the experiences made on the tour are reflected upon and thus articulated with the wider social reality through which individual tourists embed their individuality. Accordingly, the emotions generated by tourists' encounters with specific sites, or listening to particular stories during the journey, usually trigger dialogues that relate such experiences to the individual stories and identities of the tourists. Most dinner conversations among tourists do not thematise the social realities of the actual destination; instead tourists use these realities to talk about previous holidays, work and family relations back home, politics, sports and so on (Bruner, 1995; Di Giovine, 2009; Picard, 2013).

Even more significantly, once the journey home has been begun – often immediately after visiting the 'last site' – tourists frequently enter into a different 'mode'. They take no more photographs, but instead go through their digital files, pick out the best images, update blogs and craft their experiences into more stable narratives (Larsen & Urry, 2011; Picard, 2013). They also often fret about personal engagements and 'things to do' waiting for them back at home. What tourists seem to do in this phase is to reaffirm their identity in the face of Otherness (Lanfant, 1995). They delineate their identity as individuals against the exotic backdrop of the destinations. Through their conversations and their playful practices, they symbolically re-establish separations between the Self and various forms of Otherness. Through their return departure, the destination is once again separated from home. The playful re-enactment of a golden age or other myth normally reaches its end here, concluding in the separation between what society deems to be kept separate: gender, social classes, past and present temporalities, the sacred and the profane, and so on. In that way, the reintegration phase of the journey is governed by a symbolic re-alienation of the modernist Self from its 'true' or 'inner' nature, presumably found at the destination.

However, the journey can also sustainably disrupt and change this everyday order, especially when the 'liminal' is brought back home, and not interrupted – for example, when tourists get 'hooked', fall in love, bring the Other back home, become ill, or start a new life back home (Simoni, 2011). In that sense, while the journey defines a normative framework of ritualised transgression and reproduction, it is itself exposed to a risk of disruption. Contact with the Other can lead here to concrete relationships and engagements leaving deep emotional, moral traces and changes in the Self. Destinations do not only or simply respond to the tourists' projections, but also entangle and enrol tourists in their own localised struggles, issues of contention and alternative self-representations. There always is a potential for not confirming the tourists' constructions of the Other, by slightly changing them, resisting, subverting or updating them, or even proposing alternative ones. In some cases, tourists simply do not go home, but make the destination a new home or a second home, thus deeply transforming the rules of the everyday by challenging the temporary nature of liminality and, sometimes, even disrupting the social fabric of the site itself (see, for example, Frey, 1998; McKevitt, 1991).

Sympathetic Magic in Tourism and Modern Culture

Upon their return home, tourists usually integrate various types of souvenir (e.g. sand, stones, places captured in photographs, art craft objects,) within their home spaces, as if these were able to perpetuate a relation with the destination visited during the journey. Tourist souvenirs seem to follow a social life not unlike that of the relics that pilgrims use to extend an 'authentic link' (Stewart, 1993) with the specific aura of a visited shrine (Hitchcock & Teague, 2000; Morgan & Pritchard, 2005; Picard, 2013; Robinson & Picard, 2009). Indeed, as Di Giovine shows in his study of pilgrimage at the shrine of Catholic stigmatic and saint Padre Pio of Pietrelcina, religious tourists especially conflate the souvenir and the relic – spiritually and semantically. Immediately before their departure home (often on the bus to the airport), Italian and Irish pilgrims would often engage their priests and spiritual advisers to enact a form of the Catholic rite of *inventio*, converting touristic souvenirs purchased during the trip into 'relics' that can carry the sacred back home and, importantly, that can have often taumaturgic value for their friends and relatives (especially those who were too ill to make the journey to the shrine) (Di Giovine, 2012: 113–114). In the post-destination context, many returned tourists indicate that they feel that their 'inner' Self has been renewed or 'revitalised' through its immersion in the realms of the destination, as if it had been charged like one would charge a battery by connecting it to an electric current.

In this sense, the Self and the forms of Otherness encountered during the journey seem to perpetuate what the anthropologist James Frazer (1922 [1890]) terms a 'sympathetic relation'. While Frazer has been criticised for his aim to demonstrate the 'false belief' and 'cultural backwardness' of magicians and their societies, his approach to explaining the logic of magical relations from the subjective understanding of such magicians remains valuable. Frazer posits that such relations are based on either of two basic principles of sympathetic magic: 'first, that like produces like, or that an effect resembles its cause; and, second, that things which have once been in contact with each other continue to act on each other at a distance after the physical contact has been severed':

> Sympathetic magic is based on the idea that things act on each other at a distance through a secret sympathy, the impulse being transmitted from one to the other by means of what we may conceive as a kind of

invisible ether, not unlike that which is postulated by modern science for a precisely similar purpose, namely, to explain how things can physically affect each other through a space which appears to be empty. (Frazer, 2009 [1890]: 12)

In the context of tourism, the destination often imitates the décor, spatial structure and temporality of – for example – the biblical Eden or Hobbesian state of nature and, through the narrative of reintegration, their loss and the initiation of history. Although destinations such as tropical islands are not paradise, through their similarity to the collective imaginary of paradise they provide powerful metaphorical grounds to invoke and bring to life the myth of paradise. The theatrical play tourists and destinations engage in to evoke the mythical time of origin seems able to make this time feel real during the course of the journey. After the journey, the bodies of tourists that had been immersed in the material realms of the destination and also objects taken home as material fragments of the destination seem able, in the touristic understanding, to affect each other through Frazer's aforementioned 'invisible ether'. In the post-destination context, souvenirs often become part of what can be seen as post-religious living-room shrines, displays of personal 'sacred' objects – tourist souvenirs, family photos, various objects – assembled on dedicated shelves or corners. In apparent continuity with former religious practices through which such shrines established communication between persons and the divine, they seem to function as mediators between the immediacy of the here and now and the 'sacred' world of distanced Otherness (Picard, 2011; Price, 2013; Riggins, 1994).

In this way, the originally theological notions of a 'true' or 'inner' Self seem to have flowed into a broader popular culture. The modernist Self seems to be conceived here in relation to a wider mythical whole: a divine nature, a cultural ancestry, and so on, which is revived through the journey and with which it is believed to pertain to an ongoing sympathetic relationship while at home. Tourism seems governed by a ritual process that attempts to reconnect to such forms of Otherness, to revive the underlying cosmological order and re-empower the person. As a practice stemming from modernity, it thus appears to operate within a proto-religious context, evolving within the scripts and narratives of its own liturgy, invoking a specifically modernist form of the magical divine and allowing tourists to recreate the cosmological order of modern social life in general (Graburn, 1983a).

Play, Pray and the Reassertion of the *Social Contract*

Most works on the anthropology of tourism consider the ceremonialised reproduction of order operated through touristic rituals in terms of a playful practice – and, indeed, it is precisely this 'recreational' or leisurely component that has opened tourism up to criticism as a light and fluffy practice, devoid of true meaning, or a 'pseudo-event' (see Boorstin, 1987 [1961]: 77–117). In reality, when one looks at what tourists actually put themselves through, it seems more often a painful, rather than playful, experience: tourists spend otherwise unacceptably long amounts of time contained in uncomfortable airplane seats; suffer in many cases disease or illness, and extreme heat or cold; live like monks in spatially reduced hotel rooms; are constrained by their lack of intimate place-based knowledge to move freely around; engage in social activities they would otherwise avoid; eat what they deem not best for their bodies; and, of course, spend large amounts of money on their holiday. Such voluntarily engaged-in discomfort and travail seem to stem from longstanding pilgrimage practices, in which self-inflicted, purgative pain was often normatively understood to be integral – as both an expression of, and a resolution to, the human condition of suffering (Dubisch & Winkelman, 2005).

Indeed, what seems neglected in much of the current work in tourism anthropology is the aspect of self-inflicted pain and the wider forms of sacrifice, exchange and reciprocity that this appears to bring to the surface. Nelson Graburn's (1983b) study of Japanese tourism, which he asserts is based upon the three principles of 'play, pray and pay', lends itself here to the construction of a wider theory. While the aspects of 'play' (the enactment of scripts, the reappropriation and motion of the body, the interactions between people) and 'pray' (the enchantment and veneration of Otherness and the re-enchantments of Self) are relatively well understood in tourism theory, the aspect of 'pay' remains widely under-theorised. When borrowing from the simplifying narratives of economic theory, social scientists frequently portray tourists as conspicuous consumers of cash-paid-for sign experiences that are devoid of any 'deeper' meaning (Boorstin, 1987 [1961]). Their experiences are often declared as fake or naïve. Of course, tourists pay their invoices to balance their consumption, but 'tourism is a much more encompassing spatial [and social] interface than an analysis centred on money would project' (Di Giovine, 2009: 149). Indeed, there is more to tourism and the complex political economy of desires and the body it manoeuvres.

To grasp the complexity of the systems of reciprocity and repayment that operate in tourism, it may make sense here to look again at the way in which European philosophical visions of the world have flowed into the wider worldview and organisational apparatus of modernist culture, and how they materialise in tourism practice in particular. The widely mediated and socially instituted philosophical idea of a 'social contract' seems to provide here once again an overall ideological framework of modernist cosmology (Sahlins, 1972). While important variations exist among philosophers about the interpretation of its different elements, the generally accepted 'logic' associated with the idea of such a contract suggests that humans, tacitly or out of free will, gave up some of their supposedly 'natural' rights and freedoms and submitted to the authority of a ruler or other representative of the collective. Following the influential English philosopher Thomas Hobbes, 'civilised society' thus emerges as the result of the act of opposing a presumably original state of nature, defined by the absence of any wider political order (Hobbes, 1651). At the same time, by creating a social contract binding individuals together within a society, humanity forces this 'original' nature into new forms, thus initiating history as a result of human – and not divine – conditioning and agency. The ideas of the social contract thus set a wider framework that underlies the constitution of a modernist cosmology of time and conception of history (see the section on 'modernist cosmology' above). It also provides a normative framework to regulate individual behaviour in society, particularly by suppressing or regulating the satisfaction of sensual and sexual desires and the presumed 'taming' of human nature as a means to reach a higher sense of civilisation (Foucault, 1988; Callon & Latour, 1981).

Tourism and holidaymaking in a wider sense seem to be able to disrupt these forms of order. In much of modern popular culture, they are regarded as a form of 'reward' for people's docile support of the constraints of work-life, the presumed non-freedom of societal existence and the 'alienations' suffered from a presumed 'true' human nature (Graburn, 1977; Lanfant, 1972). The seduction exercised by various forms of Otherness is tacitly present in everyday life, and which eventually leads tourists to a temporary disruption of this everyday life – that is, they go on holiday – seems a fundamental element for the maintenance and reproduction of modern social life. It not only enables tourists eventually to 'recharge their batteries', to appropriate and personalise the public culture meta-narratives of time, history and being in the world, and to renew their feelings of belonging, but it also creates a critical moment for the reproduction and maintenance of social order back home. In an act of ritualised transgression, analogous to what researchers observed in other festive contexts (Caillois, 2001), the theatrical and playful realms of tourism invite tourists to engage otherwise distanced and even alienated worlds.

Tourism thus seems to reveal a more general paradox of modernity: order is maintained by the promise of, and eventual act of, its temporary suspension (Bataille, 1987; Eagleton, 1981). The various forms of Otherness consumed in tourism seem able (and are often purposely produced) to satisfy desires that are hidden or otherwise repressed in tourists' everyday lives. Tourism allows tourists to 'get dirty', to do what otherwise would be considered as socially unacceptable, or at least inappropriate (Picard & Robinson, 2006). In this sense, by temporarily suppressing one's 'actual' desires in the present, future tourists provide for a future return, enjoyed during the holiday. If individuals voluntarily restrain themselves from living a bodily life 'at full' during most of the year, the festive space of the journey turns into a kind of modern potlatch where 'society', as a personified door-keeper of nature and its original magic, pays back, or ideally overpays, the accumulated debt it has towards individuals.

In this way, the sacrificial aspect that operates in tourism is based on a time-delayed system of reciprocity governed by a social contract between individuals and the virtual institution of society (Sahlins, 1972). It is framed by what Lévi-Strauss (1949; quoted in Graburn, 2013: 174) termed a 'long cycle of exchange', based on provisions of reciprocity that are never balanced and thus allow complex permanent relations of dependency between different entities to be maintained. Because of its ability to act upon the virtual balance that marks the relation between individual and society, tourism seems a crucial institution for maintaining social solidarity and for reasserting the logic of the social contract governing modern social life. Sustaining social peace and solidarity may thus stem less from the normative power of a social contract itself than from the relations built upon expected exchanges and accumulated debts between individuals and society (see Mauss, 1990 [1950]). As long as the debt is not equalised, the relationships between borrower and receiver – here, the individual and society or God (though Durkheim famously conflates the two!) – are ongoing, and in some cases extend into the imaginary realm of the afterlife.

If all goes well (knock on wood!), the last journey of a good Christian leads to Eden, a destination that looks much like a tropical hotel garden. The modernist Self and the lifelong, aspirational sympathetic Other, periodically met during the tour or the Sunday walk, eventually reunite here for their final, ever-lasting holiday.

Notes

(1) We would like to thank readers Dean MacCannell, Elvi Whittaker, Tamas Regi, Valerio Simoni and Diana Espirito Santo for their constructive comments and suggestions on an earlier draft of this Introduction. We hope we did some justice to the historical heritage of concepts about Selfhood and generated some new ideas. We also thank the Department of Anthropology and Sociology at West Chester University for its support during the final phase of publication, and in particular its departmental assistant, Sheri Roberts, for her help in compiling the index. The work invested in the editing of this book was partly financed through national funds provided by the Portuguese Foundation for Science and Technology (FCT), Project PTDC/CSANT/114825/2009.
(2) We would like to thank readers Diana Espirito Santo, Elvi Whittaker and Dean MacCannell for pushing us in this direction.
(3) We would like to thank reader Tamas Regi for pointing out that arguments about the discontinuity of 'history' as a merely symbolic construct to articulate and socialise series of ruptures, accidents and limitations were equally noted by many other commentators (Bataille, 1987; Benjamin, 1969; Deleuze & Guattari, 1983).

References

Adler, J. (1989) Travel as performed art. *American Journal of Sociology* 94 (6), 1366–1391.

Asad, T. (1993) *Genealogies of Religion*. Baltimore, MD: Johns Hopkins University Press.

Barth, F. (1969) *Ethnic Groups and Boundaries: The Social Organization of Culture Difference*. Boston, MA: Little, Brown.

Bastide, R. (1970) *Le prochain et le lointain*. Paris: Cujas.

Bataille, G. (1987) *Eroticism*. London: Marion Boyars.

Bauman, Z. (1991) *Modernity and Ambivalence*. Ithaca, NY: Cornell University Press.

Benjamin, W. (1969) *Illuminations: Essays and Reflections* (vol. 241, no. 2). New York: Schocken.

Boorstin, D.J. (1987 [1961]) *The Image: A Guide to Pseudo-events in America*. New York: Vintage Books.

Bruner, E.M. (1991) Transformation of self in tourism. *Annals of Tourism Research* 18 (2), 238–250.

Bruner, E.M. (1995) The ethnographer/tourist in Indonesia. In M.F. Lanfant, E.M. Bruner and J.B. Allcock (eds) *International Tourism: Identity and Change* (pp. 224–241). London: Sage.

Bruner, E.M. (2004) *Culture on Tour: Ethnographies of Travel*. Chicago, IL: University of Chicago Press.

Bruner, E.M. (2005) The Balinese borderzone. In *Culture on Tour: Ethnographies of Travel* (pp. 191–210). Chicago, IL: University of Chicago Press.

Caillois, R. (2001) *Man and the Sacred*. Champaign, IL: University of Illinois Press.

Callon, M. and Latour, B. (1981) Unscrewing the big Leviathan: How actors macro-structure reality and how sociologists help them to do so. In K. Knorr-Cetina and A.V. Cicourel (eds) *Advances in Social Theory and Methodology: Toward an Integration of Micro- and Macro-Sociologies* (pp. 277–303). London: Routledge.

Chabloz, N. and Raout, J. (2009) *Tourismes: La quête de soi par la pratique des autres*. Special issue of *Cahiers d'études africaines* 193–194. Paris: Éditions de l'École des hautes études en sciences sociales.

Chadwick, H. (1998) Introduction. In Augustine of Hippo. *St Augustine: Confessions* (pp. ix–xxvi). H. Chadwick, tr. Oxford: Oxford University Press.

Chapple, E.D. and Coon, C.S. (1942) *Principles of Anthropology*. New York: Holt.

Comaroff, J.L. (1982) Dialectical systems, history and anthropology: Units of study and questions of theory. *Journal of Southern African Studies* 8 (2), 143–172.

Cronk, G. (2001) George Herbert Mead (1863–1931). Internet Encyclopedia of Philosophy. See http://www.iep.utm.edu/mead/#SH3c (accessed January 2013).

Crossley, É. (2012) Affect and moral transformations in young volunteer tourists. In D. Picard and M. Robinson (eds) *Emotion in Motion: Tourism, Affect and Transformation*, pp. 85–98. London: Ashgate.

Csordas, T.J. (1994) *The Sacred Self: A Cultural Phenomenology of Charismatic Healing*. Berkeley, CA: University of California Press.

Darwin, C. (2005 [1859]) *Origin of Species*. In *The Darwin Compendium*. New York: Barnes and Noble.

Deleuze, G. and Guattari, F. (1983) Savages, barbarians, and civilized men. From *Anti-Oedipus*.

Di Giovine, M. (2009) *The Heritage-scape: UNESCO, World Heritage, and Tourism*. Lanham, MD: Lexington Books.

Di Giovine, M. (2012) Padre Pio for sale: Souvenirs, relics, or identity markers? *International Journal of Tourism Anthropology* 2 (2), 108–127.

Donati, P.R. (1992) Political discourse analysis. In M. Diani and R. Eyerman (eds) *Studying Collective Action* (pp. 136–167). London: Sage.

Dubisch, J. and Winkelman, M. (2005) *Pilgrimage and Healing*. Tucson, AZ: University of Arizona Press.

Durkheim, E. (2008) *The Elementary Forms of the Religious Life*. New York: Dover.

Eagleton, T. (1981) *Walter Benjamin, or, Towards a Revolutionary Criticism*. London: Verso.

Eliade, M. (1959) *Cosmos and History: The Myth of the Eternal Return*. New York: Harper.

Fedele, A. and Blanes, R.L. (2011) *Encounters of Body and Soul in Contemporary Religious Practices: Anthropological Reflections*. New York: Berghahn Books.

Foucault, M. (1988) *Technologies of the Self*. Amherst, MA: University of Massachusetts Press.

Frazer, J.G. (2009 [1890]) *The Golden Bough: A Study of Magic and Religion*. New York: Cosimo.

Frenzel, F. and Koens, K. (2012) Slum tourism: Developments in a young field of interdisciplinary tourism research. *Tourism Geographies* 14 (2), 195–212.

Frey, N.L. (1998) *Pilgrim Stories: On and Off the Road to Santiago. Journeys Along an Ancient Way in Modern Spain*. Berkeley, CA: University of California Press.

Goethe, J.W. (1856) *Goethe's Faust*. Leipzig: Insel Verlag.

Gottlieb, A. (1982) Americans' vacations. *Annals of Tourism Research* 9 (2), 165–187.

Graburn, N.H. (1977) Tourism: The sacred journey. In V. Smith (ed.) *Hosts and Guests: The Anthropology of Tourism* (pp. 17–31). Philadelphia, PA: University of Pennsylvania Press.

Graburn, N.H. (ed.) (1983a) *The Anthropology of Tourism*. Special issue of *Annals of Tourism Research* 10 (1) .

Graburn, N.H. (1983b) *To Pray, Pay and Play: The Cultural Structure of Japanese Domestic Tourism*. Paris: Université de droit, d'économie et des sciences, Centre des hautes études touristiques.

Graburn, N.H. (2002) The ethnographic tourist. In G. Dann (ed.) *The Tourist as a Metaphor of the Social World* (pp. 19–39). Wallingford: CAB International..

Graburn, N.H. (2012) The dark is on the inside: The honne of Japanese exploratory tourists. In D. Picard and M. Robinson (eds) *Emotion in Motion: Tourism, Affect and Transformation* (pp. 49–72). London: Ashgate.

Graburn, N.H. (2013) Anthropology and couchsurfing – Variations on a theme. In D. Picard and S. Buchberger (eds) *Couchsurfing Cosmopolitanisms* (pp. 173–180). Bielefeld: Transcript Verlag.

Greenwood, S. (2009) *The Anthropology of Magic*. Oxford: Berg.

Heelas, P. (1996) *The New Age Movement*. Oxford: Blackwell.

Hegel, G.F. (1807) Independence and dependence of self-consciousness: Lordship and bondage. In *Phenomenology of Mind*. See http://www.waste.org/~roadrunner/Hegel/PhenSpirit/LordBondsman_FINAL.html (accessed July 2013).

Herskovits, M.J. (1958) *The Myth of the Negro Past*. Boston, MA: Beacon Press.

Hitchcock, M. and Teague, K. (2000) *Souvenirs: The Material Culture of Tourism*. London: Ashgate.

Hobbes, T. (1651) Of the natural condition of mankind as concerning their felicity, and misery. In *Leviathan*. In *The English Works of Thomas Hobbes of Malmesbury; Now First Collected and Edited by Sir William Molesworth, Bart.*, vol. 3. London: Bohn, 1839–45. See http://oll.libertyfund.org/title/585 (accessed July 2013).

Hollis, M. (1985) Of masks and men. In M. Carrithers, S. Collins and S. Lukes (eds) *The Category of the Person: Anthropology, Philosophy, History* (pp. 217–233). Cambridge: Cambridge University Press.

Howes, D. (ed.) (1991) *The Varieties of Sensory Experience: A Sourcebook in the Anthropology of the Senses*. Toronto: University of Toronto Press.

Jackson, M. (2012) *Lifeworlds: Essays in Existential Anthropology*. Chicago, IL: University of Chicago Press.

Lanfant, M.F. (1972) *Les théories du loisir*. Paris: Presses Universitaires de France.

Lanfant, M.F. (1995) Tourism, internationalization and identity. In M.F. Lanfant, J.B. Allcock and E.M. Bruner (eds) *International Tourism: Identity and Change* (pp. 24–43). London: Sage.

Larsen, J. and Urry, J. (2011) *The Tourist Gaze 3.0*. London: Sage.

Le Clézio, J.M.G. (1993) *Diego et Frida*. Paris: Stock.

Leite, N. and Graburn, N. (2009) Anthropological interventions in tourism studies. In M. Robinson and T. Jamal (eds) *The Sage Handbook of Tourism Studies* (pp. 35–64). London: Sage.

Lessing, T. (1919) *Geschichte als Sinngebung des Sinnlosen*. Munich: Beck.

Lett, J.W. (1983) Ludic and liminoid aspects of charter yacht tourism in the Caribbean. *Annals of Tourism Research* 10 (1), 35–56.

Lévi-Strauss, C. (1949) *Les structures elémentaires de la parenté [Elementary Systems of Kinship]*. Paris: Presses Universitaires de France.

Lévi-Strauss, C. (1974) *Structural Anthropology* (vol. 1). New York: Basic Books.

Lock, M. (1993) Cultivating the body: Anthropology and epistemologies of bodily practice and knowledge. *Annual Review of Anthropology* 22, 133–155.

Locke, J. (1964 [1778]) *Some Thoughts Concerning Education*. Hauppauge, NY: Barron's Educational Series.

MacCannell, D. (1976) *The Tourist: A New Theory of the Leisure Class*. New York: Schocken.

MacCannell, D. (2011) *The Ethics of Sightseeing*. Berkeley, CA: University of California Press.

Malinowski, B. (1939) The group and the individual in functional analysis. *American Journal of Sociology* 44 (6), 938–964.

Markus, R.A. (1989) *Saeculum: History and Society in the Theology of St Augustine*. Cambridge: Cambridge University Press.

Mauss, M. (1990 [1950]) *The Gift: The Form and Reason for Exchange in Archaic Societies* (trans. W. D. Halls). New York: Norton.

Mauss, M. (1985 [1938]) A category of the human mind: The notion of person; the notion of self. In M. Carrithers, S. Collins and S. Lukes (eds) *The Category of the Person: Anthropology, Philosophy, History* (pp. 1–25). Cambridge: Cambridge University Press.

McKevitt, C. (2000) San Giovanni Rotondo and the Shrine of Padre Pio. In J. Eade and M. Sallnow (eds) *Contesting the Sacred: The Anthropology of Pilgrimage* (2nd edn) (pp. 77–97). Urbana, IL: University of Illinois Press.

Mead, G.H. (1967) *Mind, Self, and Society: From the Standpoint of a Social Behaviorist*. Chicago, IL: University of Chicago Press.

Meyer, B. and Pels, P. (eds) (2003) *Magic and Modernity: Interfaces of Revelation and Concealment*. Palo Alto, CA: Stanford University Press.

Milbank, J. (2006) *Theology and Social Theory*. Malden: Blackwell.

Morgan, N. and Pritchard, A. (2005) On souvenirs and metonymy: Narratives of memory, metaphor and materiality. *Tourist Studies* 5 (1), 29–53.

Ortiz, F. (1947) *Cuban Counterpoint: Tobacco and Sugar* (trans. H. de Onís, introduction by B. Malinowski, prologue by H. Portell Vilá). New York: A.A. Knopf.

Pandian, J. and Parman, S. (2004) *The Making of Anthropology: The Semiotics of Self and Other in the Western Tradition*. New Delhi: Vedams eBooks.

Picard, D. (2011) *Tourism, Magic and Modernity: Cultivating the Human Garden*. New York: Berghahn Books.

Picard, D. (2012) Tourism, awe and inner journeys. In D. Picard and M. Robinson (eds) *Emotion in Motion: Tourism, Affect and Transformation* (pp. 163–186). London: Ashgate.

Picard, D. (2013) What it feels like to be a tourist: Exploring the meaningful experiences of ordinary mass tourists. *Ethnologia Europaea. Journal of European Ethnology* 43 (1) 5–18.

Picard, D. and Robinson, M. (2006) *Festivals, Tourism and Social Change: Remaking Worlds*. Clevedon: Channel View Publications.

Picard, M. (1996) Dance and drama in Bali: The making of an Indonesian art form. In A. Vickers (ed.) *Being Modern in Bali: Image and Change* (pp. 115–157). New Haven, CT: Yale University Press.

Pratt, M.L. (1992) *Imperial Eyes: Travel Writing and Transculturation*. New York: Routledge.

Price, C. (2013) Tokens of renewal: The picture postcard as a secular relic of re-creation and recreation. *Culture and Religion: An Interdisciplinary Journal* 14 (1), 111–130.

Radcliffe-Brown, A.R. (1961) *Structure and Function in Primitive Society: Essays and Addresses*. London: Taylor and Francis.

Reiss, T. (2002) *Mirages of the Selfe: Patterns of Personhood in Ancient and Early Modern Europe*. Palo Alto, CA: Stanford University Press.

Riggins, S.H. (1994) Fieldwork in the living room: An autoethnographic essay. In S.H. Riggins (ed.) *The Socialness of Things: Essays on the Socio-semiotics of Objects* (pp. 101–147). New York: Mouton de Gruyter.

Robinson, M. and Picard, D. (2009) Moments, magic and memories: Photographing tourists, tourist photographs and making worlds. In M. Robinson and D. Picard (eds) *The Framed World: Tourism, Tourists and Photography* (pp. 1–37). London: Ashgate.

Rousseau, J.J. (1762) *The Social Contract or Principles of Political Right* (trans. G.D.H. Cole). See http://www.constitution.org/jjr/socon.htm (accessed July 2013).

Sahlins, M. (1972) *Stone Age Economics*. Chicago, IL: Aldine-Atherton.

Sahlins, M. (1987) *Islands of History*. Chicago, IL: University of Chicago Press.

Salazar, N.B. and Graburn, N.H. (eds) (2014) *Tourism Imaginaries: Anthropological Approaches*. Oxford: Berghahn.

Seliinniemi, T. (2003) On holiday in the liminoid playground: Place, time, and self in tourism. In T.G. Bauer and B. McKercher (eds) *Sex and Tourism: Journeys of Romance, Love, and Lust* (pp. 19–34). London: Haworth.

Simoni, V. (2011) L'interculturalité comme justification: Sexe 'couleur locale' dans la Cuba touristique. In A. Lavanchy, F. Dervin and A. Gajardo (eds) *Anthropologies de l'interculturalité* (pp. 197–225). Paris: L'Harmattan.

Stewart, S. (1993) *On Longing: Narratives of the Miniature, the Gigantic, the Souvenir, the Collection*. Durham, NC: Duke University Press.

Tambiah, S.J. (1990) *Magic, Science and Religion and the Scope of Rationality* (vol. 1981). Cambridge: Cambridge University Press.

Taylor, C. (2007) *A Secular Age*. Cambridge, MA: Belknap Press of Harvard University Press.

Turner, V.W. (1972) The centre out there: Pilgrim's goal. *History of Religions* 12 (3): 191–230.

Turner, V.W. (1995 [1969]) *The Ritual Process: Structure and Anti-structure*. New York: Aldine.

van Gennep, A. (2004 [1909]) *The Rites of Passage*. London: Routledge.

Waldenfels, B. (2007) *The Question of the Other*. Albany, NY: State University of New York Press.

Walsh, G., Zema, D., Monahan, G. and Honan, D. (trans.) (1958) *St Augustine: City of God*. New York: Image Books/Doubleday.

Werbner, P. (2006) Understanding vernacular cosmopolitanism. *Anthropology News* 47 (5), 7–11.

Whittaker, E. (1992) The birth of the anthropological self and its career. *Ethos* 20 (2), 191–219.

Wygant, A. (eds) (2006) *The Meanings of Magic: From the Bible to Buffalo Bill*. Oxford: Berghahn.

Zigon, J. (2009) Within a range of possibilities: Morality and ethics in social life. *Ethnos* 75 (2), 251–276.

Part 1

Travels into a Past Golden Age

2 Through Other Times: The Politics of Heritage and the Past in the Catalan Pyrenees

Camila del Mármol

> *Eagles cannot span her in one flight*
> *And halt to rest, when bent on the ascent*
> *From based to rugged Pyrenean heights;*
> *And clouds, eager to hover round her top,*
> *Unless the stormy wings of fire uplift them,*
> *Stay instead at her feet*
> Jacint Verdaguer (1945 [1886])

Introduction

The Catalan Pyrenees, a mountain range in the north-east of Spain,[1] are often represented in terms of an ideal landscape embodying an imagined realm of authenticity that prevailed in a past rural life. The production of value in relation to the past (Kirshenblatt-Gimblett, 1998) is one of the strategic elements used in heritage politics geared towards both international tourists and domestic visitors. At first sight, the imagination of a romantic past, devoid of social conflicts, seems to channel here a need for a counterpoint to the disenchantments brought about by urban society (Clifford, 1989; Williams, 1985). However, initiatives that aim to conserve natural and cultural heritage are immersed in broader political considerations that also entail the production of new systems of economic activity, especially tourism.

This situation is not exclusive to the Catalan Pyrenees (Bensa & Fabre, 2001; Friedman, 1994; Kirshenblatt-Gimblett, 2001). Raymond Williams (1985) analyses Western representations of rural society as an ancient but continuing way of life that has nevertheless been considered to be ending in different periods, and so acts as a myth that conceals historical and local specificities. This representation of rurality as a golden age is still at work in some areas, and results in specific imaginaries that are prone to be mobilised

31

for the needs of tourism economies. Ferguson (1992: 80) argues that themes of rurality provide powerful metaphors as alternative moral images, in contrast to urban and industrial systems. The revaluation of the past, till recently considered a sign of backwardness and poverty, was made possible by a change in discourses and imaginaries. But 'the past' does not simply refer to a concrete historical moment, but rather to an extemporal reality representing a better time. In this symbolic way, it becomes imbued with moral values, in opposition to contemporary societies.

The aim of this chapter is to explore the specific politics of heritage and time that have driven this development in recent decades. I will argue that an idealised version of the past focusing on rural traditions and an allegedly bucolic countryside has been strategically cultivated and institutionalised in order to feed a regionalist political agenda. My interest specifically centres on the way in which a variety of institutions have fostered new types of attraction, reformulating the specific value of the Catalan Pyrenees region and its ability to supply images of the past. I refer to these new uses of the past as the establishment of a new moral order (MacCannell, 1999), within which the region is founded as the incarnation of a better past ready to be offered to visitors. I also examine how local populations have been affected by these changes and have adopted ways of appropriating and discussing the new structures. I will refer to the constitution of a new consciousness that integrates these new perspectives and at the same time disputes and opposes official heritage discourses.

I aim to discuss the emergence of heritage politics and specific uses of the past (Harrison, 2010) that arose following a series of social and economic transformations, and that gave rise to a new economy in the field of tourism. New ways of conceiving the territory and new uses for existing resources have been established within a changing economic model, which left behind agricultural and livestock exploitations to focus on the tourism sector. In the first section of this chapter I will discuss the body of legislation configuring a political agenda that allowed for the reconceptualisation of the region as a tourist attraction. It was oriented towards a reappraisal of the past, projecting a new rhetoric of heritage. In the second section I will deal with the constitution of a new moral order, resulting from the uses of the past set by the politics of heritage and time. I then examine how these moral structures have been discussed, opposed and integrated by the local population, and how it has led to the emergence of a novel social conscious-ness within local inhabitants.

Shaping Tourism in the Catalan Pyrenees

My research focuses on the county of Alt Urgell, which borders Andorra and is one of 11 counties (*comarques*) spread across the north of Catalonia in the north-east of Spain. Despite marked differences in the development of these counties, similar development of a tourism-based economy has been observed across the entire region. Over the past years, the Alt Urgell and the other 10 counties of the Catalan Pyrenees underwent a radical economic change, transforming the former local agricultural and livestock economy into a growing tourism industry. A new economic model emerged, offering new ways of conceiving the territory but using existing resources.

The Alt Urgell covers an area of nearly 1500 km^2 in the central section of the Catalan Pyrenees. It has a population of around 22,000, living in 19 municipalities.[2] The county is among the most impoverished in Catalonia in terms of employment, wealth creation and population growth (Aldomà Buixadé, 2003). Traditional agricultural and livestock activities and the use of forestry resources have been challenged and transformed through the region's integration with the international market economy. An intensive dairy production system replaced a subsistence poly-culture. However, the production quotas imposed by the European Union (EU) from the end of the 1980s led to the decline of this dairy economy.[3] As a result, the primary sector partly focused on new forms of production, such as extensive bovine livestock breeding (Aldomà Buixadé, 2003; Fillat, 2003).

This crisis, together with a series of previous transformations, marked the end of farming in the region, which was not replaced by any intensive agricultural model. Within a European context, the inability of certain rural areas to develop intensive an agricultural sector brought about their exclusion from the market and fostered a political will to seek production in other economic spheres. In the Catalan Pyrenees in recent decades, new measures, including the development of physical and social infrastructure, have been introduced to stimulate the formation of a tourism-based economy (Roigé & Frigolé, 2010; Vaccaro & Beltran, 2010a).

To understand the processes of change the Catalan Pyrenees, and specifically some of its most isolated areas, have undergone since the late 1980s, it is useful to focus on the 'forces' driving this new economic system. The role of the EU and its emphasis on building a Europe of regions (Narotzky & Smith, 2006) is one aspect that needs to be considered. The national and regional political contexts since the late 1970s are others, in particular the claims to emancipate a Catalan nationalism. In the framework of EU structural funds, tourism has been identified as a strategic development sector for rural and mountainous areas with otherwise weak economic and social infrastructure. In many ways, the conservative logic underlying EU rural development policy has determined the evolution of different rural areas throughout the countries of the EU (Stacul, 2003; Theodossopoulos, 2003). The discourses transforming the Pyrenees into a tourist attraction responded to the strategic objectives defined within the region's development plans. The latter are placing the region on a political agenda that integrates a series of common directives for the future of European rural areas. At the same time, this integration of the regions into a major social representation model is aimed at promoting a unified Europe, which finds in its rural areas a remnant of tradition and the roots of immanent identities. These new ways of considering the territory resulted in new uses of the past that will be analysed in the next section.

New Uses of the Past

The disappearance of traditional ways of rural life in the area has become a popular topic prone of discussion. The need to attract tourism and to consolidate a new model for exploiting resources has led to elements that had long disappeared being made into museum pieces. Different levels of local and national government have been committed to remaking and exhibiting the past in an official discourse. Within this discourse, new values and categories are being formed whose function is to resignify both the material context and the social relations.

I will refer in this section to the multifaceted processes that resulted in the promotion of the region as a tourist destination. The first steps occurred at the end of the 19th century with the creation of hiking clubs, prompted by both the Alpine clubs and the romantic ideals of the Renaixença[4] (Prats & Jiménez, 2006). These clubs, closely connected to Catalan bourgeois society, were oriented to the discovery and exploration of the region. A romantic vision of the Pyrenees took shape, under the auspices of famous writers and intellectuals close to the Renaixença. Within this the region was thought of as the incarnation of a heroic past, based upon medieval legends and tales (e.g. Verdaguer, 1945 [1886]). Certain areas of the Pyrenees have been used as holiday destinations since this time. In addition, the benefits and purity of the mountain air and springs have been invoked as remedies for pulmonary diseases and a wide range of health complications. In the earlier decades, these holiday and health visits to the area were constrained to the elite and were not available to the masses. Moreover, most of the Pyrenees have remained isolated areas, with rather low development and growth. The continuous loss of population during the 20th century, as a consequence of the industrial development of cities such as Barcelona, reinforced this image of isolation and backwardness. Contrary to the romantic image, there are other historical testimonies available, including those of progressive 19th-century politicians, that denounced the backwardness and poverty in which the inhabitants of the Pyrenees were forced to live (see Gascón, 2010).

During the 1960s, Catalonia experienced a tourist boom, in consonance with similar processes fostered by Franco's regime throughout Spain (Prats & Jiménez, 2006). The Catalan Pyrenees remained mostly unaffected, except for the areas where ski facilities could be developed, which did not include the Alt Urgell. Since then, however, over the last 30 years in particular, a specific process has shaped the region as a tourist area. This could be called a process of enchantment, in which negative considerations have been transformed into attractions that feed from romantic traditions and bucolic perspectives to entice visitors. The subsequent analysis of legislation and policies allows for a deeper understanding of how the elaboration of new representations and discourses was achieved. I refer to this process as the building of a new structure of attraction (MacCannell, 1999) that helped to turn the territory into a site of tourist interest.

The development of tourism – hitherto not an important economic activity – became part of local government plans and measures and the target of EU structural development funds, mostly from the 1980s on. The tragic reality of depopulation was thereby turned into an idyllic representation of seclusion, thought to be attractive to urban dwellers. Actions have included the creation of natural parks, a series of measures to preserve the urban landscape, the improvement of transport infrastructure, the recovery of old paths, the creation of ethnographic heritage, an increase in the appreciation of local festivals and celebrations, the founding of museums, and the restoration of churches and monuments considered to be of historical interest (see Frigolé, 2007, 2010; Frigolé & del Mármol, 2009; Vaccaro & Beltran, 2010a).

Tourism in the Alt Urgell region has been one of the most heavily promoted sectors by the local government in recent decades (del Mármol, 2012). This is reflected in legislation as well as in the different projects undertaken in the area. Nowadays, tourism-related activities employ most of the working population[5] (Hinojosa, 2008). A series of ideas began to take shape in the 1980s concerning the preservation of natural mountain areas, in opposition to previous processes of urban speculation under Franco's regime (Alsina et al., 1996). In this context, the first Comunitat de Treball del Pirineu (Pyrenees Working Committee) was founded under the auspices of the European Council. The aim of these committees was to promote relationships between the French, Spanish and Andorran Pyrenees. A group of intellectuals, politicians and important stakeholders from the area got together to encourage different projects, one of which was the MAB-6[6] programme, run by the United Nations Educational, Scientific and Cultural Organization (UNESCO), the first systematic research programme launched in the area. Hence, a series of issues that affect most mountainous areas were identified and a series of precepts were laid down to foster new ways of conceiving the region. This was a small 'body of doctrine', in the words of one of its main promoters, which gave rise to a long series of subsequent policies and initiatives.[7]

The Spanish constitution of 1978 featured a specific article concerning the special treatment that mountain regions deserve (Campillo & Villaró, 1988). The Mountain Agriculture Law was drawn up in 1982, followed a year later by Law 2/1983, for high mountain regions,[8] the first to be passed by the Generalitat de Catalunya specifically targeted at the territories of the Catalan Pyrenees. The aim was to implement a development policy that would help to mitigate the consequences of what was described as 'a current process of depopulation and systematic degradation', the most evident signs of which were 'a low per capita income level and human and cultural impoverishment'.[9] Unlike other depressed zones in the Catalan territory, this law stipulates that the high mountain regions have a 'production potential' that consists of resources that had not been 'rationally' exploited until then: livestock farming, forestry resources and tourism. This is probably one of the first legal instruments to reflect a new outlook, one which contemplates the differentiated existence of 'mountain zones', attaching new values and specific development conditions to them. Special protected-area status for mountain regions is a common feature of Spanish state legislation and it is also present in EU directives.

In 1988, the European Economic Community commissioned a report, *The Future of Rural Society*, which is seen as the first step towards rural development in Europe. This document analyses the characteristics of European rural areas and their evolution over several decades. It sets out the reduction in agriculture's relative economic importance, starting mainly during the 1970s, and highlights the situation in the Mediterranean regions adversely affected by poor agricultural structures and 'structural backwardness' (European Commission, 1988: 22–23). Different strategies were proposed to deal with the standard problems confronting the rural areas, one of them being the 'protection of the environment and development of the countryside' in order to promote the development of areas 'providing recreation and leisure for the city-dwellers' (European Commission, 1988: 32). The report also highlights the need to defend 'the cultural heritage (architecture, folklore, etc.).... Not only in its own right but also because in many areas it is the key to the development of tourism' (European Commission, 1988: 40).

The concept of heritage here parallels its inflationary use in global discourses (Heinich, 2009), as a tool that underlies the wider process of creating a new tourism destination. Thus, tourism and heritage go hand in hand, and must be considered to constitute a twofold reality.

The Leader programme (Liaison entre Activités de Développement de l'Économie Rurale), a European Commission initiative that has been operating since 1991, aims to promote development in rural areas that have suffered depopulation and agricultural crisis. The goal is to foster public and private initiatives that boost endogenous development, cover relatively small geographical areas and promote the participation of local inhabitants (Luzón & Pi, 1999). These administrative instruments reflect the new way of conceiving the territory as heritage, and aim to protect it from degradation. Although this programme is not exclusively directed at promoting tourism, most of the projects have focused on this area (Luzón & Pi, 1999).

Another important line of analysis for understanding the region's economic orientation in recent decades is the establishment of natural parks and the declaration of protected areas. The concept of natural heritage underlying these declarations in Catalonia has been analysed by various authors (Frigolé, 2010; Roigé & Estrada, 2010; Vaccaro & Beltran, 2009, 2010a, 2010b). In 1983, the Catalan government founded the Parc Natural del Cadí-Moixeró,[10] which covers an area of 41,060 hectares and runs through four municipalities of the Alt Urgell, as well as another four in Berguedà and Cerdanya. Law 12/1985, on natural spaces,[11] was passed by the Catalan parliament and sets out the Pla d'espais d'interés natural (PEIN; Plan for spaces of natural interest). This is a planning instrument for all of the territory of Catalonia. Another of the more important protected areas in the Alt Urgell region is the Parc Natural de l'Alt Pirineu, established in 2003. This is the largest natural park in Catalonia, covering 69,850 hectares, and includes territories in Pallars Sobirà and the north of Alt Urgell.

This set of policies and legislation was followed by specific measures, from the 1990s onwards, directly aimed at protecting and restoring cultural heritage. This was due to a transformation in the local government's idea of cultural management, which had hitherto focused on promoting the arts, cinema and festivals. The first measures to preserve heritage were implemented just a few years after the conservation of the area's natural resources had started. They included initiatives such as the 1997 project to create the Romanesque Route with the support of the European Union's Interreg Programme.[12] Another project promoted by the Consell Comarcal of l'Alt Urgell (the regional council) focused on the Cathar past of some of the villages in the region (see del Mármol, 2006) and echoed similar processes that had been spreading through the south of France (García &

Genieys, 2005). The idea was to hold events that would commemorate the relation between some villages' medieval past and the Cathar heresy, which was widespread throughout southern France during the 11th, 12th and 13th centuries.

One of the most important initiatives undertaken by the Consell Comarcal, and also one of its first projects, was the Trade of the Past Route (Ruta dels oficis d'Ahir). The Route takes in a series of museums that revive different trades that are considered 'traditional' and which all disappeared during the 20th century: the Loggers Museum (Museu dels Raiers), the Oliana's Ice Well (Pou de Gel d'Oliana), the Flourmill of Trobada (Farinera de la Trobada), the Mountain Vine and Wine Museum (Museu de la Vinya i del Vi de Muntanya), the Wool Fabric (Fàbrica de Llanes d'Arsèguel) and the Turpentine-Makers Museum (see Frigolé, 2005). The last is a perfect example of the idealisation of past activities. In it, the visitor can find long accounts of women turpentine-makers – of their work, the process of herb collection and turpentine production, as well as of their long trips across the mountains in order to sell their products in other regions of Catalonia. These women are presented as hallmarks of an ancient peasant society in which courage, solidarity and an ethic of hard work prevailed. The romanticised version of old rural society allow for a moral account of its features.

This cluster of policies and developmental plans has resulted in a new image for the Catalan Pyrenees and a novel orientation of the economic system, driven mainly by what could be referred to as heritage creation processes or 'heritagisation' (e.g. Bendix, 2009; Davallon, 2006; Roigé & Frigolé, 2010). With this in mind, I highlight here the complex processes that have brought about a new economic and social reality in the region; these include the mobilisation and production of resources in the context of a tourism-based model. The politics of heritage and time has been one of the main tools in this transformation and can be traced back in the political and juridical discourse. I argue that this process was necessary in order to mark the region as a tourist attraction, offering social representations and images from which to build a sightseeing destination.

We can refer to different heritage processes that illustrate these new phenomena leading to the resignification of resources. A case in point is the restoration of local churches in the Valley of la Vansa and Tuixent. When I first visited the valley in 2005, several churches from different historical periods were being restored. It was not just about maintenance works, but also about deeper interventions resulting in the resignification of the buildings. Churches were once centres of social life and worked as binding spaces for the community. The local population was directly responsible for keeping the buildings in good condition, amidst other communal work that was periodically done. The years of depopulation, however, saw the abandonment of many local churches, especially in the more isolated villages. From the 1980s on, and especially during the 1990s, many villages attracted a new kind of resident, in many cases people buying a second home but also new inhabitants looking for settlement in the countryside. Even though the area was and still is severely underpopulated, these new realities involved the restoration of houses and in general the development of civil infrastructure in the villages (roads, sewage systems, lighting, etc.). Many houses and buildings were rebuilt following new standards of beauty that were mainly oriented towards an ideal rurality. Little by little, these new aesthetic standards, bringing back an allegedly ancient appearance to the villages, were incorporated within local urban legislation governing building works. In the Valley of la Vansa and Tuixent, the restoration of churches was supported by various funds, primarily the Leader programme. Several institutions were held responsible for the restoration works, such as the Urgell Diocese – the proprietors of the churches – as well as different local and regional governments, leading to local people condemning their loss of power and control over the buildings. For many experts working on the restoration works, the churches were no longer considered as places of local communion and religiosity, but rather as heritage. They came to be perceived as historical sites, of patrimonial value, leaving aside other previous meanings.

The elements of the former local systems of production have become isolated and reinterpreted within the new social and economic contexts. In this regard, 'heritage' can be thought of as a semantic converter device, by which elements from the past that were considered obsolete are re-interpreted by means of exhibition processes that supply them with new values. Several authors highlight diverse ways in which heritage works, by isolating the object or practice from its former context, giving way for the addition of a set of whole new meanings (e.g. Kirshenblatt-Gimblett, 2006; Smith, 2006). In these processes, the elements are deprived of different meanings to nullify their multivocality and retain a unique interpretation. According to Narotzky (2004: 130), heritage processes generate reifications of aspects of the past and allow elements to be presented without the social relations that produced them. Hence, it can be considered that the production of heritage is a process of decontextualisation, which works by overshadowing the intrinsic production conditions.

For a better understanding of the production of meaning related to heritage politics, we can think of heritage as a representation of the past: a symbol. A sign has the specific ability of signifying, while a symbol represents – it takes the place of something else and evokes it (Benveniste, 1977). An old, rusty, misshapen vessel for storing herbs that is exhibited in a local museum extends its meaning through the patina that relates it to a wider past. It becomes worthy of being exhibited as it is, in itself, a representation of the past. According to Barthes's (1957) analysis of the production of the myth, the past can be thought of as being seized by heritage and used as an object, from which a new signification process sprouts. Heritage is, then, a symbol that evokes an image of the past, which is remade in the process. The whole region is produced as an isolated place that has remained untouched by the distorting influence of modern history. If the past is a foreign country (Lowenthal, 1985), then some regions are being shaped as the materialisation of that past, a sort of Neverland.

Heritage discourses often make use of an enchanted imaginary related to romantic visions of the past. Nostalgia and collage are central assets in heritage policies, as well as being central to the production and reproduction of images in post-capitalist societies (Harvey, 1990). I refer to imagined nostalgias (Appadurai, 1996), the longing for idealised representations of a world we have never inhabited. As Clifford (1989) has pointed out, there is a pastoral version of the salvage paradigm, a pervasive ideological complex that reflects a desire to reach more authentic realities situated somewhere else. Whether this is an exotic land or a traditional rural setting is a matter of context. But rurality needs to be built out of the contemporary situation of rural territories, producing an image of an eternal past. A bewitching incarnation of the past in a specific place is intended to seduce urban inhabitants out from their daily life. But it also imposes a set of new values with which the local population has to cope.

The impact on the region of the above measures has been manifold. Several areas of social life have been deeply affected. This can be observed, for example, in natural parks, in that they limit human activities in order to produce a landscape of wild nature. The dramatic decrease in intensive agriculture and livestock breeding has meant the abandonment of cultivated land, leaving room for the forests to expand. The above-mentioned legislation had effects also at the urban level, principally in limiting the construction of housing. In the case of the small villages, the aim was to protect the 'old' and 'traditional' aspects of rural settlements, though this restricted the possibilities of widening old houses, for example, and increased construction costs because of the new requirement to use 'traditional' materials such as stone. In the same vein, new projects for restoring heritage buildings upstaged former proposals, such as the construction of social housing.

The structure of attraction is built upon an image of the past, which marks the direction of local development. It supposed a moral involvement with public representations of the past, as an idealised region inhabited by a better society. To understand the role of the past as an authoritative element, the new meanings of this concept in contemporary societies have to be considered, especially regarding its seductive character. The production of a place that is worth visiting is not just about promoting beauty; the past, represented as traditional ways of life and wild landscapes, offers a web of dense meanings that shroud territories with mystery. This process entails recovering a specific past, selecting features and creating an idealised image that is not always in accordance with other uses of the past in the local context.

The tourism-focused local economy now promotes a rural world that is regarded mainly as a residential, recreational and landscape area. Specific policies to develop tourism are being encouraged in rural areas all over Europe, where the former economic and social structures have been transformed dramatically or have disappeared. An alternative way of visualising the region and exploiting local resources is emerging within a new economic model. Vaccaro and Beltran (2007) argue that the new meanings of rurality are related to the bond established between collective imaginaries and new markets. These imaginaries are related to different discourses, mostly focusing on bucolic ideas of the past and essentialist interpretations of nature. The new structure of attraction projects a nostalgic imaginary and is designed particularly to attract the urban middle classes. An important tool has been the implementation of a rhetoric of heritage, which leads to the resignification of several aspects of social reality as 'patrimony'. In this sense, I argued that the past, or at least its newly idealised version, is the main key to build the structure of attraction, offering a new way to interpret the region. This, in turn, supposed the implementation of a new moral order, within which an idealised past was established as the centre point of the discourses of attraction. In the next section I will dwell on these processes and discuss how they have affected local populations.

Engaging with the Past

The outline of a new moral order of attraction, defined in this region through the constitution of a new political and legal framework that supports the reorientation of the economic system, has been expressed mainly in the shaping and exhibition of a specific past. This process has dislocated previous local considerations about the past and the way people build on it. The new uses of the past are based on a moral structure that projects a definition of aspects of social reality and elements of material culture that are suitable for protection, reappraisal and exhibition. Wider aspects of local culture, ranging from its social relations and production system to cultural ties with nature, have been thoroughly examined to create a new moral order that aims to define appropriate ways with which to engage modern realities. Thus, these processes have important repercussions at different levels of social and cultural relations, resulting in a conflictive equilibrium that is continuously in a state of jeopardy.

The moral order acts in different ways, defining new imaginaries within which the region can be reconsidered but also stipulating new ways of relating to the resources available, offering local inhabitants a shared symbolic ground from where to build social relations (Picard, 2010). On the one hand, the territory is shaped to incarnate the essence of a better past, in order to attract visitors. That results in the creation of museums that reappraise aspects of the past, in the preservation of 'traditional' architecture, as well as in the conservation of a pristine nature, and so on. But, on the other hand, it also has specific consequences in the way the locality is being produced and represented (Appadurai, 1996). The past has turned into a reference from where to build new moral structures that directly affect people's lives.

Building on Zigon's (2009) discussion of concepts of morality and the complicated relations established between social groups, individuals and institutions, the processes in the Catalan Pyrenees can be described as deliberate transformations of the moral structure. Zigon (2009: 258) refers to three aspects of morality, constituted respectively by institutions, public discourses and embodied dispositions. In the case analysed here, it was mostly an institutional transformation of moral values that acted by rendering new symbolisms of rurality and shaping the territory as a tourist attraction. In this section I will discuss the way these various levels of morality influence and inform each other, in an attempt to reach a clear understanding of the processes involved in the restructuring of moral orders.

My aim is to approach the different ways in which individual aspects of morality engaged with the institutional models available. My interest focuses on how this transformation impacts at a local level, working on the different ways people coped with social and political transformations. If the territory became the incarnation of a better past, individuals were forced to adhere to this new image. This symbolic construction results in specific processes that exclude the local population from the management of different aspects of their social life and environment. The conservation of nature as a pristine landscape untouched by human labour means the exclusion of the local population from its administration. Similarly, the new urban measures oriented to preserve an ideal version of rural towns limits people's opportunities to refine their homes or construct new one on their own land. Although state regulation of social life is by no means a new phenomenon (Stacul, 2003), I argue that the new structures of attraction act as constrictions in rural settings.

Governments and local populations do not usually question actions and discourses about the preservation of heritage. Guillaume (1990) refers to the 'naturalisation' of heritage, in its both cultural and natural scope; it becomes internalised and joins new ways of framing social realities. Nonetheless, specific policies and legislation that have been influenced by these discourses are controversial, including the creation of natural parks, urban measures designed to conserve landscapes and the opening of new museums. It is thus important to identify the intrinsic political character of heritage discourses, and the way they are adopted, rejected or assumed by the local population. The aim is to find ways to overcome the isolation of notions of heritage, to break away from constructed myths and to reposition the discourse within the specific conditions of production and circulation.

The establishment of visions of the past as heritage has set new limits to the interpretation of reality. The appraisal processes within heritage politics are powerful ways of instituting an official monopoly over people's lives and histories. Likewise, the processes involved in the official declaration of heritage should be highlighted (both by international institutions, such as UNESCO, and by local governments), as it is usually these that transfer local control over certain elements to non-local administrations (see Kirshenblatt-Gimblett, 2006). As examples, several projects can be cited that have led to the loss of local prerogatives over, for example, the restoration of old churches, due to official declarations that resulted in the surrendering of control over the buildings and, perhaps more controversially, the monopoly that natural parks and related organisations have over a variety of former local ways of engaging with the environment.

In my field studies I met people in their late 60s who recalled a different view of the past: 'Before, things were not so protected'.[13] This statement is more than a simple consideration: it represents a radical distinction in the conceptualisation of the past. Furthermore, it reminds us that not everyone has the same access to the production of authoritative discourses about the past. The analysis should not be simplified by focusing on dominant processes that institute new social realities; inequalities and differences in the dynamic of power, which require a detailed knowledge of the social structure of the local population, should also be referred to.

The politics of heritage and time have aroused both rejection and complacency. They have become fields prone to clashes and confrontations, in which different sectors of society make efforts to impose diverse perspectives and political interests. An analysis of these processes can shed light on the ways in which different administrations operate, and how this affects the production of social practices and representations. Furthermore, this can lead to discussions on the construction of a new moral order, based on the new uses of the past.

Therefore, the defining potential of the politics of heritage and time arouses different reactions. As mentioned above, many of the official practices are aimed at the promotion of a new economic, tourism-based model that builds on the past as a producer of value in the present. In my fieldwork, I could identify two major threads in people's discourses. Firstly, there has been a considerable increase in criticism and debates that attempt to examine and reject these new processes. Secondly, a considerable level of consensus has been found, with official practices being mainly accepted and even internalised and embodied.

First, I will dwell on the criticism and debates related to new uses of the past within the politics of heritage. In this respect, the new rhetoric about the past might be experienced as paradoxical. When older ways of life, which are now 'protected', were at risk of disappearing, institutional help was lacking and support to overcome the economic crisis never arrived. This experience of oblivion is often juxtaposed with the recent initiatives that foster the idealisation of traditional life. People who work in 'traditional trades' that were not 'protected' until they were properly extinct might experience these situations as deeply contradictory. Several complaints focus on the institutional emphasis on celebrating the past without providing solutions for current problems, considering that the actions taken do not respond properly to current difficulties. Many local inhabitants do not easily acknowledge the retrieval of the past as an appropriate measure for combating depopulation and the lack of business opportunities. The expression 'we cannot live from the past'[14] might be heard in different situations, mostly in criticism of the considerable amount of money invested in promoting heritage politics. In addition, some people are angry about the restrictions accompanying natural parks. An older woman, a farm owner, expressed her grievance as she could not take advantage of the woods on her land due to institutional regulations: 'It's not fair – we are no longer masters of our lands',[15] she told me. The criticism of new uses of nature actually reflects tension with the politics of heritage and time.

Moreover, some conflicts have arisen in relation to the selection of specific versions of the past on which there is no consensus.[16] Many situations have caused such struggles, in which sectors of the local population oppose and reject the official versions of the past, linked to specific institutional plans and actions. Examples include complaints about trades that have been condemned to oblivion, while others that received less praise before are currently being transformed into museum themes. In addition, tension can arise about the silence that looms over relatively recent events that were directly experienced by large sectors of the local population, such as the Civil War and the Franco dictatorship. The institutional tendency towards the preservation and celebration of the past does not affect crucial events in recent history that have an important place in people's memory, configuring an official history of silence (Narotzky, 2004). We should recognise within these criticisms people's manoeuvring to maintain control of the symbolic means of producing their own past and strategies to prevent the dispossession of key elements of cultural production. These kinds of critiques are specifically directed at a version of the past, but could be analysed as broader complaints that are being expressed in the hegemonic idiom of heritage politics.

One night, over beers in a crowded bar in la Seu d'Urgell, a middle-aged man who was aware of my research, as he put it, 'on the Pyrenean specimens', told me in a philosophical tone accentuated by alcohol that 'if all this', with a broad sweep of his arm to indicate the whole county, 'is a reservation, Tuixent is a bastion'.[17] Criticism of the new model is not rare, and the fear that the Pyrenees region is being turned into what several locals and non-locals refer to as a theme park is expressed regardless of whether or not they are associated with tourism. Nevertheless, the conversion of these judgements into wider ideological and political confrontation is difficult to achieve, since it would be contrary to what has become, in certain ways, a hegemonic dimension of social reality. Organising coherent criticism of the new tourism-based economy would go against what it has already turned into hegemonic values.

But not everything is criticism. The hegemonic character gained by the politics of heritage and time in recent years reveals itself when expressed in different contexts, as resources to achieve several goals. In addition to old trades being made into museum pieces, festivals from the past are being retrieved and restaged, houses are being decorated following rules allegedly from the past, and old objects are being recovered from junk rooms. Reference to the past has been consolidated as a legitimation device in multiple contexts. Old is fashionable. Even conflicts that are clearly a result of contemporary situations are in many cases expressed in the idiomatic uses of the past. Hegemonic processes are essentially dialectics, since they are burdened with the ferment of criticism and contradiction. Nonetheless, as they are hegemonic, they have to be assimilated and experienced as a part of social reality; they need to become integrated and at the same time to be active engineers of new moral orders.

During my fieldwork, I was able to record several examples of this longing for a traditional rural life that went beyond official discourses of the past:

the treatment of private houses as museums, daily speeches legitimating old practices and ways of doing things, the use of old recipes, the recovery of lost paths through the woods, and so on (and on). Many people who live in or who are frequent visitors to the area quickly gain vast knowledge about older times. Comments on how old cooking methods gave food a better taste, on the happiness of festivals after long hours of work and on the beauty of the landscape when it was cultivated rather than left as woods are not just official discourses promoted in institutional contexts such as museums. Rather, these opinions are frequently expressed in bars and at family meals, during daily routines, and are recalled by different sectors of the population. In the case of elderly people, the new relevance of the past is confronted with the memories of their experienced history, in which the territory was considered to be abandoned and to have fallen into neglect. In many cases, the appraisal of the past reaches high levels of consensus due to its ability to empower old inhabitants, who can relate their experiences of these former ways of life. Jaumet, who was in his early 80s, told me about old songs that were sung in the village and that were forgotten for decades until new attempts were made to recover traditional music. Every time he is asked to sing them again, he remembers the time when no one was interested: 'This country used to be so lonely...',[18] he said in a weary tone of voice. Official uses of the past within the politics of heritage and time became hegemonic not just as a consequence of institutional discourses but also because, beyond criticism, they can be thought of as ways to thwart the oblivion to which the territory had previously been condemned.

The adoption of ideological frames of reference promoted by institutional practices in the field of heritage works as a strategy for asserting social power (Woost, 1993). Thus, the configuration of hegemonies is key to understanding the interrelation between different levels or aspects of moralities and how they interact to construct a new social order. In the Catalan Pyrenees, a variety of practices that fluctuate between negotiation and refusal can be identified, giving rise to different uses of the past.

At the intersection of these opposite reactions to contemporary modes of relation to the past, the tensions involved in the definition of new moral orders can be recognised. As Zigon (2009: 271) stressed, the concept of morality should not be limited to the classical classification of bad and good, but can also 'refer to the way people and institutions are able to existentially be in the social world comfortably'. In this sense, pressures that result in the configuration of a new image for the territory can be seen as the result of cultural changes in the administration of the politics of heritage and time. While many activities in the field of heritage promote suspicion, distrust and even denial, other are supported and further incentivised by different sectors of the local population. I do not refer to a radical opposition dividing the social structure, but rather to diverse realignments in which the same people can be found defending contradictory discourses, depending on the context. In the centre of these complex processes the configuring of a new moral order is to be found.

Conclusion

In recent years, policies and developmental plans have been implemented in the Catalan Pyrenees triggering a new tourism-based economy. An extensive political, legal and administrative corpus has been created that covers different regions in which a generalist and inclusive perspective is applied. I have argued that the promotion of a politics of heritage and time was crucial for the definition of a new productive system, mainly designed to attract urban consumers.

These processes are the outcome of trends that affect the Alt Urgell, but also the broader area of the Catalan Pyrenees. This chapter has discussed the politics of heritage and time that has developed in the past decades, as a result of the changing political, economic and social context. The way the region has been oriented towards a rural past, focusing on traditions and images of wild nature, has changed cultural imaginaries, affected social relationships and given rise to a new moral order.

The new moral regime defines an appropriate way of relating to the past, which has been fostered by institutional discourses but which has also involved conflicting processes and resulted in new social hegemonies. Heritage processes have strengthened new practices, social discourses, values and ideas about the past and the future. They have boosted new economic models and discussion. Ethnographic examples help to explain the multiple processes that converge when material conditions are redesigned, and allow us to acknowledge the interconnectedness of these conditions and local culture.

Heritage discourses and practices benefit from social legitimacy generated at global level, which facilitates its adoption by local populations. This legitimacy is in turn transferred to a new economic model. Nevertheless, I have also focused on the conflicts that arise in the intersecting aspects of moralities, defined as the tensions between social groups, institutions and individuals that result in the production of new consciousness and practices. I have referred to these processes as the constitution of a new moral order that is mobilised in the realm of tourism.

Notes

(1) My research in the Catalan Pyrenees dates back to 2005, when I started long-term ethnographic fieldwork in the region, involving three stays over a period of 14 months. The fieldwork was the basis for a PhD dissertation submitted in 2010. This study was carried out as part of a project entitled 'Patrimonio y redefinición de la ruralidad. Nuevos usos del patrimonio local', which was funded by the Spanish Ministry of Education and Science and the FEDER Programme (CSO2011-29413). I thank Joan Frigolé for his many insights, and especially David Picard for his valuable inputs and for throwing new light in my research.

(2) Source: Institut d'Estadística de Catalunya, 2008 (http://www.idescat.es).

(3) From 1992, the year in which the quotas for milk production were applied in Spain, to 2010, the number milk farms in the region fell by 86% (Observatori de la Llet, 2010).

(4) Catalan cultural movement oriented to the restoration of Catalan culture and language. It flourished throughout the second half of the 19th century and was related to the ideals of romanticism.

(5) In 2012, 70.7% of the Alt Urgell working population was employed in the service industry, especially tourism-related activities. Source: Institut d'Estadística de Catalunya.

(6) The UNESCO Man and the Biosphere (MAB) Programme is an intergovernmental scientific programme that proposes an interdisciplinary research agenda and capacity building that targets the ecological, social and economic dimensions of biodiversity loss.

(7) During my fieldwork, I interviewed several Catalan politicians whose activities have been influential in the Pyrenees.

(8) Llei 2/1983, de 9 de març, d'alta muntanya (DOGC 312, de 16/03/1983).

(9) *Ibid.*

(10) Decret 353/1983, de 15 de juliol, de declaració del Parc Natural del Cadí-Moixeró (DOGC 357, 24/09/1983).

(11) Llei 12/1985 de 13 de juny, d'espais naturals (DOGC 556, 28/06/1985).

(12) An EU-funded programme that helps Europe's regions to form partnerships and work together on common projects.

(13) 'Abans les coses no es guardaven tant' (fieldnotes).

(14) 'No podem viure del passat' (fieldnotes).

(15) 'No és just, ja no som amos de les nostres terres' (fieldnotes).

(16) In other works I have analysed situations that exemplify these positions, such as the struggles around the recovery of the Cathar past of the different villages (see above) and conflicts caused by the restoration of Romanesque churches (del Mármol, 2010). Joan Frigolé has conducted long-term research on the creation of museums (Frigolé, 2005) and related topics.

(17) 'Si tota això és una reserva, Tuixent és un reducte' (fieldnotes).

(18) 'Aquest país va estar tan sol…' (fieldnotes).

References

Aldomà Buixadé, I. (2003) Evolució del model econòmic de la muntanya. *Espais Etno-gràfics, La muntanya a Catalunya, Revista del Departament de Política Territorial i Obres Públiques* 49, 66–73.

Alsina i Cases, G., García Osuna, M. and Pérez López, R. (1996) Els GAP: Fruit d'una època. Actuacions per a la defensa de l'Alt Pirineu. *Treballs de la Societat Catalana de Geografia* 42, 9–36.

Applauder, A. (1996) *Modernity at Large: Cultural Dimensions of Globalization*. Minneapolis, MN: University of Minnesota Press.

Barthes, R. (1957) *Mythologies*. Paris: Éditions du Seuil.

Bendix, R. (2009) Heritage between economy and politics. An assessment from the perspective of cultural anthropology. In L. Smith and N. Akawaga (eds) *Intangible Heritage* (pp. 253–269). London: Routledge.

Bensa, A. and Fabre, D. (eds) (2001) *Une histoire à soi. Figurations du passé et localités*. Paris: Édtions de la Maison des Sciences de l'Homme.

Benveniste, E. (1977) *Problemas de lingüística general II*. Buenos Aires: Siglo XXI.

Campillo, X. and Villaró, A. (1988) Introducció al programa MAB-6 Alt Pirineu: L'area d'estudi. *Documents d'Anàlisi Geogràfica* 12, 7–19.

Clifford, J. (1989) The Others: Beyond the 'salvage' paradigm. *Third Text: Third World Perspectives on Contemporary Art and Culture* 6, 73–77.

Davallon, J. (2006) *Le don du patrimoine: Une approche communicationnelle de la patrimonialisation*. Paris: Hermès Sciences-Lavoisier.

del Mármol, C. (2006) Escenificando tradiciones. Una aproximación a los usos del pasado cátaro en los pirineos catalanes. In J. Frigolé and X. Roigé (eds) *Globalización y localidad. Perspectiva etnográfica* (pp. 121–144). Barcelona: Publicacions i Edicions de la Universitat de Barcelona.

del Mármol, C. (2010) Iglesias: De la liturgia a la exhibición. Los procesos de patrimonialización en un valle del Pirineo Catalán. In C. del Mármol, J. Frigolé and S. Narotzky (eds) *Los Lindes del patrimonio: Consumo y valores del pasado* (pp. 335–354). Barcelona: Icaria.

del Mármol, C. (2012) *Pasados locales, políticas globales. Los procesos de patrimonialización en un valle del Pirineo catalán*. Valencia: Editorial Germanías AVA.

European Commission (1988) *Future of the Rural Society*. Commission communication transmitted to the Council and to the European Parliament on 29 July 1988. COM(88) 501 final 1988. *Bulletin of the European Communities*, supplement 4/88.

Ferguson, J. (1992) The country and the city on the copperbelt. *Cultural Anthropology* 7 (1), 80–92.

Fillat, F. (2003) La intensificació ramadera i l'abandó, dues tendències dels Pirineus espanyols al començament del segle XXI. *Espais Monogràfics, La Muntanya a Catalunya, Revista del departament de Política territorial i Obres Públiques* 49, 8–14.

Friedman, J. (1994) *Cultural Identity and Global Process*. London: Sage.

Frigolé, J. (2005) *Dones que anaven pel món. Estudi etnogràfic de les trementinaires de la Vall de la Vansa i Tuixent (Alt Urgell)*. Barcelona: Generalitat de Catalunya.

Frigolé, J. (2007) Producció cultural de lloc, memòria i terciarització de l'economia en una vall del Prepirineu. *Revista d'Etnologia de Catalunya* 30, 70–80.

Frigolé, J. (2010) Rusticity, wild flora and fauna patterns, and identity in a valley of Cadí. In I. Vaccaro and O. Beltran (eds) *Social and Ecological History of the Pyrenees: State, Market, and Landscape*. Walknut Creek, CA: Left Coast Press.

Frigolé, J. and del Mármol, C. (2009) Localization of global discourses: Cultural heritage, nature, and authenticity in the Catalan Pyrenees. *Revue du Modys: En cours* 11, 45–52.

García, M.C. and Genieys, W. (2005) *L'invention du Pays Cathare: Essai sur la constitution d'un territoire imaginé*. Paris: L'Harmattan.

Gascón, C. (2010) *Comarques oblidades. Josep Zulueta i el Pirineu l'any 1890*. La Seu d'Urgell: Edicions Salòria.

Guillaume, M. (1990) Inventions et stratégies du patrimoine. In H. Jeudy (dir.) *Patrimoines en folie* (pp. 13–20). París: Éditions de la Maison des Sciences de l'Homme.

Harrison, R. (2010) *Understanding the Politics of Heritage*. Manchester: Manchester University Press.

Harvey, D. (1990) *The Condition of Postmodernity: An Enquiry into the Origins of Cultural Change*. Oxford: Blackwell.

Heinich, N. (2009) *La fabrique du patrimoine: De la cathédrale à la petite cuillère*. Paris: Maison des Sciences de l'Homme.

Hinojosa, A. (2008) *Estudi estadístic dels municipis de l'Alt Urgell*. Barcelona: Universitat Politècnica de Catalunya.

Kirshenblatt-Gimblett, B. (1998) *Destination Culture: Tourism, Museums, and Heritage*. Berkeley, CA: University of California Press.

Kirshenblatt-Gimblett, B. (2001) La cultura de les destinacions: Teoritzar el patrimoni. *Revista d'Etnologia de Catalunya* 19, 44–61.

Kirshenblatt-Gimblett, B. (2006) World heritage and cultural economics. In I. Karp, A. Kratz, L. Szwaja and T. Ybarra-Frausto (eds) *Museum Frictions: Public Cultures/Global Transformations* (pp. 161–202). Durham, NC: Duke University Press.

Lowenthal, D. (1985) *The Past is a Foreign Country*. Cambridge: Cambridge University Press.

Luzón, J.L. and Pi, C. (1999) La iniciativa comunitaria Leader de desarrollo rural en Europa: La experiencia de Catalunya. *Revista Econômica do Nordeste* 30 (2), 162–177.

MacCannell, D. (1999) *The Tourist: A New Theory of the Leisure Class*. Berkeley, CA: University of California Press.

Narotzky, S. (2004) Una historia necesaria: Ética, política y responsabilidad en la práctica antropológica. *Relaciones* 25 (98), 109–145.

Narotzky, S. and Smith, G. (2006) *Immediate Struggles: People, Power, and Place in Rural Spain*. Berkeley, CA: University of California Press.

Observatori de la Llet (2010) *Informe anual: Evolució de nombre d'explotacions a Catalunya per comarques, 2000–2010*. Informe núm. 23/10. Barcelona: Departament d'Agricultura, Alimentació i Acció Rural, Generalitat de Catalunya.

Picard, D. (2010) 'Being a model for the world': performing Creoleness is La Réunion. *Social Anthropology* 18 (3), 302–315.

Prats, L. and Jiménez, S. (2006) El turismo en Catalunya: Evolución histórica y retos de futuro. *A Pasos: Revista de Turismo y Patrimonio Cultural* 4 (2), 153–174.

Roigé, X. and Estrada, F. (2010) Socio-economic use of cultural heritage in a natural park: The Montseny mountains (Catalonia). In X. Roigé and J. Frigolé (eds) *Constructing Cultural and Natural Heritage: Parks, Museums and Rural Heritage* (pp. 77–90). Girona: ICRPC Llibres.

Roigé, X. and Frigolé J. (eds) (2010) *Constructing Cultural and Natural Heritage: Parks, Museums and Rural Heritage*. Girona: ICRPC Llibres.

Smith, L. (2006) *Uses of Heritage*. London: Routledge.

Stacul, J. (2003) *The Bounded Field: Localism and Local Identity in an Italian Alpine Valley*. New York: Berghahn Books.

Theodossopoulos, D. (2003) *Troubles with Turtles: Cultural Understandings of the Environment on a Greek Island*. New York: Berghahn Books.

Vaccaro, I. and Beltran, O. (2007) Consuming space, nature and culture: Patrimonial discussions in the hyper-modern era. *Journal of Tourism Geographies* 9 (3), 254–274.

Vaccaro, I. and Beltran, O. (2009) Livestock versus 'wild beasts': The contradictions of the natural patrimonialization of the Pyrenees. *Geographical Review* 99 (4), 499–516.

Vaccaro, I. and Beltran, O. (eds) (2010a) *Social and Ecological History of the Pyrenees: State, Market, and Landscape*. Walknut Creek, CA: Left Coast Press.

Vaccaro, I. and Beltran, O. (2010b) From scenic beauty to biodiversity. The patrimonialization of nature in the Pallars Sobirà (Catalan Pyrenees). In X. Roigé and J. Frigolé (eds) *Constructing Cultural and Natural Heritage: Parks, Museums and Rural Heritage* (pp. 63–74). Girona: ICRPC Llibres.

Verdaguer, J. (1945 [1886]) *Canigó*. Vic: Llibreria Sala.

Williams, R. (1985) *The Country and the City*. London: Hogarth Press.

Woost, M. (1993) Nationalizing the local past in Sri Lanka: Histories of nation and development in a Sinhalese village. *American Ethnologist* 20 (3), 502–521.

Zigon, J. (2009) Within a range of possibilities: Morality and ethics in social life. *Ethnos* 74 (2), 251–276.

3 Calling Upon the Lost Empire: The Evocative Power of Miniatures in a Portuguese Nationalist Theme Park

Paula Mota Santos

Introduction

Portugal dos Pequenitos is a theme park located in the city of Coimbra, central Portugal. In an area of 2.5 hectares, it assembles a large number of miniatures of vernacular architecture associated with the country's regional provinces and its (now former) overseas colonial possessions. The park was officially opened in 1940 as part of the celebrations marking the 800th anniversary of Portugal's foundation and the 300th anniversary of regaining national sovereignty from Spanish domination. It was completed in 1962, when, through its displays and settings, it provided António Salazar's Estado Novo (New State) regime, a right-wing dictatorship, with a holistic narrative of Portugal as colonial empire.[1] Today, more than 70 years after its official opening, this theme park remains one of the most visited tourist attractions in Coimbra, a city not without other major historical attractions, including one of the oldest universities in the Western world.[2]

Portugal dos Pequenitos is a place that I visited several times when I was a child growing up in Portugal. I went there with my parents and siblings while on holidays, and also as part of field trips while at primary school. My childhood memories of the place are all about having fun. I remember enjoying getting in and out of the little houses while my parents, due to their height, had to stand outside, gazing on. Because my memories of Portugal dos Pequenitos as a child were of enjoyment, I took my children there when they were small. It was the first time I had revisited the place. It was then, as an adult, and as an early career academic, that I realised that it had more to it than being simply a 'play place'.

Some years later, in 2008, in the context of my work as a university lecturer, I set a course assignment to a group of undergraduate architecture students to visit the park and write a reflective report on the experience. While reading over the 20 or so personal accounts by the students, I noticed the frequent occurrence of sentences such as 'and I felt proud to belong to the nation that has shown the world to the world'. These sentences seemed indicative of a strong emotional attachment to the Portugal on display in the park. I was surprised to see such strong feelings, because all of these students had been born well after the demise of the Portuguese colonial empire, some 40 years ago.[3] If the park's material structure has been left almost untouched since its completion in 1962, the world it represents has undergone dramatic changes. Since the end of the Portuguese colonial era in 1975 and the transformation of the colonies into sovereign nations, the world on display at Portugal dos Pequenitos is no longer presented as the colonial empire but as the member states of the Community of Portuguese-Speaking Countries (the Lusophone world).

My curiosity about the reasons for this strong emotional attachment shown by my students started me on what became a new research project: exploring the meanings of the site for contemporary domestic and international tourists. Apart from learning that Portugal dos Pequenitos was, apparently, the most visited tourist site in Coimbra,[4] my initial findings showed that the majority of visitors to the park were over 13 years old, and not primary school children as I had initially assumed. Portugal dos Pequenitos seems, then, to be a children's place that is visited mostly by non-children.[5] At a more general level, I wanted to know why and how a place that pertains to an era associated with the ideology of a right-wing dictatorship manages to continue exerting an evocative power over its present-day visitors.

All but two of the Portuguese architecture students who since 2008 have attended my lectures and gone to visit the park had visited Portugal dos Pequenitos when they were children.[6] Also, almost all of them were revisiting the park for the first time since having been there as children. In addition to the observations made by these students, I also gained access to the perspectives of non-Portuguese students on the park; these were mostly students from the University of California, Berkeley, who since 2007 attended my lectures on Portugal dos Pequenitos as part of their summer school programme.[7] In addition, I have undertaken several visits to the park, including a two-day on-site observation of tourists in June 2012, during which I conducted a visitor survey.[8] This chapter draws on these observations, the data collected by the survey and the conversations held with different visitors to the park, as well as on my students' experiences as written down in their reports and as discussed in the classroom.[9]

The Miniature and the Gigantic in the Process of Enchantment

Portugal dos Pequenitos is entered through a fairy-tale castle-like gateway (Figure 3.1). The park essentially comprises five themed areas (Figure 3.2), which are accessed in a particular order. The first is built around the general topic of 'Overseas Portugal'. This area is set out with miniature buildings of houses representing Cape Verde, Guinea-Bissau, Sao Tome and Principe, Angola, Mozambique, Macao, East Timor and the Portuguese State of India.[10] The second theme is 'Insular Portugal'. In this area the archipelagos of the Azores and Madeira are represented by one building each, both surrounded by a small waterway symbolising the Atlantic. The third area, 'Monumental Portugal', assembles a pastiche of the major historical monuments of mainland Portugal, with the Lisbon-based replicas holding a prominent place. This is followed by the 'Coimbra Ensemble', with a selection of iconic buildings, mostly from the city's old town and university. The last and largest area – 'Mainland Portugal' – brings together one 'typical' house for each of Portugal's 11 provinces (which in 1940 constituted the mainland territory).[11]

The building of colonial theme parks and exhibitions (or fairs) like Portugal dos Pequenitos can be seen as part of a wider trend observed in most European colonial empires of the 19th and early 20th century. First developed in the Netherlands in 1883, such parks and exhibitions proved highly popular and attracted large numbers of national and international visitors. Throughout the final decades of the 19th century and the first half of the 20th, they provided increasingly sophisticated displays for nations to showcase their 'wealth'. At the same time, they significantly contributed to the vulgarisation of exoticism as an appealing quality of faraway Others. The colonial sections of these exhibitions, with their replicas of exotic architecture and displays of exotic people, were described by many of their visitors as a 'veritable land of dreams' (Rydell, 1993: 61).[12]

The effect of appearing like 'a land of dreams' stems from a strategic effort by the parks' 'imagineers',[13] in particular through the use of rhetorical devices in the organisation of space. The dream-like character of Portugal dos Pequenitos, for instance, stems not only from its mimetic quality (i.e. the use of replicas of real buildings) but also, more importantly, from the use it makes of scale. In fact, the replicas displayed here are not life-size, as in other parks whose theme is the nation – like El Poble Espanyol (The Spanish Village) in Barcelona, built in 1929, or Taman Mini Indonesia Inda (Beautiful Miniature Indonesia) in Jakarta, Indonesia, built in 1975. The buildings in Portugal dos Pequenitos are scaled-down miniatures of the originals. Despite

Figure 3.1 Entrance to Portugal dos Pequenitos (author's photograph)

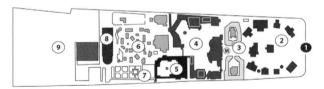

1. Entrance	6. Mainland Portugal
2. Overseas Portugal	(Regional Houses*)
(Portuguese Speaking Countries*)	7. Formal Gardens
3. Insular Portugal	8. Childrens' House
(Azores and Madeira)	9. Playground Area
4. Monumental Portugal	
5. Coimbra Ensemble	M. World Map

* present day designation of the area

Figure 3.2 Map of the park showing the five themed areas
Source: FundaÇao Bissaya Barreto/Portugal dos Pequenitos.
© Lynn Salt and Paula Mota Santos.

their reduced size, almost all of them can be accessed. Thus, the miniature scale of Portugal dos Pequenitos allows visitors to experience the different objects as 'lived in' rather than just gazed at.

Since the power of a tourist place to move the visitor emotionally can be usefully explained by the concept of magic approached from a phenomenological perspective (Picard, 2011: 10), the visit to the park and its enduring attraction will be taken in the sense of *experientiation*.[14] According to the phenomenological approach (Merleau-Ponty, 1989 [1962]), magical properties stem from subjective perception, which itself can be theorised as 'a reciprocity between the sentient body and the entities that surround it in a continuous dialogue that unfolds far below, or even independently of the subject's verbal awareness' (Abram, 1996: 52). Magical consciousness, a mythopoetic, expanded aspect of awareness, can thus be experienced by anyone (Greenwood, 2009: 4). It will be argued here that the often referred to magical quality of the park, that is, the seductive power the displays in the park apparently exercise over its visitors, stems from the specific use of the miniature and of the gigantic, and the underlying rhetoric these forms mediate.[15] Rhetoric is the art of using form to convince others of the validity and/or truthfulness of one's arguments. In the following sections, I will look specifically at how the miniature and the gigantic, as particular forms, are deployed in the process of enchanting visitors and subtly convincing them of the truthfulness and goodness of the narratives staged in the park.

The miniature

The miniature constitutes a specific form of representation of and mode of experiencing the nature of a wider reality or order. The creation of the miniature creates an impossible world, and by that very act of making it exist, the miniature denies the very impossibility of the existence of that impossible world. This ability of the miniature to overturn the impossibility of existence laid out by the laws of the commonsense world enters the realm of the magical. Stein (1990 [1987]) suggests that the specific 'powers' of the miniature lie in the effects of 'skillfulness' and of 'wholeness in smallness' and in its power of depiction. In the following sections I will build on Stein's and Stewart's (1997 [1984]) analysis, to investigate the role of the miniature as a form of representation at play in Portugal dos Pequenitos.

The miniature experiments with the limits of skill. The gestures and actions behind the creation of the minute speak of craft and discipline (Stewart, 1997 [1984]: 39). Far from being simply an accidental quality (a makeshift due to lack of space) smallness enhances the value of the object. This attribution of value to the miniaturised reality can be found, for instance, in the old tradition of miniature gardens in Chinese and Chinese-influenced cultures, such as Japan, Vietnam and Thailand, where gardens in containers were and still are highly valued, holding aesthetic, philosophical and magical properties (Stein, 1990 [1987]).[16] Portugal dos Pequenitos is often quoted and visited by architects and architecture students precisely because of the skilful quality of its replicas, while visitors often speak in wonderment of the minutiae of the buildings.

> Monumental Portugal is undoubtedly the area that impresses the most, by its dimension and presence.... I felt that although the scale was not that of the monuments, it respected them and those buildings seemed as if they were the real monuments ... leaving us with a message, recalling Portugal's past and the greatest of its historic virtues. (Architecture student, male, 22 years old, 2011)

Through the skilfulness of producing the very small, the miniature produces awe inasmuch as it produces a fabulous and fantastic world. Gell's (1992: 47) description of his encounter as an 11-year old with a matchstick model of Salisbury Cathedral while visiting the original clearly illustrates the miniature's ability to affect those who behold it. Additionally, and according to Gell, the power of art objects stems from the technical process that they objectively embody: 'the *technology of enchantment* is founded on the *enchantment of technology*' (Gell, 1992: 44, original emphasis). This 'enchantment of technology' is definitely at play at Portugal dos Pequenitos. In his report, a student explained his feelings when walking into the Monumental Portugal area:

> I am in awe. I fell in love with this area: an extraordinary architectural accuracy ... parts of Portuguese monuments representing the grandiosity of the Nation. (Architecture student, male, 40 years old, 2012)

The miniature enables a clear perception of the totality of the observed object. In her 1997 book, the poet and critic Susan Stewart dwells on, among other subjects, the relation of body to scale and to narrative through the analysis of micrographia. The earliest examples of micrographia were of texts with social importance. Small enough to be carried close to the body, miniature books often had a pedagogical aim: in a small quantity of physical space the reader had available important information.[17] Portugal dos Pequenitos can be taken as an example of micrographia, inasmuch as it depicts, narrates and conveys important information in a compressed time–space: limited in physical space and yet fantastic in its content; a place of wonderment.

Miniature worlds as microcosms are an encapsulation of macrocosms. In Portugal dos Pequenitos as a miniature world (the theme park), via a single experience (the visit), we are able to grasp and to learn about a wholeness that is gigantic (the colonial empire or the Community of Portuguese-Speaking Countries), that, were it to be learnt through visiting the real places that the replicas represent, would probably never be acquired.[18]

> In just one hour we can undertake a fantastic journey through the whole of the country, comparing houses and monuments and being surprised by details that in the real place would go unnoticed. (Architecture student, female, 19 years old, 2008)

In 2007, as a group of Berkeley students that I was accompanying on a visit to the park was leaving the Monumental Portugal section, a student coming out of the Lisbon replicas jokingly said, 'We do not need to go to these places now: we have seen them all already!'

Magic is an element often recognised in the production of art: from European prehistory to aboriginal rock art, the depiction of scenes or symbols is assumed to partake of religious and magical systems of knowledge and practice (Layton, 1992; Leroi-Gourhan, 1964). It is truly magical to make something exist through the ability to depict it. Stein (1990 [1987]: 51) refers both to the ability of Chin dynasty magicians to create rivers by drawing them on the ground, and to hermits who, although confined to the narrow world of their retreat, had access to the entire universe: if they wanted to go on a wandering journey, all they needed to do was to create the place they wanted to go to through the simple act of drawing it on the floor of their abode.

This magical ability of making something exist by simply depicting it is not unfamiliar in Western contexts. In fact, the very popular Disney-produced children's film *Mary Poppins* (1964) has one such situation. It is the musical piece 'Jolly Holiday', in which Mary Poppins, Bert and the two children jump into a fantasy world by stepping onto coloured chalk scenes drawn on the pavement. The jolly outing is eventually interrupted by a rainstorm, which washes away the chalk drawings, thus returning the travellers to the pavement and the real world. As one of the students put it in her visit report:

> It's like a magical place when we were children, and even when we re-visit it, that magic is still there, taking us to past and treasured times.... (Architecture student, female, 19 years old, 2011)

The gigantic

At the time of its final completion in 1962, Portugal dos Pequenitos objectified the nation in an overblown way, i.e. as the empire. Today, it presents itself as an intriguing tourist space inasmuch as it holds in itself a paradox. The most striking feature ascribed to the park is the use of the miniature. However, the park is actually inhabited by two metaphoric entities: the miniature (the form used) and the gigantic (the theme being displayed, be it the colonial empire or the Community of Portuguese-Speaking Countries). The gigantic, in the same way as the miniature, feeds on exaggeration. But while the exaggeration of the miniature results in the very small, the exaggeration in the gigantic produces the opposite: the very large.

If miniature speaks of structure, the gigantic speaks of agency (Stewart, 1997 [1984]). Giants transformed the landscape. Folktales often speak of geographical features that have resulted from the actions of giants: large lakes are formed when giants leave a footprint in the earth to be filled by rain; large boulders scattered on the countryside suggest giants at play; and streams are formed from tears of a giant (Stewart, 1997 [1984]: 72–73). The colonial project is about action and transformation: by moving away from its original geography (Europe), the colonial power (Portugal) went to change the world ('discovering' new lands and 'civilising' 'savage' natives). According to Stewart (1997 [1984]: 79) pre-industrial culture locates the gigantic in nature, while the rise of industrial capitalism relocates the gigantic within the abstraction of an exchange economy. If the appropriation of the gigantic out of the natural world into the urban milieu of market relations marks a transition from the ambivalent forces of the natural (productive and destructive) to the reproductive forces of class societies (Stewart, 1997 [1984]: 79–84), then the colonial project is truly gigantic, inasmuch as class society is both an essence and a consequence of the nature and fate of the colonial endeavour.

The reality on display at Portugal dos Pequenitos is thus gigantic, both as empire and as the Community of Portuguese-Speaking Countries: while the former is the nation overblown, a body enlarged beyond its 'natural' limits (its European borders and geography), the latter encompasses approximately 250 million people spread throughout the world.[19] This gigantic quality of the world on display in Portugal dos Pequenitos is most clearly objectified in one particular element of the park: the world map, approximately 7 × 4 metres, displayed on the wall that separates the overseas section (the now former colonies, and the Azores and Madeira archipelagos) from the mainland-based representations (Monumental Portugal, Coimbra Ensemble and Mainland Portugal). This is a gigantic world map in which

Figure 3.3 The world map at Portugal dos Pequenitos (author's photograph)

both the 'discovery' routes travelled by the Portuguese and the territories constituting the empire are displayed (Figure 3.3). On the right-hand side of this representation of the world sits a statue of Henry the Navigator, the Portuguese prince who led the nation into maritime adventure in the 15th century and thus initiated the Portugal's colonial destiny. According to Stewart, the gigantic exteriorises and communalises, being analogous to abstract institutions such as state or religion: 'it envelops us and encloses us in its shadow' (1997: 71), and that is precisely the effect of the photos (frequently) taken by the park's visitors against the backdrop of this Portuguese-led world map.

In this particular spectacle of the gigantic, Henry is depicted sitting in a regal way, in a commanding pose, larger than life-size. He is gigantic in both his demeanour and volume, as gigantic as the world map next to him, on which the gigantic colonial endeavour of the Portuguese nation is so clearly laid out. And because aesthetic size cannot be seen as separate from social function and values, the gigantic displayed at Portugal dos Pequenitos is also grand, majestic.

Suddenly we are faced with a map of the voyages of discovery. Grandiose and immense, objectifying the importance of this Nation in world history. (Architecture student, male, 30 years old, 2011)

The ethnographic observation of the visitors to the park confirmed the central role this map of a Portuguese-led world has in the visitor's experientiation of the park. The park's path layout makes it impossible for visitors to avoid facing this massive world map, and their reaction to it is always of interest. They stop, they gaze at it, they read the information, they track the routes displayed, they pinpoint places (Portuguese parents teach their small children where Portugal is; teachers ask pupils to point to places they should be familiar with; foreign visitors find their places of origin and track the maritime routes, and so on), and finally they turn their backs to it in order to have a group photo taken against this massive Portuguese-led world map with the larger than life statue of Henry as a gentle custodian.

In 2012, on yet another visit to the park, but this time with Erasmus exchange students, I found one of them – a male Czech, and a marketing major – gazing at this world map. When I asked him what he thought of it, he said that he was very surprised: 'I had no idea that Portugal, such a small country, had done all this! … such a small country … all these places!' We talked a bit more and I left him to go to find the other students. A few minutes later I returned and went by the world map area again. He was still there, gazing at it.

Representational Space and the Moral Order of Attractions

When I first returned to Portugal dos Pequenitos as an adult, I remember being particularly struck by the blatant colonial representation present in the park's first section (Overseas Portugal), namely of the Other as embodied in the African identity (Figure 3.4).[20] This was something I had no recollection of as a child. My memories of the park were mostly of the regional houses (Mainland Portugal) and Monumental Portugal. Most of the Portuguese students referred to here, whose study visit to the park was their first since having been there as children, frequently refer to having no recollection of the colonial section. This can also be explained by the different nature of these houses. Not only are they bigger than the regional houses, but their interior works as a museum of sorts: ethnographic objects from the colony/ African country are on display in old-fashioned glass and wooden frame cases. This is in stark contrast to the empty interiors of the regional houses, through which children can run freely.

Figure 3.4 The Other as embodied in the African identity (author's photograph)

On my adult visits to the park I frequently saw children running eagerly into the interior of the houses in Overseas Portugal (the colonial section) and then immediately run out of them, while voicing their lack of interest in the interior of those buildings. The displays in that section, with their objects and written explanations, were designed for an older audience and thus do not appeal as much to the younger children. As one student wrote in her report:

This [colonial] part is the one of which I have less recollection. Perhaps because it is like a museum, and thus one of the least interesting parts when we are children, because although the buildings are smaller than the originals, the truth is that that scale feels big to children. I now find the objects in them interesting, but I have no recollection whatsoever of having seen them before; it is that part [of the park] which does not interest you when you are a child: we can't touch things, play with them, thus we don't care about them. (Architecture student, female, 19 years old, 2011)[21]

Perhaps this play-place quality of Portugal dos Pequenitos might explain the particular place the park seems to have in Portuguese society.[22] Most of the adult Portuguese visitors I talked to during the two days of on-site observation referred to revisiting the park. These would be grandparents with their grandchildren and young adult parents of very small children. They were all showing a place that they had known themselves as children, but in addition to this shared situation, the young parents quite often expressed the intention of returning to the park once the children were a bit older, so that they would remember it better and learn more from it.[23] Young people with no children, when asked about returning to the park, quite often replied that they would if they went on holiday with friends who might not know the place, or later in life, if they ever became parents.[24]

It is a fact that most of my informants were Portuguese citizens. This Portuguese quality bears on the research inasmuch as it relates to socialisation processes, namely the role of the Portuguese schooling system and the way Portuguese history is taught.[25] However, my initial curiosity as to the elements behind the emotional impact of this place is not fully explained by this social factor alone, since the place seems also (although not equally) to please foreign tourists. Following MacCannell's (1976) idea that tourist places and touristic sightseeing imply a moral order of attractions, the question to ask is: what can be said about Portugal do Pequenitos's moral order of attraction in the present day?

Portugal dos Pequenitos is a themed place, and as such it has the quality of evoking and bringing alive a set of narratives. Narratives are about closure and ellipses. The boundaries of the events (in this case, the actual boundaries of the park and the theme on display – the colonial empire and/ or Community of Portuguese-Speaking Countries) together with the order in which they are told (in this case, the order in which the different spaces unfold before us as we walk through the park) form the ideological basis for the interpretation of their significance. The park's original entrance was not where it stands today: it was by the Mainland Portugal (regional houses) section, the only one built when the park was officially opened in 1940.[26]

When asked to think about the meaning that the structured space of the park produced as one walked from the entrance (Overseas Portugal) to the opposite end of the park (Mainland Portugal), some students referred to the fact that the park presented an inverted chronology, inasmuch as it displayed first more recent events within Portuguese history (the colonial endeavour) and then spatially proceeded back towards the nation's origin (Mainland Portugal). The spatial ordering (i.e. the structure) of the elements on display produced a specific meaning, that is, a narrative, one of 'origins':

> This disposition [of the different sections of the park] can be seen as a holistic view of the History of Portugal; it starts in a wider view (colonies/countries of Portuguese language) to move along the general elements of Portuguese culture and its historical monuments to then proceed to the different regions that characterise the origins of each one of us. (Architecture student, male, 20 years old, 2012)[27]

It can be argued that narrative never describes lived experience but only the conventions for organising and interpreting that experience. Portugal dos Pequenitos describes and narrates a world. But descriptions must rely on an economy of significance, and thus they display a hierarchical organisation of information. For at least some the park's visitors, that hierarchy – the way the different scenarios are presented for the visitors to experience – apparently produced an origins narrative. However, in addition to structure, one must consider another element of the park's rhetoric of space: the mode, that is, the style of the representations.

Portugal dos Pequenitos displays two different modes of representational styles: a hyper-realistic mode (the four sections related to non-colonial spaces – Insular and Monumental Portugal, Coimbra Ensemble and Mainland Portugal) (Figure 3.5) and an 'Orientalism' mode (Said, 2003 [1978]) applied to the colonial area (Figure 3.6). In the latter, the buildings representing each colonial possession are strongly marked by a modernist aesthetic where the architectural elements of 'exotic' cultures are interpreted by Western codes resulting in imagined Africas, Indias and Far Easts. But nevertheless, the quality and faithfulness of the 'Portuguese' replicas in Portugal dos Pequenitos, namely in the Monumental Portugal, Coimbra Ensemble, Insular and Mainland Portugal, together with the fact that Mainland Portugal, with its regional houses, seems to be the section that strikes the visitor's imagination the most, make Portugal dos Pequenitos a place of heightened *realism*.

As far as genres go, realism implies that the organisation of the information must clearly resemble the organisation of information in daily life, but in fact what realism does is not to be mimetic of everyday life, but of its hierarchisation of information. By taking the world of the miniature as a metaphorical world (Stewart, 1997: 44) and not as a metonymic world, we can see that Portugal dos Pequenitos acquires the quality of an emblem. Thus, functioning in the same way as family photographs in front of the Christmas tree (Bourdieu, 1965), Portugal dos Pequenitos is a space that

Figure 3.5 Hyper-realistic mode – Coimbra Ensemble (author's photograph)

articulates the individual and the historic according to a set of conventions. Limited in space (a small version of the colonial empire and/or of the Community of Portuguese-Speaking Countries), Portugal dos Pequenitos as miniature offers the closure of the description: it offers a *tableau*.

A tableau speaks to the distance between the narrated context (in this case the park itself, be it as the empire and/or as the Community) and the context at hand (the historical conditions of their production). Tableaux 'are only possible through representation since [they] offer a complete closure of a text framed off from the ongoing reality that surrounds it' (Stewart, 1997 [1984]: 48). The positive qualities of the colonial and its history frequently mentioned by Portuguese students and visitors are possible only insofar as the representation offered by Portugal dos Pequenitos hides the historical conditions of the empire. Portugal dos Pequenitos as a representational space is thus also a *myth* in Roland Barthes's (1976) sense, that is, a type of speech, a form that aims not at explanation but at persuasion.

It is because Portugal dos Pequenitos naturalises the empire/Lusophone world by hiding the historical and material conditions of its production that

Figure 3.6 'Orientalism' mode – Guinea Bissau (author's photograph)

it assumes the qualities of Stewart's (1997 [1984]) *tableau* and of Barthes's (1976) *myth*, two concepts imbued with a timeless time. The latter is most clearly a feature of Portugal dos Pequenitos as a ritualised place and as a tourist space. The park as a narrative not only has a point of view but also has its own story time. The closure of the narrative offered by Portugal dos Pequenitos is thus set outside the temporality of everyday lives. The physical permanence of the ordered space that is the park creates an ahistorical time, giving the quality of timelessness to the world depicted, to the world therein created.

Hochbruck and Schlehe (2010: 8), writing on nation-themed parks, state that 'what is staged in themed environments is either the creation of a history of a nation ... as an offer to the visitor as an imaginative identification, *or*[28] it is the creation of a seemingly exotic Other, juxtaposed to the Self and serving to stabilize and position it in the global world'. As a theme park whose theme is the nation, Portugal dos Pequenitos is unusual inasmuch as it carries out not just one but actually both the functions described by Hochbruck and Schlehe. Portugal dos Pequenitos is not a colonial space that, as time and history have moved on, has shed its colonial skin and has acquired a new one constituted by qualities of both the post-colonial (objectifying the Lusophone world) and high modernity (the themed place: 'the oldest theme park in Portugal', as the official website of the park states). In fact, Portugal dos Pequenitos incorporates (at least) these two skins. This makes the park a multidimensional and multivocal place, with these two characteristics dependent on the personal and social history of the tourist visiting it, elements that will impinge on the visitor's experientiation of the place.

Place is the most fundamental form of embodied experience – the site of a powerful fusion of self, space and time (Feld & Basso, 1996). In this vein, a non-purpose-built tourist place is initially 'just a place' to which, at some point, the value of being a tourist-worthy site was added. Such processes of touristic socialisation of places was what, in the 17th and 18th centuries, transformed many Italian cities into must-see places for members of the European upper classes (especially the British aristocracy); from then onwards, cities such as Florence and Rome were not just places where Italians lived – they became also nodal points of the Grand Tour. Thus, tourist places are usually sites of encountering the Other.

Portugal dos Pequenitos, in that respect, is an out-of-the-ordinary tourist place, inasmuch as the Other being gazed at is frequently part of the Us who gaze at it. However, the colonial empire (whose motto was *Uno e multiracial*: unified and multiracial) and the Lusophone Community are entities that participate strongly in the Us, that is, in *Portugueseness*.[29] Portugal dos Pequenitos as a miniature offers a world clearly limited in space but also a frozen space, a place of nostalgia and timeless history, as the quoted excerpts from the students' reports show. In processes of nostalgia, the reconstruction carried out by the present is denied and the past takes on an authenticity of being. Portugal dos Pequenitos is thus a place-time of ontological and unchangeable (continuously reproducing) identity.

The park's rhetoric of space presents the nation in an exaggerated way because it is compressed in time and space (the visit to the park). Also, it presents the intricate and diverse Lusophone world (previously the empire), and this intricacy adds to the size of the object's significance. Portugal dos Pequenitos assumes the quality of a large place as far as symbolism and representation are concerned. Its grandeur, its gigantic nature as produced reality is actually, and paradoxically, reinforced by its material reduction, by the miniature in it. This dialectical co-habiting of two opposing metaphors (the miniature and the gigantic) together with the felicitous encounter of the park with high-modern times inhabited by the post-tourist[30] work towards the ability this colonial space has to attract and seduce visitors in a post-colonial era, thus successfully negotiating the moral orders of attraction (MacCannell, 1976). But it is argued here that more than this historical contingency, it is the particular use the park makes of the miniature, and the way the latter impinges on the visitor's experientiation of the place, that allows for a successful negotiation of the moral orders of attraction.

In this realm of the rhetoric of space and its entanglement with the phenomenological stance, it is necessary to bring into focus the way Portugal dos Pequenitos makes use of the miniature. Contrary to Bekonscot (late 1920s, Beaconsfield, UK) or Splendid China (1989, Shenzen, People's Republic of China) – two theme parks that also present miniature replicas of real buildings (but in a size too small for visitors to enter them) – the scale used in Portugal dos Pequenitos allows for visitors to enter the buildings.[31] Children can do it with no effort, while adults can enter the smaller houses if they stoop, although only small children can get into the houses in the Mainland Portugal section. It is argued here that these effects of the miniature as phenomenologically experienced through the sentient body is the main element that is related to the successful negotiation of the moral orders of attraction being objectified in the frequently expressed magical quality of the experience of visiting Portugal dos Pequenitos.

Portugal dos Pequenitos represents and objectifies *Portugueseness*. It offers its visitors the wholeness of *Portuguese-as-identity* (be it the empire or the Community) through the possibility of the impossibility of wholeness in smallness. As already argued, in the miniature the effects of skilfulness, of wholeness in smallness, and the power of depiction are all at work in the experientiation of visiting the park. Besides these effects, as Sontag (1979 [1977]) stated in relation to the photograph, miniaturisation has the ability to enhance the sense of appropriation, which in turn helps to produce a sense of identification, inasmuch as what I feel to be mine can be perceived as part of me.

By displaying a world so small that the only thing visitors can do is to point at the miniature replicas 'down there', both Bekonscot and Splendid China produce what I call a *Lilliputian* experientiation of space, while Portugal dos Pequenitos produces a *Carrollian* experientiation.[32] By accessing the interior of the little houses via the ability to make one's body fit within the available space (even if with difficulty), visitors to Portugal dos Pequenitos go through an experience akin to Alice's experientiation of magical changes of body size in Lewis Carroll's *Alice in Wonderland*, but, most importantly, this ability to access the interior of the miniaturised buildings allows the park's visitors (children, teenagers and adults) to really participate in the world on display. And through this ability to be on the inside of those miniaturised buildings, that world is no longer a fantasy: it is a reality.

One final element must be added to the ones already addressed if we want to achieve a full explanation of the 'powers' of Portugal dos Pequenitos' miniatures in captivating the park's visitors. Gell describes the power of the beautifully and skilfully carved prow-boards of the *kula* canoes that 'are supposed to dazzle the beholder and weaken his grip on himself' (Gell, 1992: 44) making him behave with unexpected generosity, that is, more willing to offer the visiting *kula* partners the higher quality *kula* items available to him (Gell, 1992: 46). This willingness to offer his best *kula* items to the visiting *kula* partner is akin to empathy. And empathy is what the visitors to Portugal dos Pequenitos experience when they express their liking for the place, their enjoyment of the visit. The exquisitely carved *kula* prow-boards have the magical capacity to deprive those who behold them of their reason (Gell, 1992: 46). For Gell, this magical power, that is, the efficacy of the art object as a component of the technology of enchantment, is in itself a result of the enchantment of technology since 'It is the way an art object is construed as having come to the world which is the source of the power such objects have over us – their becoming rather than their being' (Gell, 1992: 46).

The skilfulness and intricacy of the miniature world brought into existence in Portugal dos Pequenitos, together with the perception of the high level of difficulty its construction surely involved, makes the park's existence and its experientiation magical inasmuch as the technical processes that transcend one's understanding force us to construe it as magical (Gell, 1992: 49). Just as the captivating powers of the *kula* canoe prow-boards make you surrender your reason and give to the visiting *kula* partner your best *kula* objects, Portugal dos Pequenitos, through its dazzling appearance and artistic quality, seduces its visitors, making them behave with unexpected generosity, surrendering to the park's narrative their higher constituent of the self, their heart:

[to tell now] how I felt about the place ... the representation of the maritime expansion ... it transmits [to] me great pride since it portrays one of the greatest times in Portuguese history: the conquests. To me it signifies and glorifies the Motherland, it pays homage to the Portuguese men who lost their lives in the seas while in search of new lands, new territories, new cultures. In this way their splendour will always be present in our lives ... I loved the visit, and if I already loved my country, I love it more now.... (Architecture student, female, 19 years old, 2008)

Notes

(1) The Estado Novo regime ruled Portugal from 1926 to 1974. Due to the connection to that regime and its politics of national identity, the park has been frequently written about in terms of its past (Babo, 1997; Matos, 2006; Paulo, 1990; Porto, 1994; Silva, 2010). It has been written about less often in terms of its present (Matos, 2010; Santos, 2014).

(2) Coimbra University was founded in 1290. The buildings of the so-called Old University are one of the tourist attractions of the city.

(3) Portuguese former colonies obtained independence in 1975, one year after the democratic revolution of 1974.

(4) That Portugal dos Pequenitos is the most visited tourist attraction in Coimbra is regularly mentioned by the park's director, Lúcia Monteiro, and is also widely mentioned in web commentaries about the park. Although there are no reliable long-term statistics concerning visitors to the different places in Coimbra, the two most popular entry-paying places are the Old University and Portugal dos Pequenitos. In 2008, the Old University registered 190,000 visitors (Universidade de Coimbra 2009: 41) while the park registered 300,000 (information supplied by the park's director). In 2008, a study on tourist activity in Coimbra was carried out by Fortuna et al. (2012). According to this study (data collected by a questionnaire given between the months of August and October 2008), 64.1% of non-first-time visitors had previously visited the Old University and 62.4% had visited Portugal dos Pequenitos. When asked about places to go and (re)visit, 66.5% referred to the Old University and 23.4% to Portugal dos Pequenitos (Fortuna et al., 2012: 76–77). The reason for this difference is related to the fact that the sample design was constructed in order to capture the flux of tourists who were looking for the Historic Centre (Fortuna et al., 2012: 76), which makes this study fall slightly off centre as far as this research is concerned. It should be noted that Portugal dos Pequenitos is located on the south bank of the Mondego River, while the old city of Coimbra is located on the north bank.

(5) Individuals aged between 14 and 65 years pay the full price for an entry ticket. In 2008, 52% of tickets sold were full price (information supplied by the park's director).

(6) Just to give an idea of the park's standing in Portuguese society, within my circle of relatives, friends, acquaintances and fellow Portuguese academics (for what it is worth as a source of information), I have not come across more than three people who had not visited Portugal dos Pequenitos as a child.

(7) I am indebted here to Deolinda Adão, the Executive Director of the Portuguese Studies Program of the University of California at Berkeley, who in 2007, when faced with my enthusiasm for the park, challenged me to make Portugal dos Pequenitos the theme for one of my lectures. This challenge was the one that truly set me upon this research path.

(8) The number of questionnaires obtained was 40.

(9) For this research, apart from the comments of US and Portuguese students, I have also benefited from the perspective on Portugal dos Pequenitos of European students on the Erasmus exchange programme who attended my lectures. I am in debt to all of my students for their discussion of the park and for their sharing their experiences of visiting it.

(10) The Portuguese State of India comprised Goa, Daman and Diu.

(11) There is no complete agreement between authors over the order in which these park's sections were built. Matos (2010: 8) indicates the order of completion as follows: Mainland Portugal (1940); Coimbra Ensemble and Overseas Portugal (early 1940s); Monumental Portugal (1950–62). Silva (2010: 7) gives a slightly different account: Mainland Portugal and Coimbra Ensemble (1938–40); Monumental Portugal (1941–49); Insular and Overseas Portugal (throughout the 1950s). The important point, however, is that the park was built in stages over 24 years. For nearly the whole period a single architect, Cassiano Branco, was in charge of the design and construction of the park.

(12) The year of Portugal dos Pequenitos's official opening was also the year in which the six-month Exposição do Mundo Português (Exhibition of the Portuguese World) was staged in Lisbon, being one of the main events of the Estado Novo's national identity policy. For a more detailed analysis of the relationship of Portugal dos Pequenitos to international fairs and colonial exhibitions see Santos (2014).

(13) Using here the term the Disney Corporation prefers when referring to its parks' designers/creators. On Disney's 'imagineers' see Zukin (1991).

(14) *Experientiation* is used in Kant's sense of knowledge of place as genuinely local knowledge that 'is in itself experiential in the manner of *Erlebnis*, "lived experience", rather than of *Erfahrung*, the already elapsed experience' (Casey, 1996: 18).

(15) My students, Portuguese and non-Portuguese, who visited the park and the visitors to whom I talked to throughout this research all expressed a strong liking for the place. I only came across only a single case of a negative reaction to the reality displayed at the park. This was from a US student who, having visited Elmina Castle (a Portuguese-built slave-trade fortress from the late 1400s, in present-day Ghana) found the African section of 'Overseas Portugal' – which actually has two examples of military architecture – eerily reminiscent of that dark tourism place. In Figure 3.1, to the right of the main entrance, part of an example of such military architecture can just be seen.

(16) In relation to Portugal dos Pequenitos, there is one particular instance where this high value of skilfulness involved in the miniature is overtly displayed. This is a plaque stating the name of the master stone mason (Valentino Azevedo) who carved the miniature replica of one of the most celebrated Portuguese works, in late Gothic style: the Manueline window of the Christ Covent, Tomar. All the other works are anonymous to the park's visitors.

(17) It is thus not surprising that the earliest examples of miniature books were religious texts such as the Bible and books of hours (Stewart, 1997: 39).

(18) The data collected by the 2012 survey revealed an average of 1–2 hours for the duration of the visit (the most relevant variable for the time spent visiting the park was if the respondent was accompanied by children or not).

(19) Data for the year 2010. Information taken from http://www.publico.pt/cultura/falantes-de-portugues-irao-aumentar-para-335-milhoes-em-2050-1429372.

(20) Apart from the statues of Bissaya Barreto (the park's founder), of Henry the Navigator, and another four statues of eminent people from Portuguese history located at the back end of the park (and thus less visible than the first two mentioned here), all the human figures present in the park are of African bodies (mostly male) and always scantily dressed. Since the 'correct' attire (i.e. Western attire) was a measure of 'civilisation', the embodiment of the African identity displayed at Portugal dos Pequenitos is strongly marked by the European concept of the 'savage'. For a more detailed analysis of this argument see Santos (2014).

(21) For a more detailed discussion of the pedagogical role of the park as intended by its founder, Bissaya Barreto, see Santos (2014).

(22) See notes 6 and 15. Also, when I have presented my work on Portugal dos Pequenitos in Portuguese academic fora, fellow academics and students have occasionally come to me after the presentation and mentioned their enjoyment of the place and stated that the material presented made them want to go back and revisit the park, something most of them had done only as children. No one ever came to me to express a less sympathetic view of the place. This does not mean that such individuals do not exist, as they may simply be less inclined to express their views than the ones who have a pleasant memory of the place.

(23) This is most likely a result of the young parents having much younger children with them (from babies to toddlers) than the grandparents did (the grandchildren tended to be close to or already in their early teens).

(24) Foreign tourists, if adults, would express no intention of returning to Portugal dos Pequenitos, not because they had disliked it but because, once visited, there was no need to visit it again; those who had small children mentioned that if they happened to be back in the area they might return, since it was a very good place for children.

(25) For a more detailed analysis of this role of the teaching of history, see Santos (2014).

(26) The original entrance is still there but is rarely noticed by the park's visitors.

(27) The students' reports also showed how the narrative read from Portugal dos Pequenitos is linked to the spatial progression from the entrance to the opposite end of the park, since the walk back to the entry point (which is also the exit of the park) is absolutely absent from their accounts of the experientiation of the place.

(28) My emphasis.

(29) The term is here used in the most broad and polyphonic way, as an 'empty' referent that is 'filled up' with different meanings across differentially contextualised utterances.

(30) The post-tourist is a tourist who is unconcerned with authenticity and who knows that '[The world is a stage and [she or he] can delight in the multitude of games to be played' (Urry, 1990: 91).

(31) Splendid China's replicas are built at a scale of 1:15. In Portugal dos Pequenitos there are two scales, 1:5 (Mainland Portugal) and 1:2.5 (Overseas Portugal).

(32) Using here terms derived from Jonathan Swift's novel *Gulliver's Travels* (Lilliput: the imagined island nation inhabited by people who are approximately one-twelfth the height of ordinary human beings) and from Lewis Carroll, author of *Alice in Wonderland*.

References

Abram, D. (1996) *The Spell of the Sensuous*. New York: Vintage Books.

Babo, M.A. (1997) A naturalização da cultura. Uma representação arquitectónica do mundo: O Portugal dos Pequenitos. *Vértice*, Segunda Série (Maio/Junho), 89–93.

Barthes, R. (1976) O Mito, hoje. In *Mitologias* (pp. 249–298). Lisboa: Edições 70.

Bourdieu, P. (ed.) (1965) *Un art moyen – essai sur les usages sociaux de la photographie*. Paris: Éditions Minuit.

Casey, E.S. (1996) How to get from space to place in a fairly short stretch of time – phenomenological prolegomena. In S. Feld and K. Basso (eds) *Senses of Place* (pp. 13–52). Santa Fé, NM: SAR Press.

Feld, S. and Basso, K. (1996) Introduction. In S. Feld and K. Basso (eds) *Senses of Place* (pp. 3–11). Santa Fé, NM: SAR Press.

Fortuna, C., Gomes, C., Ferreira, C., Abreu, P. and Peixoto, P. (2012) *A cidade e o turismo – Dinâmicas e desafios do turismo urbano em Coimbra*. Coimbra: Edições Almedina.

Gell, A. (1992) The technology of enchantment and the enchantment of technology. In J. Coote and A. Shelton (eds) *Anthropology, Art and Aesthetics* (pp. 40–66). Oxford: Clarendon.

Greenwood, S. (2009) *The Anthropology of Magic*. Oxford: Berg.

Hochbruck, W. and Schlehe, J. (2010). Introduction: Staging the past. In J. Schlehe, C. Oesterle and W. Hochbruck (eds) *Staging the Past: Theme Environments in Transcultural Perspectives* (pp. 7–20). Bielefeld: Transcript Verlag.

Layton, R. (1992) *Australian Rock Art: A New Synthesis*. Cambridge: Cambridge University Press.

Leroi-Gourhan, A. (1964) *Les religions de la Préhistoire*. Paris: PUF.

MacCannell, D. (1976) *The Tourist – A New Theory of the Leisure Class*. New York: Schocken Books.

Matos, P.F. (2006) *As côres do império – representações raciais no império colonial português*. Lisboa: ICS.

Matos, P.F. (2010) A história e os mitos: Manifestações da ideologia colonial na construção do Portugal dos Pequenitos em Coimbra. In *7th Congresso Ibérico de Estudos Africanos, 9, Lisboa, 2010 – 50 anos das independências africanas: desafios para a modernidade*. Lisboa: CEA, 2010. See http://repositorio-iul.iscte.pt/handle/10071/2194 (accessed August 2013).

Merleau-Ponty, M, (1989 [1962]) *The Phenomenology of Perception*. London: Routledge.

Paulo, H. (1990) Portugal dos Pequenitos: Uma obra ideológico-social de um professor de Coimbra. *Revista de História da Ideias* 12, 395–413.

Picard, D. (2011) *Tourism, Magic and Modernity. Cultivating the Human Garden*. New York: Bergham Books.

Porto, N. (1994) *Uma introdução à antropologia* (Aula teórica-prática no âmbito das Provas de Aptidão Pedagógica e Capacidade Científica). Departamento de Antropologia, Faculdade de Ciências e Tecnologia, Universidade de Coimbra.

Rydell, R. (1993) *World of Fairs. The Century-of-Progress Expositions*. Chicago, IL: University of Chicago Press.

Said, E. (2003 [1978]) *Orientalism*. London: Penguin Books.

Santos, P. M. (2014) The imagined nation: The mystery of the endurance of the colonial imaginary in postcolonial times. In Noel B. Salazar and Nelson H. H. Graburn (eds) *Tourism Imaginaries – Anthropological Approaches*. Oxford: Berghahn Books.

Silva, C.E.R. (2010) Portugal Pequenino. Resdomus, Grupo FCT Atlas da Casa, Centro de Estudos de Arquitectura e Urbanismo. Porto. 1–19. See http://resdomus.blogspot.pt/2010/03/portugal-pequenino.html (accessed August 2013).

Sontag, S. (1979 [1977]) *On Photography*. London: Penguin Books.

Stein, R.A. (1990 [1987]) *The World in Miniature. Container Gardens and Dwellings in Far Eastern Religious Thought* (trans. P. Brooks). Stanford, CA, Stanford University Press.

Stewart, S. (1984) *On Longing: Narratives of the Miniature, the Gigantic, the Souvenir, the Collection*. Durham, NC: Duke University Press.

Universidade de Coimbra, (2009) *UC em números*. See http://www.uc.pt/sobrenos/ucnumeros (accessed August 2013).

Urry, J. (1990) *The Tourist Gaze: Leisure and Travel in Contemporary Societies*. London: Sage.

Zukin, S. (1991) *Landscapes of Power – From Detroit to Disney World*. Berkeley, CA: University of California Press.

4 Tourism and Post-socialist Heterotopias: Eastern Europe as an Imagined Rural Past

Mathilde Verschaeve and Hannah C. Wadle

Introduction

In the mid-1990s, Marc Augé wrote that the countries of Eastern Europe 'retain a measure of exoticism' for the Western, globalised world. He explained this exoticism with 'the simple reason that they do not yet have all the necessary means to accede to the world-wide consumption space' (Augé, 1995: 107). Since then, the former socialist countries of Eastern Europe have undergone rapid transformation, which has brought about a set of contradictory, yet deeply entangled claims, asserting, on the one hand, participation in a global modernity and cultivating, on the other, a sense of longing for a lost condition or state associated with the former regimes. Tourism represents here a particular field of practice in which these incongruous claims are pulled to the surface, meet and enter into dialogue. Specifically, the historical legacy and continued promotion of a Western European imaginary of Eastern Europe as a backwardly exotic space, as earlier observed by Marc Augé, contributes here to the development of an inherently ambiguous sense of place and identity.

In this chapter, we will use the results of two ethnographic field studies on tourism development in Maramures in Romania (Mathilde) and Masuria in Poland (Hannah) to explore the transformations of Eastern Europe as a Western European tourist destination. We will focus in particular on rural areas, which seem to constitute a tourism reality different from that of urban centres, whose socialist heritage sites have become a major attraction for a younger generation of Western tourists (Light & Young, 2006). By comparing the results of these studies, we are able to discuss the wider cultural frameworks in which tourism imaginaries are produced, performed and institutionalised, and how they challenge identity processes among stakeholders and populations involved in the tourism sector in destinations.

The chapter thus aims to contribute to a wider debate on the touristic production and consumption of places, local identity construction processes in post-socialist Europe and power relations in post-Cold War united Europe.

During the Cold War, countries like Poland or Romania never managed to become popular destinations for tourists from Western Europe. This is why for many contemporary Western European tourists such destinations lacked positive cultural memory and social prestige. One of our informants, for instance, a retired bank director from former West Germany, explained that it had been difficult for him to convince his wife to spend their holiday in a former socialist state. Yet, he affirmed, they eventually wanted to give the 'former socialist states another chance'. Studies have observed that, after 1989, tourism to Eastern Europe has often been driven by motives of (re-)discovery and construction, and contest national and religious identities in the post-socialist states (e.g. Galbraith, 2000; Klekot, 2010; Light, 2011). At the same time, authors like Câmpeanu (2008), Peleikis (2006a) and Wadle (2012) suggest these new forms of tourism are arenas in which processes of cultural pluralisation emerge, often from and around the legacies of the Second World War (Feldman, 2008; Fendl, 1998). In this work, we argue that these travel motives and the pluralisation processes they induce can be considered as two complementary facets of Western tourism, in which local populations have different stakes. Mathilde Verschaeve observes in her work that Maramures, a small county in the north of Romania, seems to embody for many Romanians the 'essence' of the country, because the inhabitants have, according to their discourses, 'preserved' 'their' traditions and are 'still' living 'as' their ancestors had, in little wooden houses, wearing the same ancient costumes. In a way, the commoditisation of culture for tourists becomes here a specific means to cultivate and discuss local identities, an observation Simone Abram (1996) had already made in the 1990s, in her study on rural France. In a similar vein, Hannah Wadle encounters a seeming contradiction between the secluded lakes and quietude promised in her travel books and the reality met when visiting the Masurian Lake District in the county of Warmia and Mazury during a road trip through Poland in summer 2004. Stuck in traffic jams between vehicles from Warsaw and from Stuttgart, she found that there were far more cars and coaches with German number plates than elsewhere in Poland, together with pension-aged cyclists, sailing yachts on the lakes and canoes on the rivers. Masuria was a destination for many, creating a fusion of tourisms that Wadle did not quite understand. Leisure centres in the socialist tradition coexisted with private accommodation in apartment blocks, neo-classical second-home villas, Catholic scout camps and renovated period estates managed by German owners.

In the following sections, we first explore the tourism imaginaries related to rural Romania and north-east Poland, and then investigate how these imaginaries are encountered and transformed by different stakeholders in the two locales studied.

Finding a Lost Countryside in Romania

One of the most visible slogans of the 2009 tourism campaign run by the Romanian ministry of tourism asked the rhetorical question: 'You know nothing about Romania, do you?' The aim of the campaign was to change the often negative stereotypes from which the country suffered abroad. In France, for instance, representations of Romania, mediated by reports on television and in the newspapers, often involve images of miserable orphanages, poverty, corruption and gypsy people begging. To stimulate the growing rural tourism market, the Romanian tourism campaign focused on the countryside. One of the brochures produced by the National Authority for Tourism explained that, in the Romanian countryside, 'there still endures a life full of centuries-old customs and beliefs, which are otherwise known to the people of today only through museums.... You can spend a holiday reminiscent of the times when your grandparents were children.'

Such a description evokes the image of an uncommon, preserved way of life that has otherwise been 'lost' elsewhere, in other places, in particular those of the potential tourists addressed here. This image is intimately bound to the ethnological gaze that national and foreign ethnographers and folklorists in Romania have fixed upon rural customs, legends and material culture. Similar to the way in which other rural areas in Europe – like the Auvergne, studied by Abram (1996: 175) – are made to embody a place of imagined origin for the national self, the rural county of Maramures, in northern Romania, is 'considered by many to be the heart and soul of rural Romania', as the tourism promotion website of the county council explains (http://www.visitmaramures.ro). One of the most common themes is here that of a land of preserved traditions. Many of the ethnographic studies from the 19th century onwards (among them the works by Romanian philosopher Mircea Eliade, 1970) state that the intangible and material cultural heritage of Maramures dates back to the pre-Roman Dacian epoch, thus transforming this specific space into a large theatrical setting in which a national narrative of historical filiation is made to unfold. Many of the discourses produced by these works refer to historical religious and holiday practices, carved wooden gates and churches (eight of the wooden churches are listed as World Heritage Sites by the United Nations Educational, Scientific and Cultural Organization, UNESCO), textiles, particularly carpets and blankets, and traditional costumes. The image of a remote and somehow backward place is equally being taken up by guidebooks. For instance, the Lonely Planet online guide portrays the entrance to the region as follows:

> Dismount from the horse-drawn cart and tip your chauffeur in cigarettes. You've found one of the last places where rural European medieval life remains intact. Where peasants live off the land as countless generations did before them. (http://www.lonelyplanet.com/romania/maramures)

In the same vein, a few television documentaries broadcast in France have depicted Maramures as an isolated, rustic place, embedded in a wild, pre-modern atmosphere. These films play an important role for the mediation of specific place-related tourism imageries (Beeton, 2005), as witnessed by the comment posted by a member of the online forum from the travel website www.routard.com. After watching a documentary about a steam locomotive in Maramures, the latter asked whether there actually are such places in the Carpathians, as the report suggested: 'Are there, sorry for the word, delightfully underdeveloped spots with no electricity, but charcoal and wood fires? Are there still bears and wolves?' Similar desires to flee from a modernity perceived as noxious are illustrated by the experience of Nathalie, from the Romanian field study. (She and her husband decided to live a whole year with their three children in a house in Maramures, an initiative of their own that is particularly uncommon.) She explained that 'we wanted our children to experience a real life, without TV, without the pressure of the city life, to allow them to live close to nature and make friends in another environment, to be happy with simple things. It is really fun; it is like acting in *Little House on the Prairie*.'

Such an imaginary points at a more general idea about Maramures, popular among tourists, that, by undertaking a journey there, people will encounter a kind of living museum, showcasing a shared European past. Andrei, an experienced Romanian guide and travel agency manager, explained that many foreign pensioners visit the region because 'they feel comfortable there. For them, it is like travelling through time. It reminds them of their childhood.' Similarly, Monique, in her fifties, was one of many tourists who associated Maramures with an image of a France from the past. She came to Romania to visit her son, a student in Bucharest, and, armed with her guidebook, she took a trip to the north. Maramures 'reminds' her of how she pictures her mother's childhood in the 1930s, acknowledging the strong influence of the church, the presence of carts and horses, and the use of weaving looms.

The bucolic image of Maramures is not a recent invention. It has in fact long been part of a wider national tradition of elevating rural village life that finds its root in the German Romantic conception of the nation brought to Romania during the 1848 revolutions. Throughout the 20th century, but most particularly during the inter-war period, the idea of the Romanian village was a political tool to formulate, express and celebrate national Romanian identity (Mihailescu, 1999). Today, this historical imaginary seems to have changed little in form and, to a certain extent, even in function. According to the tourism industry, guidebooks, tourists and also to many Romanians, Maramures, in a widely consensual way, does embody and make visible a quintessence of the countryside and of a wider 'Romanian spirit' at large.

Sehnsucht Masuren and Ostpreußen in Poland

'Where did you tell your friends and family at home that you are going on holiday?', Rainer, the guide of a cycle holiday he organised, asked his participants. They were sitting at the marina of Gizycko, formerly Lötzen, in Poland, having a beer. 'I simply said, I am going to "Ostpreußen" (East Prussia), in particular to Masuria. That's the order, in which I put it', one of the participants, a man in his early forties responded. 'I said, I am going to Poland *but* to Masuria', a women in her mid-fifties chipped in. Rainer grinned: 'This is what most tourists have told me, openly and honestly'. 'Usually', he explained, 'if you go, let's say to Burgundy, you say, I am going to France, to Burgundy. But nobody shouts about going to Poland. Instead, people say, "I'm going to Masuren". With Poland, people intuitively antici-pate a stupid answer like "in that poor country you won't bring your car back with you".... These old stereotypes are still active', he concluded. The group nodded, seemingly approving Rainer's analysis.

While 'Poland' often seems to leave a stale aftertaste in the mind of most German tourists, Masuren and Ostpreußen appear to appeal to them. Why is that so? An answer may be found in the observation that, unlike 'Poland', Masuren and Ostpreußen refer to a highly poeticised space (Mai, 2005: 323) and time; a product of cultural memory, of German literature by notable authors from East Prussia, perpetuated through numerous travel documentaries produced by German regional channels, travel books and reports, and often also ancestral or individual memories. Asking 'Why does East Prussia still look so East Prussian?', the sociologist Günther Beck (2000) argues that the mental map of East Prussia is fixed through a set of stable places with high cultural symbolism and an interacting community who share these imaginaries. Masuren and Ostpreußen are known as a land 'of dark forests and crystal clear lakes', a 'land with no hurry that liked to sleep away time', phrases that reappear regularly in television travel documentaries broadcast in contemporary Germany. Masuren is thus stylised as a rural idyll, in which people live in 'tune' with the seasons in their red-brick houses with gabled roofs.

In these narratives, the portrait of the Masuren in East Prussia is different from that of 'Mazury', the Polish word that describes what is basically the same place and that constitutes an important domestic tourism destination. While the representations associated with Mazury in Poland evoke an atmosphere of action, youth and adventure with yachts, motorcyclists and summer festivals, the German 'Masuren und Ostpreußen' is filled with nostalgia and quietude, embodied in images of empty natural landscapes, remote villages, storks, cornfields and horse-drawn carriages on cobblestone avenues. The imaginary cultivated among many German tourists responds to an emotional quest for yearning, *Sehnsucht*. *Sehnsucht Masuren* (Yearning for/of Masuria) is a slogan that has been repeatedly used in German media reports and travel brochures, thus appealing to a specific, historically rooted emotional geography. Ulrich Mai (2005: 310) argues that the East–West divide in Europe during the Soviet period and the resulting exclusion of the then West Germans from the area contributed to the preservation, among the latter, of a romanticised, nostalgic image of Masuren. Part of the image is expressed in the ascription of Masuren as a German *Schicksalsland* (land of fate), a notion that loosely points to the trauma of separation of the area from Germany after the Second World War (a significant German population had to flee, thereby losing their homes and belongings) and also to its preceding presence during and even before the German Nazi regime.

These culturally shaped, nationally specific affects for the area by German tourists often incur the unease of the Polish population. In his essay *Ziemiec (Earthling)*, Polish poet Kaziemierz Brakoniecki (2005) describes the feeling of national contest that the imagined geographies of Masuren and Ostpreußen evoke in contemporary Poland. He resents in particular the emotional ambivalence of Warmia i Mazury (the Polish province of Warmia-Masuria). In his eyes the Masuren's landscapes of memory and emotions hang like 'German tapestries over the Polish patriotic table and TV'. German tourism to the area, marked by two different and often opposing national histories, evokes and nurtures this feeling of emotional ambivalence among the Polish local and tourism populations.

Among German tourists, the sense of nostalgia associated with Masuren often has very different meanings. If most seem to agree that they are on a quest for a lost time and space, the specific configuration of such a space varies greatly. It seems to depend in particular on their age, the duration of their relationship to Masuria, the body of knowledge they have about East Prussia or Poland and also their specific political viewpoints. Until the late

1990s, Masuria was primarily visited by German tourists called *Heimweh-touristen* (homesick tourists), in search of their lost *Heimat* (Burachovič, 2002; Fendl, 1998; Peleikis, 2009; Stennert, 1995). Verena Schmitt-Roschmann (2010: 10) describes *Heimat* as a 'longed for emotional state of quietude' and as deeply German. Many of these *Heimattourists* felt that they had lost their *Heimat* when their families were forced to flee their homes in Ostpreußen at the end of the Second World War II. Gerda, for example, a 74-year-old woman who was born in Masuria, yet later grew up in West Germany, set off to search for 'her childhood' and find her old family house.

Most German tourists interviewed as part of this research rejected this form of *Heimweh* tourism and did not want to be associated with it. In many ways, this is also the case for those who come to look for their former family houses – like Gerda. Most tourists associate the idea of *Heimweh* for Masuria and East Prussia with the revanchist German claims to pre-war properties, which in their eyes are politically incorrect. Andrea from Düsseldorf, in her late fifties, explained that 'When the Berlin Wall fell, I had tears in my eyes and said to myself: "Now you can go to East Prussia and see everything yourself".' She came to search for a German past which had been silenced in her history classes in West German schools during the 1960s, and which she later studied independently through books. East Prussian architecture and landscapes, and the monuments of German history, such as Hitler's headquarters, provided her with evidence that this past had been real. At the same time, the rural landscape she encountered reminded her of her childhood in the 1950s in the West Germany. Other German tourists are far less interested in Masuria as a historical landscape, rather stressing its aspects of rural tranquil. Thirty-five-year-old Heiko explained that he was searching for the purity and calmness of nature, which Masuria seemed to provide with its lakes and forests. While he was not explicitly searching for monuments of the German past, he was still finding some of them and visited them. His travel motive was less a quest for the national historical/ cultural landscape of Masuren than, rather, a search for the more abstract German tourism image of Masuria, as a place of timelessness, where he could escape from the rush of his work life.

Producing and Performing Maramures and Masuria

The ways in which these different French and German tourists respectively conceive of Maramures in Romania and Masuria in Poland radically diverge from the immediate social environments of these two post-socialist locales. Both are narratively located in a rural pre-war past that has been built in contrast to the tourists' worlds of the present. In both cases, the tourist images and projections of the two places appropriate and transform earlier existing cultural representations and thus form wider collective imaginaries. In a wider sense, they demonstrate that Western European tourism to Central Europe constitutes an important element in the processes of reordering national identities after the Cold War, not only for the post-socialist states, but also for Western European countries themselves. In the case of Maramures in Romania, a variety of social actors, including tourists, policymakers and local populations, seem to share a widely consensual image of the place. Most of them seem to consider Maramures and its land-scapes, objects and lifestyles as quintessentially part of a wider Romanian being. In the case of Masuria in Poland, these place-related images are less homogeneous, especially where they are subjected to competing national-isms between German and Polish tourists and other stakeholders.

If the production and consumption of Maramures and Masuria seem based on a similar heterotopia (Foucault, 1986) of lost time and space, there are significant differences in the way in which this is rooted in local self-perceptions and tourist perceptions of space. These differences are il-lustrated by a personal experience of Hannah Wadle (one of the authors). One day, when she came home in the evening to her Polish hosts after having spent the day following a German group, she was unable to tell them where she had actually been. The places she and the German tourists had visited during the day all had German names, and these were mostly unknown to her hosts. Most German tourists and tour guides who travel through Masuria use German maps. These have recently become available on the growing Polish tourism map market, and were made available for sale in the tourism information centre of Gizycko. The maps mostly use the German toponyms, which the different places had carried before the Second World War, when East Prussia and its part of Masuria had administratively belonged to the German Reich. For most German tourists, these maps fulfil three main functions: they facilitate the pronunciation and remembering of the places; they allow them to 'find' and 'recognise' places of the ancestral or national pasts; and they enable to dive into a familiar imagined cultural and natural landscape of 'Masuren' and 'Ostpreußen', rather than into the Polish 'Mazury'. Navigating through the tourist space with the help of these historical maps, most German tourists and tour guides follow a route taking them to the historical monuments of pre-war times and suggesting that they enjoy the 'wide blue East Prussian sky' and the 'Masurian villages'. 'Luckily, people in the villages are too poor to reconstruct their houses and too well-off to let them decay totally', a German tourist noted while gazing at 'Masuren' through the window of the coach. 'If we still had Masuria, it would now be tidied up and there would be sausage stands and beer gardens everywhere', another tourist commented, seeming to enjoy the fact that the area was natural and non-commodified and grateful for the 'neglect' exercised by the Polish population and public institutions.

The performance of the search for Masuria is equally helped, if not framed, by German-language books on East Prussia and Masuria, made available in many German-led hotels and holiday homes. In front of the decaying East Prussian manor of Steinort, tour guides often quote from Marion Dönhoff's essay on Masuria. Dönhoff is worshipped by both Germans and Poles for her principle to 'be able to love without owning', which describes how she dealt with the loss of her own East Prussian *Heimat*. The German tourists also visit members of the local population, often former East Prussians, Germans or German-speaking Poles who have been featured in German television travel documentaries. Some of these own renovated local estates and have opened hotels that respond to the dominant German imaginary of Masuren. Others offer activities, such as punting or driving through the landscape on a horse-drawn carriage.

Among many members of the local Polish populations, German tourists are often known for their non-consumption and their lack of engagement in the local economy. German groups of cyclists are often accused of taking packed lunches with them, which they eat during their breaks, instead of going to a local inn. Similarly, coach tourists are reproached for being catered for by the coach drivers, who provide frankfurters or even self-prepared picnics. In fact, for many tour operators, the provision of food and beverages on board coaches is a means not only to save time, but also to remain independent from local tourism infrastructures. Instead, they can organise breaks in remote villages, at picturesque manors or hidden lakes. The observed reluctance of German tourists to dine in local facilities leads to a general suspicion among the local populations that Germans are stingy, if not distrustful with regard to the hygiene and quality of local food.

Some German tourism performances of 'Masuren' are, however, taken up by the local tourism industry. The most prominent one is cycling. Cycling is a very popular way for German tourists to experience Masuren. They love cycling through the old, 'typical' Masurian avenues, stop for swims in the lake and move through the landscape with all their senses. The German practice of cycling, and the organisation of cycle trips through the Masurian Lake District by German tour operators, has popularised this form of tourism activity also among local Polish tourism entrepreneurs. Thanks to the centrality of nature and movement, cycling tourism is reconcilable with the Polish concept of *turystyka aktywna* (active tourism), as it is promoted by local authorities and by Polish guidebooks for Mazury. In the case of cycling, German and Polish tourism cultures of Masuria are beginning to merge.

Similar to their overall importance for the structuring of tourism experiences in Masuria in Poland, guidebooks equally play a central role in the mediation of those sites that, in sum, are made to constitute Maramures in Romania. Stéphane, a French tourist, explained that he got to know about Maramures through travel guides. He said, 'as many guidebooks write, time has stopped here, although it is beginning to make up for it. Coming from our industrial, capitalistic, modern culture, it is still a shock. Let's hope they manage to keep their authenticity and their know-how.' In keeping with the romanticist, folkloristic and later touristic descriptions of the area as an open-air living museum, tourists like Stéphane performed and reproduced Maramures as a specific set of sceneries. In a similar vein, Anne-Marie, who had visited Maramures in 2005, enthusiastically described her car excursions through the region:

> We discovered many wonderful little valleys in which the inhabitants live from the earth and the craft, with working methods and tools dating back from the last war. I enjoyed photographing them in their working suit and their Sunday best. Every character is typical, whether it is the old lady spinning the wool or the washerwomen at the river taking advantage of a waterfall that they use as a washing machine.

The dominant aesthetics of a preserved place where nothing has changed for ages eventually met with opposition from the local population. The recent appearance of young entrepreneurs who built modern, colourful guest-houses set in concrete and PVC challenged the widely consensual imaginary of the eternal Romanian village. Reports in the national mass media and interventions by public intellectuals deplored the showy aspect of these modern and foreign elements and appealed to a 'return' to traditions, authenticity and ethno-folklore heritage. These public reactions created a feeling of unease within the tourism profession. In an interview, the president of a major association of rural tourism stated:

> many journalists and intellectuals are surprised that such houses have been built.... According to them, one should respect the traditional style, or regional style as far as possible. But you can't! Obviously, you may preserve the style, but all the houses don't have to follow a rustic style.

She contested the fact that tradition has to be followed to the letter or conform to any 'frozen past':

> Many are surprised that there are pizzerias in the countryside, but come on! There are young people there, and nowadays people eat pizzas.

We live in the 21st century – we are not in the Village Ethnographic Museum. Time travel is strictly impossible!

Although they have become a controversial topic at the local level, these signs of a global modernity were seldom mentioned by the French tourists interviewed. Most of them consumed the destination's culture by buying handicrafts that their hosts or guidebooks referred to as traditional or, as in Anne-Marie's case, by recognising and appreciating the signs of geographical and historical remoteness. When 'modernity' was mentioned in their accounts, it was mostly in a sense of wonder about how long 'it would take before the pre-modern elements' that they were enjoying disappeared. These tourists mainly engaged sentimentally with this region by expressing their fear that it would start looking like Western Europe and lose its difference, as Stéphane's comment attest:

Maramures has kept its cultural identity, but when you see hypermarkets growing everywhere in Romania, fast cars on the roads, it seems that the Romanians are eager to make up for lost time. Let's hope that they become aware that a fast progress is most certainly not the best option…. We should warn them about the mistakes we've made.

In both regions, Maramures in Romania and Masuria in Poland, Marc Augé's observation of a Western European quest for the exotic as a means to compensate for the perceived shortcomings of globalisation is a central element of the heterotopia. In Maramures, the pre-modern destination is performed by the gaze of the French tourists, enthusiastic about recognising in it elements from the past, in compliance with local tourism stakeholders. Contestations, principally with regard to local aesthetics, emerge only in a hidden way, usually behind the backs of the tourists. Such contestations about 'traditional' or 'modern' aesthetics pull to the surface a wider paradox that frames the post-socialist identity-making processes. The latter oscillates between a national project of reinvention of tradition (Hobsbawm & Ranger, 1983) and the simultaneous desire to participate in global practices of consumption. In north-east Poland, German tourist performances often willingly ignore the presence of local spaces of tourism consumption that, *a priori*, would challenge their pre-war imaginary of the area. In doing so, they perform their destination as a pristine space in a highly self-sufficient way.

The performative projection of a space lacking consumption visibly contrasts with the existing local tourism infrastructures, thus playing out a separate culture of space. It thereby creates a new tourism sector with its own set of performances and aesthetics. Yet there are some performances, such as cycling, which contribute to a merging of domestic and foreign tourism cultures and economies.

Locating Tourism Seduction in Place

Anja Peleikis (2006b) sees tourism as a stage for a very specific process of reunification after the Cold War. For her it allows the (re-)encounter of Western imaginaries of cultural landscapes with the physical, material realities in the toured Eastern Europe. This encounter does not always happen as desired by the Western tourists – sometimes, they are proved to have been bitterly deceived. In this section, we will explore the threat that social changes in Maramures and Masuria represent for a form of tourism that is based on the idealisation of an unspoiled past. As argued earlier, in north-east Poland, German tourists frequently search for a space that corresponds to a specific nostalgic image of Masuren. However, we will also show that tourists should not be seen as passive consumers of material places. What they imagine and desire in a place is important for understanding the development of aesthetics and the creation of places in rural Masuria and Maramures.

When Gerda, for instance, eventually found her 'lost home', a house in ruin near Kaliningrad in the Russian part of former East Prussia, she was disappointed. While she was sad about the overgrown fields in the Kaliningrad region, she enjoyed Masuria, where she perceived the landscape as more ordered and cultivated. During her trip, which was part of an organised journey, the tour guide stopped at a hotel called Christel's. Christel, the owner, was of German Masurian descent. She and her husband fluently spoke the East Prussian dialect. The couple served what they advertised as 'typical' food, organised folk dance evenings and even ran a small Masurian museum, with items from everyday life that had been used in the past. In doing so, they had created a space in which *Heimattourists* and German-speaking Masures could meet and commemorate their sense of belonging.

However, most German visitors to Masuria are more interested in finding the imagined geography and landscape of Masuren and Ostpreußen rather than an imagined community of former East Prussians or Masures. Andrea, for instance, had witnessed the challenges that many other tourists experience on their search for such an idealised geography:

My dream has always been to travel to East Prussia and, I believe, I am already a bit too late to see the real old thing. We went to Nikolajken, which you often read about, and I thought – I could have left that out of the programme. It turned out to be just another tourism resort with souvenir stalls and restaurants.... I am sure in 10 years it will be much more developed here.

The longed for, imagined geography is challenged not only by recent and anticipated future tourist developments but sometimes as well by the more immediate socialist past of urbanisation. 'I had imagined everything [to look] like the small villages. The towns are horrible, take only Gizycko, Lötzen', emphasised Andrea. Gizycko was one of the most popular Masurian tourism resorts, which attracted people with its music festivals, marina and pleasure beach. Yet, for people searching for pre-war Masuren, the post-war architecture of Gizycko was out of place. Andrea added: 'The socialist blocks you can see, they are poor – it looks just terrible'. Yet, in other respects, the search for the reality of lost times and spaces was successful. She said, 'But the landscape, the old avenues, they are so beautiful. If you want, you can visit a castle of the Teutonic Knights in every small town.' In other circumstances, tourists actually find places that correspond to their imaginings. In another occasion, Andrea recounted, 'Now we are just back from a village, Nida, where it was just like I imagined it. There you had buildings in the old Masurian style. Some of them had been renovated, and I very much liked that.' Andrea had been to an area in which many wealthy Warsavians had renovated or built second homes with a nostalgic rural aesthetic, which in many regards corresponded to the German idea of 'Masuren und Ostpreußen'.

Nearby, there is one of the most popular Masurian tourist attractions for German visitors, a former hunter's lodge. Trans-located from its previous place, it has been cleansed of the socialist layers of its past. It is largely kept alive through income generated from the wealthy urban elite from Warsaw. A young Polish-German entrepreneur owns it and manages it as a rustic pub with homemade dishes, as a conference centre and as a guest-house. On the first floor, his German mother established a big library with literature and CDs on Masuria, East Prussia and Poland – in German and Polish. There are pictures of the East Prussian gentry and one of its members, journalist and author Marion Dönhoff, to whom the room is devoted. The library and memorial room confirm visitors' imagined geographies of the cultural landscape of Masuren and East Prussia and gives them permission for, and moral instruction about, the nature of their yearning.

We stated earlier that the local controversy over 'modern' or 'traditional' house architecture is commonly ignored by the tourists in the Romanian Maramures. Yet, here as well, the idyllic visual imaginary of a lost paradise projected by these tourists is frequently disturbed. Stéphane, for example, who we mentioned earlier, regretted the pollution that he had seen during his stay. He said, 'When I saw the rivers, the fields and the streets contaminated with all kind of rubbish, I thought that they are on their way to the progress–waste vicious circle'. To keep the tourists happy and to participate in the realms of the tourism-generated modernity, many local hosts in Maramures actively engage in a process of adapting the built environment to the ideals of tourist fantasies and, at the same time, to the Romanian myth of a timeless village.

In the middle of the 1990s, when rural tourism in guest-houses appeared in Maramures, a Belgian–French non-governmental organisation (NGO), Opération Villages Roumains (OVR), helped to set up a selection of cultural features that had to be displayed in a tourist-facing way: beautiful landscapes, wooden architecture and a cultural wealth, revealed mostly in handicrafts. Bogdan, one of OVR's local leaders and the owner of a guest-house, mentioned the 'good taste education course', as he called it, that he had initiated to help guest-house owners adapt their houses for tourists. He had suggested in particular a review of the decoration, especially the removal of all 'kitsch' items and, instead, the integration of Maramures-like elements, such as a carved wooden gate. He also advocated the use of wood as a building and decoration material. By identifying with a lost natural world and lost cultural practices, local stakeholders had developed innovative ways of redefining the local identity, a phenomenon that has equally been noticed by Serban Vaetisi (2006) in the Romanian Apuseni Mountains.

In Botiza, a village nearby, a similar re-creation of folkloric elements has taken place. Victoria, the priest's wife and owner of a guest-house, was well known for the role she had played in the revitalisation of traditional carpet-weaving techniques. In 1974, when she moved to the place, she was surprised that people had abandoned the Maramures patterns and the natural dying techniques, and replaced them with flowers and bright industrial colours that were not native to Maramures. She had reintroduced techniques she considered to be specific to the village. She explained that she had studied these patterns in the local museums and read about historical Romanian carpet manufacturing. She had also discovered ancient vegetable dying techniques and so, she said, set up, once again, the old tradition. She noted that, following her interventions, the village had progressively changed 'back to the past':

> In 1974, the villagers used to sell their embroidered costumes to people coming from the cities. I bought some of them and on Sundays, my daughters and I used to wear the traditional costume.... And then the villagers found their taste for traditions again.... I have altered the face of the village.

Anthropologist Chiara Cipollari argues that, in Botiza, 'tourists and locals together create a landscape through a self-referential game in which they each provide the other with the contrivance they expect to see' (Cipollari, 2010: 24). Beyond a merely commercial aspect, by appropriating the folklorists' discourse, by perpetuating or reinventing traditions, the pioneers of rural tourism thus gave substance to the national myth of an eternal rural Romania. Foreign tourists assimilate and reproduce the aesthetics of Maramures that they have been introduced to, and therefore play a central role in its legitimisation.

The appreciation of a specific tourism place is often altered, especially where tourists perceive signs that they consider counter to their expectations. These may be evidence of contemporary tourist developments, forms of post-war socialist urbanisation or signs of environmental pollution. Yet, in both regions studied here, the German and French tourists mostly found what they were looking for, be it only in special spots and marginal locales purposefully 'protected' against the 'threat' of modernity.

As such, tourism induces processes of protection and even purification of desired sign-worlds from undesired change. The utopia of a 'lost state of the past' is kept alive through the heterotopia of tourism places. Both case studies show that this heterotopia is built on a process of co-construction, involving tourists, tourism agents, local populations and other local stakeholders. In Masuria, German tourists now treasure the newly renovated buildings that recreate an old East Prussian atmosphere and they consume culturally comfortable tourism in a rustic inn decorated with East Prussian memorabilia. In Maramures, French tourists find in their hosts' efforts to recreate a mythical setting a haven to escape from their day-to-day modernity. In both cases, the tensions between tourism as performed art (Adler, 1989), of un-ambivalent space, and as an economic system for local populations became visible. In Maramures, the economic benefits generated by tourism provided an argument for the increasing folklorisation and preservation of the area for tourists. In Masuria, different tourism performances of space contest with each other. In both cases, the economic dimension is inseparable from the dimension of national identities and local adherence to them.

Conclusion

Our discussion of French and German tourism in post-socialist rural north Romania and north-east Poland demonstrates that tourism imaginaries are significant elements for the construction of spatial identities and the production of places in post-socialist Eastern Europe. It shows that tourism imaginaries of Eastern Europe are hybrid constructs of shared ideas about the 'East' and varying culturally rooted senses of belonging and locally specific allures.

French and German tourists imagine their travel destinations in rural Eastern Europe as 'frozen' in past times, somehow outside the globalised world. Maramures and Masuria appeal to them as spaces in which they can encounter themselves in another time and enjoy thereby a familiar difference. This gap between a cultural familiarity and a temporal distance creates a particular relation between the tourists and their travel destination, which Saskia Cousin (2010) calls 'in-between otherness'. Made familiar through ethnographic or historical discourses, this otherness is a lure to French and German tourists: in their trips to Eastern Europe, many are in search of an imagined self-in-the-other, rather than an exotic and totally different 'other'.

Despite these similarities, tourist imaginaries of Maramures and Masuria are not generic, arbitrary products of tourism marketing, but are deeply embedded in political and cultural traditions and in national narratives of belonging. The example of German tourism to Masuria in particular shows that tourist appeals evolve along the lines of changing cultural attitudes and biographical experiences.

Western tourism clearly affects the nature of late post-socialist transformation processes and shapes future spatial identities in the two studied areas of rural Eastern Europe. While Western Europeans use tourism to Maramures and Masuria in their search for a non-globalised haven, for local stakeholders tourism is an important realm to engage with and through which to participate in a united, shared Europe (Picard, 2011). In both north-east Poland and north Romania, this also leads to discord and friction. Tourism imaginaries and performances are noticed by permanent residents and entail differently perceived social, cultural and economic consequences for them. The authors therefore recommend looking at local politics of place and processes of place-making from a trans-national point of view. Such a perspective allows researchers to grasp the active participation of Western tourism imaginaries in the construction of spatial orders and identities in Eastern Europe.

The ethnographic evidence shows that Marc Augé's observation of Eastern Europe is still relevant and resonates strongly in the analysed tourism imaginaries and heterotopias. The image of Eastern Europe as a space lacking access to globalisation forms the basis for Western tourism imaginaries. Nowadays, however, the image no longer belongs solely to the Western gaze and to the Western tourism imaginary, but also shapes local politics of place in rural Eastern Europe and merges with questions of national identity, tradition and economic revenue. At the same time, it is deeply embedded in contexts of national and trans-national discourses about culture and history, and therefore varies greatly within different areas of Eastern Europe. By seeking to preserve and reproduce the tourism imaginary of a pre-modern space, tourism heterotopias in Eastern Europe have turned Augé's observation into a self-fulfilling prophecy and paradox of post-socialist transformation.

Acknowledgements

We wish to thank David Picard for his comments on our first draft of the chapter and Ian Hague for his skilful and empathic proofreading of the text. We also thank all our informants for the time they let us participate in their lives, for their trust in our research and their patience. The last thank you goes to Skype, by means of which we were able to write this chapter across the Channel.

References

Abram, S. (1996) Reactions to tourism: A view from the deep green heart of France. In J. Boissevain (ed.) *Coping with Tourists: European Reactions to Mass Tourism* (pp. 174–203). Oxford: Berghahn Books.
Adler, J. (1989) Travel as performed art. *American Journal of Sociology* 94 (6), 1366–1391.
Augé, M. (1995) *Non-places: Introduction to an Anthropology of Supermodernity*. London: Verso.
Beck, G. (2000) Warum sieht Ostpreußen (immer noch) so ostpreußisch aus? Anmerkungen zur mentalen Repräsentation regionaler Einheiten. *Zeitschrift für Kultur- und Bildungswissenschaften* 10, 79–87.
Beeton, S. (2005) *Film-Induced Tourism*. Clevedon: Channel View Publications.
Brakoniecki, K. (2005) *Ziemiec – prowincjałki rowerowe*. Olsztyn: Borussia.
Burachovič, S. (2002) Gedanken zum Sudetendeutschen Heimwehtourismus aus tschechischer Sicht. In E. Fendl ed.) *Zur Ikonographie des Heimwehs* (pp. 223–244). Freiburg: Johannes Künzig Institut.
Câmpeanu, N. (2008) Material desires: Cultural production, post-socialist transformations, and heritage tourism in a Transylvanian town. PhD thesis, University of Texas at Austin.
Cipollari, C. (2010) Can tourists purchase 'the past'? The past as a commodity in tourist sites. *Anthropological Notebooks* 16 (1), 23–35.
Cousin, S. (2010) In-between otherness: Seductions of ethnography in tourism. Paper delivered at the conference Tourism and Seductions of Difference, organised by the Centro em Rede de Investigação em Antropologia (CRIA) in cooperation with Tourism Contact Culture Research Network (TOCOCU) and the Centre for Tourism and Cultural Change (CTCC). Lisbon.
Eliade, M. (1970) *De Zalmoxis à Gengis-Khan: Études comparatives sur les religions et le folklore de la Dacie et de l'Europe orientale*. Paris: Payot.
Feldman, J. (2008) *Above the Death Pits, Beneath the Flag: Jewish Youth Voyages to Poland and Performances of Israeli National Identity*. New York: Berghahn Books.

Fendl, E. (1998) Reisen in die verlorene Vergangenheit. Überlegungen zum 'Heimweh-tourismus'. *Jahrbuch für deutsche und osteuropäische Volkskunde* 41, 85–100.

Foucault, M. (1986) Of other spaces. *Diacritics* 16 (1), 22–27.

Galbraith, M.H. (2000) On the road to Czestochowa: Rhetoric and experience on a Polish pilgrimage. *Anthropological Quarterly* 73 (2), 61–73.

Hobsbawn, E. and Ranger, T.O. (eds) (1983) *The Invention of Tradition*. Cambridge: Cambridge University Press.

Klekot, E. (2010) La visite du patrimoine national: Entre politique et tourisme. *Ethnologie Française* 40 (2), 273–284.

Light, D. (2011) *The Dracula Dilemma: Tourism, Identity, and the State in Romania*. Aldershot: Ashgate.

Light, D. and Young, C. (2006) Communist heritage tourism: Between economic development and European integration. In D. Hassenpflug, B. Kolbmüller and S. Schröder-Esch (eds) *Heritage and Media in Europe – Contributing Towards Integration and Regional Development* (pp. 249–263). Weimar: Bauhaus Universität Weimar.

Mai, U. (2005) 'Das einfache Leben': Zur Wahrnehmung der masurischen Landschaft unter Neusiedlern. In U. Mai (ed.) *Masuren: Trauma, Sehnsucht, leichtes Leben. Zur Gefühlswelt einer Landschaft* (pp. 310–330). Münster: LIT Verlag.

Mihailescu, V. (1999) Le monde enchanté de la culture populaire. Une lecture du discours ethnologique roumain à travers ses enjeux idéologiques. *Ethnologies* 21 (2), 27–45.

Peleikis, A. (2006a) Whose heritage? Legal pluralism and the politics of the past. A case study from the Curonian Spit (Lithuania). *Journal of Legal Pluralism* 53–54, 209–237.

Peleikis, A. (2006b) Tourism and the making of cultural heritage. The case of Nida (Curonian Spit), Lithuania. *Acta Historica Universitatis Klaipedensis* 12, 101–114.

Peleikis, A. (2009) Reisen in die Vergangenheit. Deutsche Heimattouristen auf der Kurischen Nehrung Voyage. In W. Kolbe, C. Noack and H. Spode (eds) *Tourismusgeschichte(n)* (pp. 85–97). München: Profil Verlag.

Picard, D. (2011) *Tourism, Magic and Modernity: Cultivating the Human Garden*. New York: Berghahn Books.

Schmitt-Roschmann, V. (2010) *Heimat: Neuentdeckung eines verpönten Gefühls*. München: Gütersloher Verlagshaus.

Stennert, D. (1995) Reisen zum Wiedersehen und Neuerleben. Aspekte des 'Heimweh-tourismus' dargestellt am Beispiel der Grafschaft Glatzer. In K. Dröge (ed.) *Alltagskulturen zwischen Erinnerung und Geschichte. Beiträge zur Volkeskunde der Deutschen im und aus dem östlichen Europa* (pp. 83–93). Oldenburg: Oldenburger Wissenschafts Verlag.

Vaetisi, S. (2006) Rural tourism in the Apuseni Mountains, Romania: An anthropological research on using natural and cultural resources in developing a poor region. In B.P. George and D. Nigam (eds) *Tourists and Tourism* (pp. 40–50). New Delhi: Abhijeet Publications.

Wadle, H. (2012) Von Fragmenten der Ortsintimität zu einem Konzept des performa-tiven deutsch-polnischen Kulturerbes. Ethnographische Nahaufnahmen von Schloss Sztynort/Steinort. In J. Drejer and P. Zalewski (eds) *Deutsch-Polnisches Kulturerbe und die Zivilgesellschaft im heutigen Polen* (pp. 142–159). Warszawa: Wydawnictwo Naukowe.

Part 2
Tourism and Others in Dialogue

5 Frozen Vodka and White Skin in Tourist Goa

Pamila Gupta

Introduction

On the narrow lanes that lead towards the Anjuna flea market, impromptu convoys of motorbikes and scooters weave around the ubiquitous cows and bump over the potholes, heading in the direction of the beach. Their riders are an odd mix: the hippies, semi-naked with their intricate tattoos and wraparound shades, straddling old Enfield bullets, studiously ignoring the fat, pink, middle-aged package tourists clinging nervously to their scooter handlebars and wishing they were sipping their first cool Kingfisher beer of the day. These men, too, have discarded their shirts, preferring to expose their beer bellies to the sun; the women favour strappy vest tops and shorts that ruck up around the thighs. If they notice the cold stares they receive from some of the local people who move among them, it does not show. The sun is bakingly hot, sitting high in the deep blue sky above the coconut palms, the light glinting off the waves rolling gently on to the sand. This is the Goa most people know: the relaxed, freewheeling former Portuguese colony that opens it arms to visitors of all kinds and so appealed to the hippies who flocked here in the late 1960s that some have never left. Yet something poisonous has entered Eden. A spate of high-profile attacks on western tourists ... is the most obvious symptom of the malaise. A state-sponsored land grab of expatriates' properties, the influx of Russian and Indian property developers, and even a threat to ban the wearing of bikinis has convinced many long-term stayers that the time to leave has come. (Chamberlain, 2010)

This is an excerpt from a recent article entitled 'The party's over for Goa's expats', written by Gethin Chamberlain for the *Guardian Weekly* (23 April

2010). I start my chapter with his evocative description both to introduce the central theme of this volume, but also to think about the seedy and sordid underbelly of the seemingly sublime that the art of seduction requires, but is very often kept hidden from the tourist view. The following chapter is organised in a series of vignettes or 'thick descriptions' (Geertz, 1973) of ethnographic encounters taken from my own experiences as an anthropologist and tourist (Crick, 1995) visiting Goa in November 2009, a place that receives approximately 2 million tourists annually, including half a million foreign visitors (IBN Live, 2010). That I lived in Goa for 14 months during 1999–2000 while conducting ethnographic and archival research on a different yet inter-related topic, and have continued to visit what is popularly described as a 'tiny emerald' (IndiaLine, 2012) in the Indian Ocean repeatedly over the past decade, also allows me a unique perspective on the dramatically changing tourism landscape of Goa. I tell these everyday tales of 'contact zones' (Pratt, 1992) to reveal the numerous ways in which the 'tourist gaze' (Urry, 1990) in Goa is a complicated and complicating one – where it cannot be tied down to one form of touristic spectatorship, but rather involves everyday processes of looking at others and being looked at in a mutually constituting field of visual reciprocity (Schneider & Wright, 2006: 18).

It is a pendulum of 'friction' in Anna Tsing's sense of the word, that has been shifting back and forth for quite some time now, in 'the grip of worldly encounter' wherein 'heterogeneous and unequal encounters can lead to new arrangements of culture and power' (Tsing, 2005: 1–5) and which in some ways foreshadows the disquieting (yet very real) cosmopolitan tourist scene found in Goa today. And I tell these stories as incomplete/uncompleted ethnographic moments in space and time, as fragmented and fragmentary, because, as Tsing (2005: 271) argues, this is precisely *how* and *where* global connections are made. Specifically, the 'fragment' encapsulates a methodology for conducting fieldwork in increasingly globalised settings and on the subject of globalisation itself, that is, it enables a way of capturing the complexity of the globalised world *ethnographically*, through an immersion in the 'contests and engagements of the present' (Tsing, 2005: 271). It operates in much the same way as Bruno Latour's shift from conducting fieldwork in (impossibly discrete) territories to studying 'networks' (Latour, 2005). And, finally, it works by interrupting a story of totalising or unified (global) success. Thus, if we take into account that Western foreigners increasingly no longer feel welcome in this tropical paradise, enough to feel the 'frictions' at play, those bubbling under its sublime surface, then this is a far cry from Goa's hedonistic early days as a global destination for hippy tourism and 'psychedelic trance'. I ask: is the party really over?

More generally, the central problematic in this chapter is to address the varying historical and cultural 'imaginaries' (Salazar, 2010) of seduction that are at play in the tourist scene that is Goa today, and by way of a series of colliding or dialectical 'fragments' as I have defined them here. What makes these tourist imaginaries so compelling is that, for the case of Goa, we are perhaps close to the end of a cycle of seduction, when its promises as a seducer, once so successful, are increasingly wearing thin, for a variety of reasons, as will become evident in the following analysis. However, the reality is that Goa is dependent on tourism for its economic livelihood. In other words, we are perched on a precarious ethnographic edge, watching curiously to see who (among the already seduced) is slowly losing interest in what Goa has on touristic offer, and in what manner, just as it searches anew for alternative forms, cycles and audiences ripe for seduction.

Fragment 1: Frozen Vodka

Take any taxi motorbike in Goa and ask the driver what he thinks about the Russian girls and he'll say 'very sexy!' and more. Russian girls go to the markets in bikinis, drive around in revealing outfits and basically do all they can to upset the conservative religious and cultural values of India. Either they don't know or they don't care – but in any case they look good, so we're not complaining. (GoaGuide, 2010)

I arrive straight from Dabolim Airport in South Goa to the Regal Palms Resort and apartment complex located in North Goa, in a popular tourist area named Candolim, where my friend Angeline, a local travel agent, has arranged for me stay for the next two weeks. It is a huge complex, set off from the main road but still central enough for everything required for a package tourist – the beach, the liquor shop, the grocery store, the shopping stalls, all in walking distance. It is immaculately clean, with numerous sets of three-storey buildings organised around various swimming pools, the requisite colourful beach towels drying on the surrounding balconies. It is the height of the tourist season in Goa (September–March). It is the next morning when I decide to venture to the pool-side to have a day of what Goa is most popularly known for, a bit of sun, surf and *soçegado*, all qualities of excess, with the last term a carryover from its Portuguese colonial days and which translates into 'leisure' or 'relaxation', and includes drinking and a love of music and diversion.[1]

I carefully lay out my beach towel on one of the numerous empty lawn chairs that have an attached umbrella. Just as I am starting to truly relax, an overweight British man appears out of nowhere to tell me that I cannot sit there, his thick northern England accent immediately apparent. He informs me that that particular umbrella is reserved for someone who resides in the complex permanently. I sit up a bit perplexed, and immediately offer to move if and when a person who has seniority over me within the hierarchy of the complex rules arrives. He refuses my request and so I spend the rest of my pool-side days sitting on one of the few umbrella-less chairs, getting sunburnt, and surrounded of course by a sea of empty umbrella chairs, but knowing and feeling that he is observing me, ready to pounce on me for any infraction. But I, in turn, spend my pool-side days watching *him*, this British expat, package tourist and Goan long-term resident. Like clockwork, this man's days consist of getting up for a morning swim, checking on any repairs that need to be done (and which includes yelling at the gardening staff if they are not doing something properly), having a Kingfisher beer over lunch and a game of cards with his retired British friends who also reside in the complex, followed by an afternoon Latin-type siesta that Goa is known for, also due its Portuguese colonial past, and then another dip in the pool before it is time to dress for dinner and a night out on the town with his wife and buddies.

The attitude as well as story of the nameless British pensioner living out his retirement in Goa, whom I encountered during my two-week visit, is now a familiar one, as Goa has long been a popular destination for international, charter and domestic tourists, and for a variety of reasons having to do with its Portuguese colonial legacy, and the nature of its late decolonisation and forced integration into the Indian nation state after 1961 (Cahen *et al.*, 2000). In some sense, Goa's tourist industry developed in the historical and cultural space leftover by Portuguese colonialism, wherein Goa was labelled 'India for Beginners'; it was considered less dirty and impoverished than other parts of India. As well, pork and beef were more readily available, as was alcohol, due to the history of a strong Portuguese presence (Newman, 2001). With a state population close to 1.4 million, of whom 400,000 are dependent on tourism for their livelihood – the majority of these in turn from Goa's Catholic population, the direct inheritors of many Portuguese buildings and cultural traits (Trichur, 2000) – Goa annually takes in approximately 400,000 foreign tourists (half of whom historically came from Great Britain) and another million domestic tourists. Tourism is very much part of Goa's sense of itself (Pearson, 2003: 274).

'Tom' (as I have now decided to name my neighbour in the complex) is one of many British tourists who, taking advantage of the competitively priced charter tours now available – remarkably, 50% of all charter flights to India are to Goa (Pinto, 2006) – visit Goa on an annual basis. Like many others before and after him, Tom comes less to experience 'incredible India' (as the incredibly successful recent advertising campaign has labelled it) and its attendant spiritualism, first made popular by The Beatles' frequent visits to India in the 1960s, but rather to avoid it, opting for Goa instead, as a cheap, faceless, commodified beach destination, a cosmopolitan 'non-place' (Augé, 1995) and form of 'enclave tourism' (Pearson, 2003) where British tourists have little interaction with locals beyond a service industry, and where their pounds, underwritten by a pension fund, can potentially go a long(er) way. However, it is not only the cheap beer and the search for a perfect suntan that seduces them to come to Goa, aspects confirmed both by the tourists I spoke with and by my travel agent friend Angeline. It was she who also suggested to me that Goa's popularity is very much tied to the complicated relationship that British tourists reluctantly have to bear when traveling in the rest of (formerly British) India. Goa, then, given its Portuguese past, becomes in contradistinction, a place to visit without this added burden (of guilt) weighing on their sunburnt shoulders.[2]

More recently, however, there has been a massive influx of Russian package tourists who are flying in straight from Moscow, bottles of frozen vodka lining the bottoms of their suitcases in order to be opened upon arrival, perfectly chilled and ready to be served,[3] no doubt previous tourists (and friends) on the Goa tourist circuit having informed them of the exorbitant prices for purchasing imported alcohol in India. With rates far more competitive than Europe, nearly 40,000 Russians have been hitting Goa's beaches over the last five years. They are a noticeable group, particularly in the relatively newly developed beach area of Morjim, in North Goa, recently dubbed 'Little Russia', where they tend to congregate (IBN Live, 2010). According to one news report, Russian tourists were poised to become the largest component of foreign tourists to Goa during the season 2009–10, displacing for the first time the number of British tourists, who had been coming here for over a decade (*Deccan Herald*, 2013); one recent report has suggested a reduction by 20% of the number of British tourists countered by some 80,000 Russian tourists arriving for Goa's high season in the year 2012 (*Deccan Herald*, 2013). Interestingly, for these package tourists, in contrast to the British, it is less about the burden of a colonial past that makes them travel to Goa (considered a part of India) and more a sense of curiosity to see the world, precisely because this was something denied to earlier generations of Russians. Thus, like the British, they are making up for their past in a way as well, only it is a very different past they are responding to, an insight provided once again by Angeline.

I find myself one day on the beach at Palolem, sunbathing (considered here an integral part of fieldwork) like the rest of the tourist hoards who have come to Goa during the height of its season. I cannot help but notice an increased amount of topless sunbathing among the Russian female tourists, something I did not see 10 years ago. I feel embarrassed, not only for those guilty parties indulging in such an act (perhaps they *really* didn't know, but then how ignorant could they be?), but for the Goans (mostly male), who cannot help but stare at their exposed breasts, and are seemingly enjoying the act. At this same beach, I get harassed for a massage. Just as I am about to say no thank you to at least the tenth sari-clad woman who has come by, I notice all of them suddenly fleeing. I sit up from my beach chair and watch as a stream of vendors run and disappear into the mangroves. It is truly a spectacle. Five minutes later, I see a plainclothes policeman strolling along the beach, checking the permits of those unfortunate few who had not caught wind of his arrival in time to escape persecution. Just as the sun starts to dip below the horizon, and I am one of the few tourists remaining, about to pack up my beach bag, I notice a slight Rajasthani woman meticulously picking up the day's accumulated garbage; she, like the many others who are increasingly travelling to Goa from other parts of India in the hope of finding seasonal work and who, as a result, are slowly changing Goa's profile, no doubt lives off Goa's tourism leftovers.

As I am walking to dinner one night, I see a group of tall blond Russian women, skimpily dressed, smoking, talking and walking. I notice the placard outside advertising Goan specialities like *sorpatel* (a spicy Goan pork curry) and *vindaloo* (either chicken or lamb cooked in spices, garlic and wine) in Russian, something I have never seen before this particular visit. It brings back memories during fieldwork 10 years ago of isolated pockets of Israeli tourists, many of whom came to imbibe Goa's excess after the confinement of their nation's obligatory military service. They tended to reside in some of North Goa's less populated beaches, a few even going so far as to set up impromptu food stalls with signs in Hebrew advertising *hummus* and *falafel*. Among the Russians, however, what I observe is on a much larger scale. I see thick wads of cash being pulled out of jacket pockets, to pay for small things like a drink or a packet of cigarettes. I hear from my expat British and diasporic Indian friends who are now living in Goa permanently[4] – my source of all Goan gossip – about the rumours flying around concerning the Russians' mafia connections, as well as their attempts to buy up whole swathes of buildings for tourism development. I hear stories of rape, rage and violence, amid concerns over the safety of female tourists.[5] I find numerous editorials in the local newspaper, the *Navhind Times*, written by middle-class Goans as well as conservative politicians (members of the Bharatiya Janata Party, BJP) voicing their concerns over Goa's recent so-called 'Russian invasion' (*Deccan Herald*, 2010).

I return briefly here to the quote that I relied on at the outset of this 'fragment' to suggest that the contrasting image of a bikini-clad Russian girl versus an overweight British pensioner points to the different forms of seduction that are rubbing up against one another in Goa today. While some are seduced, others are less so, particularly those individuals (tourists and locals alike) who choose to move beyond the powers of seduction in order to see what lies underneath in order to make this scene possible.

Fragment 2: The River Princess

The Princess, which had ruled the seas, had no answer as she got entangled in the sandbar, and no amount of maneuvering could wrest her off the bank. The Princess, now turned pauper, was hoping for a Prince to rescue her and free her from her entanglement. Some tried to but failed. (Merinews, 2010)

Perched very close to Candolim, one of Goa's most popular beaches, the *River Princess* is an ore carrier, 240 metres long, that became grounded there on 6 June 2000 (Figure 5.1). Carrying a dead-weight cargo of over 100,000 metric tonnes, it drifted from the high seas in the midst of a heavy storm and got stuck in Goa's coastal waters (Goa Blog, 2010). Abandoned by its owners, Salgaonkar Mining Industries, the Goan government spent a decade trying to remove it, without success. Fresh bids for its disposal were renewed once again in 2009, after several shipping companies tried and failed to remove the hulk of metal. Worse yet, parts of the ship's corroded steel are being washed ashore periodically; it is wreaking long-term damage on the surrounding seabed – it has now settled 8–10 metres into the seabed and has taken in 30,000–40,000 tonnes of sand – altering the sea current, polluting the surrounding waters and threatening bathers (Merinews, 2010). To me, the *River Princess* is a bizarre oddity: a now a strangely familiar tourist spectacle but an eyesore on Goa's tourist image of pristine beaches, particularly as some continue to swim in close proximity to the ship whilst others derive pleasure from its use as a high-platform diving board into the Indian Ocean.[6] Rumours abound, a fresh set of new ones each time I come back for a visit: for example, that some homeless children have found a place to live on its balconies; that the locals are quietly dismantling the ship for scrap metal to sell as parts; that it is government corruption that is preventing its removal. Recent reports confirm that, after 12 years of being run aground, it is finally in the process of being dismantled by a Mumbai-based ship-breaking company, with a scheduled completion for January 2013,

Figure 5.1 Goa beach scene © Pamila Gupta 2009

only now there is an added worry of long-term sand erosion and additional tourist drownings as a result of a depression in the seabed caused by its removal (Digital Goa, 2013).

The story of the marooned *River Princess* is just one example among many that raises larger environmental concerns that have been percolating underneath the surface of the tourist bubble that is Goa since the late 1960s. As Michael Pearson notes, the ecological effects have been dire. He writes:

> There are now at least fifty swimming pools in the tiny Calangute–Baga strip alone, when thirty years ago there were none. The government privileges hotels over local rice farmers when it allocates water, so that the swimming pools will be full, and the lawns green. The three Taj hotels at Fort Aguada take more water than that available to the population of all the local villages of Calangute.... 'Development' has been uncontrolled, leading to massive violations of the environment,

such as building far too close to the maximum high tide level, discharge of sewage into the ocean, and mounds of discarded plastic containers disfiguring the sand. (Pearson, 2003: 275)

And, of course, with approximately one-third of Goa's population dependent on the tourism industry for their livelihood (Pearson, 2003: 274), the danger remains not only that Goa will be less idyllic in the future, and fall out of global tourist favour, but that Goa's economy will suffer disastrously as a result if it does not *take care* (Noronha, 1999; Routledge, 2001; Rubinoff, 1998). The case of the *River Princess* as a second 'fragment' thus allows us to see the complexity of environmental concerns in Goa today, which are fast becoming frighteningly real as they affect basic necessities such as food and water, for tourist and local alike. As its beaches and coastline slowly erode, which perhaps is not so far off as imagined, Goa's seductive abilities to attract tourists will also wane, unless of course it finds more sustainable forms of 'development', masked as aesthetic choices and practices.

Fragment 3: 'Psychedelic White'

So, while the history of psychedelic dance culture [in Anjuna] is an entanglement of trajectories of sounds, travellers, drugs, and scenes, its tendency toward whiteness has not only remained intact, but has perhaps become stronger, as the music became dark and serious like mother-fucking cancer. (Saldanha, 2007: 43)

It is a Wednesday, and I decide to head out to the Anjuna flea market. It is *the* event in Goa – one not to be missed by its visitors. It is where one goes on 'pilgrimage' (Gupta, 2005) to pay homage to Goa's remarkable and distinct history of tourism, first as a hippy haven, from the 1960s onwards, which involved living in beach shacks and massive drug consumption (Pearson, 2008: 3), and then as centre of psychedelic trance music, from the 1990s onwards, which involved hordes of travelling ravers from the UK, Israel, Germany, France and Japan (Pearson, 2008: 10). More generally, it is the continued overlapping of these two distinct forms of tourism that makes Anjuna so compelling as a destination for a wide range of Western tourists, its *mise-en-scène* very much as cultural geographer Arun Saldanha describes it from his own field-notes: He writes:

Goa trance parties traditionally happen … on the beaches, in forests, and on hills. They are normally free, going on till late morning, keeping the village awake with the throbbing kick drum. Goa trance music is a fast, hypnotic kind of techno, with fluctuating streams of bleeps, squelches and soundscapes vaguely reminiscent of Eastern harmonics. Anjuna's hippie past is reflected in the fluorescent paintings and performances to match the music's heavy psychedelic thrust, further enhanced by the use of illegal drugs like LSD, Ecstasy, hashish – this music isn't called trance for nothing. (Saldanha, 'Fear and loathing in Goa: Tourism and Goan society', quoted in Pearson, 2008)

I arrive in Anjuna by taxi, only to find myself in the midst of a massive traffic jam, and still two kilometres from the centre. I decide to go by foot the rest of the way, as it would take just as long to continue by car. I arrive, sweating and breathless but ready to do some serious shopping, my bargaining tools honed for the special occasion. I start with what looks like an endless row of vendors selling trinkets and jewellery. I see the sun glinting off the Arabian Sea in the background. Several rows later, when the silver bracelets and anklets sold by the Kashmiri women[7] start to all look the same, I decide to take a much-needed break. I venture towards the food area, where I find a German tourist selling homemade brownies and cakes; I bite into one as I sip a homemade Indian chai.[8] I fall in love with a pair of sandals from an Israeli vendor. He won't budge on the price; I buy them anyway, despite my misgivings both for not having struck a bargain and for not contributing to Goa's local economy more directly.[9] As the sun sets, and day turns to evening, I stay to watch the changing scene unfolding in front of me. With Anjuna's various vendors packing up their wares, this famed beach is transformed from an outdoor flea market to a party scene.

It is just starting to gather momentum; the music starts up. I notice that the vendors (both Goan and non-Goan) have quietly disappeared; left are Anjuna's most dedicated partiers, in for the long overnight haul. I am reminded of Arun Saldanha's assertion that 'psy-trance's psychedelic drive ... [is] still geared to self-alienation, still recognizably "white"' (Saldanha, 2007: 43). I look around me and cannot help but concur. The whiteness of Goa's tourist circuit is reinforced through other examples, such as the organised tours (with packaged Western food included) to visit other white tourists who have been arrested and made an example of for illegal drug possession and who are serving harsh sentences in one of Goa's worst prisons, Fort Aguada, a former Portuguese fort.[10] Here I want to extend Saldanha's point, to suggest that the whiteness of Goa's trance scene is a striking one, in relation to the increased globalisation (and heterogeneity) of tourists and tourism more generally. Moreover, its politics of exclusion operate through a variety of subtle mechanisms – historical, economic, cultural and social.

Thus, it is less about a prohibition against Indian (or other non-white) tourists from participating in the scene, but rather about a habitus that largely makes only white privileged Western tourists feel comfortable in this liminal yet delimiting space.

Specifically, there is a history and culture to trance that are at work here, and that operate at the level of self-censorship. So much of the 'scene' is about seeing and being seen, which is reliant on cultural cues in order to be recognised; it also requires a lot of time and investment in serious partying, including money to buy hash, long periods of free time to contemplate, do nothing and dance, and, finally, a willingness to meet other partiers while under the influence of a hashish haze. I would argue that it is difficult to react to an ideology if one doesn't understand what that ideology is about in the first place. Trance, in other words, is inescapably a white ideological phenomenon, purely by the fact that it was set up in contradistinction to (and as a reaction to) a certain kind of restrained Western lifestyle. This third 'fragment' shows how the Anjuna flea market and trance scene in Goa is very much reliant on a particular kind of whiteness that is both put on display and increasingly under threat, precisely because it works through subtle mechanisms of seduction, including music, dance, drugs and material goods in a space of visual reciprocity.

Fragment 4: 'Monsoon Wedding'

> [Goa's beaches] had become to the Indians what the burning ghats were to the foreigners, mostly a place to watch others lose their dignity. (Mehta, 1979: 174)

There is a famous Bollywood film entitled *Bombay to Goa* (directed by S. Ramanathan). Produced in 1972, this adventure-cum-comedy Hindi film, starring a very young and innocent looking Amitabh Bachchan (one of Bollywood's biggest stars), tells the story of Mala, a young female from a respectable north Indian family who is on the run after having witnessed a murder. She takes the first available bus to Goa and is followed by an admirer (and unbeknownst to her, he is the man whom her parents have arranged for her to marry); what follows is a tale of romantic love (but set within the confines of arranged marriage), with Goa during its monsoon season as its backdrop (May to September). It is 'raindrop' tourism (Pearson, 2008) at its best, with scenes of Goa's lush greenery providing the backdrop for endless stills of wet saris and near chaste kisses. This film, alongside a more recent one directed by Mira Nair, and which is also centred on rain and romance (but set in Mumbai), entitled *Monsoon Wedding* (2001), in many senses captures what I am interested in discussing in this last 'fragment': Goa as a historical site of domestic tourism, where Indians from the north, numbering more than 1 million annually (Pearson, 2003: 274), have continued to visit (both during and outside the monsoon season) this exoticised 'internal other' to gaze upon Western-ness in all its excessive forms (Gupta, 2009), and where they allow themselves to indulge in and experiment with ideals of romance, sexuality and alterity in an affordable manner, particularly if travel to the West is not a feasible destination in the near future. As Michael Pearson notes, even middle-class Indians two decades ago were lured to Goa by brochures for bus sightseeing tours which promised beaches where 'naked hippies [would] be seen' (Pearson, 2003: 274), a detail that very much mirrors the acerbic line from Gita Mehta's tale of tourism in India that I rely on at the beginning of this section. In other words, this form of domestic tourism (which includes both honeymooners as well as packs of young Indian males) is equally dependent on the international tourism for its seductive powers; it is only when Goa is filled to capacity with foreigners doing their tourist thing, that is, in their habitus, that it fulfils their idealised desires – the honeymooners feeling that they can express their physical love more freely as a result of the context (and away from the confines of family and watchful parents), and the young men learning lessons in the art of seduction through the casual act of seeing.

This fourth and last 'fragment' addresses the ways in which Goa is made to appear more 'different' from the rest of India to satisfy two distinct groups of tourists who are interpellated by each other as they simultaneously gaze upon one another – Western tourists coming to Goa as a much needed break away from 'spiritual' India and a return to the (modern) conveniences of home (or at least a close approximation), and Indian domestic tourists coming to Goa to affordably experience the West (both Goa itself and the Western tourists who temporarily inhabit the space, thus marking it as fittingly Western) without having to travel very far. This duality (but very much marked by its unevenness or economic disparity) also conveniently sets up Goa's Portuguese heritage as distinct from India's British colonial legacy, allowing Goa's 'packaging' for two different kinds of visitors simultaneously. Each tourist group is further exoticised and popularised by its distinction from the other, which, in turn, bolsters tourism in India more generally.

Conclusion

> Anjuna Beach ... is an anthropologist's dream. (Mehta, 1979: 179)

By way of conclusion, I return full circle to the *Guardian Weekly* article that I started with. The author, Gethin Chamberlain, interviewed a Westerner caught up in Goa's recent backlash against foreigners, a man named Cooper. He said: 'Now you get called a white bastard and white trash. When we moved here it was like living in paradise. Now we are being held hostage. We want to sell up and go home. It's not a safe place to be anymore' (Chamberlain, 2010: 28). The tourist gaze continues to oscillate in Goa, creating new sparks of 'friction' along the way, but I don't think the party is over, at least not quite yet.

The montage of ethnographic 'fragments' on display here picks up on a variety of different themes tied to the tourist scene in Goa today. It shows snippets of stories that focus on the multiple powers (and disavowals) of the art of seduction: of beer-swilling British pensioners, suitcases lined with frozen vodka, topless Russian female sunbathers, a beached whale of a ship stuck in Goa's coastal waters, thrifty shoppers, hippies and drug-tripping hipsters engaged in trance, packs of horny Indian males and romantic honeymooners and, finally, a female anthropologist sitting by a pool in a sea of empty umbrella chairs. These 'fragments' work by way of their incompleteness, following Tsing (2005), seducing the reader (and tourist) to feel a compulsion, both a nostalgic desire for what Goa once was (a tourist paradise) but also a realisation of its costs and benefits, which continually shapes anew its cosmopolitan sense of self. It is a tale of neither global tourism's totalising success nor failure, but rather one that sheds light on how careful the balance is in fact between seducer and seduced that tourism requires on an everyday basis.

Notes

(1) Interestingly, these characteristics had been used to describe and deride the Portuguese during colonial times; however, in the postcolonial context, these same character traits are now reconfigured in tourism discourses as the positive influences of the legacy of the Portuguese, and displaced onto their former colonial subjects, the Goans themselves, and packaged as Goa's essentialised and commodified 'traditions'. See Gupta (2009).

(2) Interview with Angeline Lobo, tourism agent, 25 November 2009.

(3) Interview with Angeline Lobo, 25 November 2009.

(4) This is also another ethnographic 'fragment' that is part of Goa's tourism scene, and could potentially be explored further. I have several friends who run bookshops, cafes and lifestyle shops that cater to all kinds of tourist elites (Western and Indian).

There is also a large art, cultural and literary scene that is fuelled by a large number of diasporic and wealthy Bombayites who own second homes in Goa. Most recently, India's only international film festival was moved to Goa in 2009.

(5) There have been several high-profile crimes in Goa which have made the headlines: the rape of a 25-year-old Russian woman in December 2009; the rape of a nine-year-old Russian girl in January 2010; the mysterious murder of a Russian teenager in May 2009. See 'Russian tourists bad for Goa: BJP leader', at http://ibnlive.in.com/news/russian-tourists-bad-for-goa-bjp-leader/110482-3.html (accessed August 2010). The gang rape of a woman on a bus in Delhi in December 2012 who subsequently died from her injuries both sparked riots and demonstrations in Delhi and raised awareness of the high incidence of rape (and sexual abuse) in the country more generally.

(6) Conversation (2011 November, in New York) with a Danish tourist named Ana who had done just that, during her trip to Goa, three years earlier.

(7) They are seasonal vendors who sell their wares on the Western tourist circuit. Typically, they station themselves in Manali, north India, during the June–September tourist season (which is Goa's monsoon season), and then come to Goa for September–May (which is Manali's winter, when the tourist season is at a low). Once, on a visit to Manali, I noticed the same woman selling the same things that I had seen in Goa several months earlier. August, 1999. Also, the influx of Kashmiris to Goa is tied to what is going on politically in the contested state of Kashmir.

(8) Goa has a comparatively long history of tourism, having received German and British tourists from the 1960s, many of whom stayed on in Goa. They became integral to Goa's the industry, setting up shops, flea markets and restaurants, and catering to the continuous flow of Western tourists (and selling distinctly Western goods) and in some sense setting the standards by which locals set up their own tourist businesses.

(9) Many of the resident Western vendors will not engage in bargaining, standing firmly by the price (for goods usually handcrafted by themselves – for example, in the case of the sandals they were Indian in style, modelled along the lines of a *chappal*, but Western in their comfort and fit), and in some ways setting themselves off from the Indian vendors who think bargaining is part of the respectful art of shopping.

(10) The British consulate spends quite a bit of its time dealing with these drug cases (hiring lawyers, bringing the families over), as well as the deaths of their nationals in Goa (usually accidental, or related to drug overdose). The latter involves issuing a death certificate, as well as organising the shipping of the corpse to the individual's family in the UK. Interview in January 2005 with Rita, a Goan who worked at British Council at the time.

References

Augé, M. (1995) *Non-Places: Introduction to an Anthropology of Supermodernity*. John Howe (transl) London: Verso.

Cahen, M., Couto, D., de Souza, P.R., Marrou, L. and Siqueira, A. (2000) Introduction: Issues of Asian Portuguese-speaking spaces and Lusotopias. *Lusotopie*, 137–158.

Chamberlain, G. (2010) The party's over for Goa's expats. *Guardian Weekly*, 23 April, pp. 28–29.

Crick, M. (1995) The anthropologist as tourist: An identity in question. In M.F. Lanfant,

J. Allcock and E. Bruner (eds) *International Tourism: Identity and Change* (pp. 205–223). London: Sage.

Deccan Herald (2013) Goa set for big spurt in Russian tourists. See http://www.deccanherald.com/content/30056/goa-set-big-spurt-russian.html (accessed January 2013).

Digital Goa (2013) River Princess to finally vanish after 12 years. See http://www.digitalgoa.com/ca_disp.php?id=2051 (accessed January 2013).

Geertz, C. (1973) *The Interpretation of Cultures*. New York: Basic Books.

Goa Guide (2010) Russian tourists. See http://www.goaguide.org/russians.html (accessed August 2010).

Goablog (2010) Goa: Fresh bids to remove River Princess from the shore. See http://www.goablog.org/posts/goa-fresh-bids-to-remove-river-princess-from-the-shore (accessed August 2010).

Gupta, P. (2005) The corporeal and the carnivalesque: The exposition of St Francis Xavier and the consumption of history in Goa (India). Unpublished paper.

Gupta, P. (2009) Goa Dourada, the internal exotic in South Asia: Discourses of colonialism and tourism. In A. Phukan, and V.G. Rajan (eds) *Reading the Exotic: South Asia and Its Others* (pp. 123–148). Cambridge: Cambridge Scholars Press.

IBN Live (2010) Russian tourists bad for Goa: BJP leader. See http://ibnlive.in.com/news/russian-tourists-bad-for-goa-bjp-leader/110482-3.html (accessed August 2010).

IndiaLine (2010) Goa tourism guide. See http://www.indialine.com/travel/goa (accessed August 2010).

Latour, B. (2005) *Reassembling the Social: An Introduction to Actor-Network-Theory*. Oxford: Oxford University Press.

Mehta, G. (1979) *Karma Cola*. London: Penguin Books.

Merinews (2010) Goa: Grounded River Princess raises ecological concerns. See http://www.merinews.com/article/goa-grounded-river-princess-raises-ecological-concerns/129970.shtml (accessed August 2010).

Newman, R. (2001) *Of Umbrellas, Goddesses and Dreams: Essays on Goan Culture and Society*. Mapusa: Other India Press.

Noronha, F. (1999) Ten years later, Goa still uneasy over the impact of tourism. *International Journal of Contemporary Hospitality Management* 11 (2/3), 100–106.

Pearson, M. (2003) *The Indian Ocean*. London: Routledge.

Pearson, M. (2008) An overview of tourism in Goa. Unpublished paper.

Pinto, J. (2006) *Reflected in Water: Writings on Goa*. New Delhi: Penguin Books.

Pratt, M. (1992) *Travel Writing and Transculturation*. New York: Routledge.

Routledge, P. (2001) Selling the rain, resisting the sale: Resistant identities and the conflict over tourism in Goa. *Social and Cultural Geography* 2 (2), 221–240.

Rubinoff, A. (1998) *The Construction of a Political Community: Integration and Identity in Goa*. New Delhi: Sage.

Salazar, N. (2010) *Envisioning Eden: Mobilizing Imaginaries in Tourism and Beyond*. New York: Berghahn Books.

Saldanha, A. (2007) *Psychedelic White: Goa Trance and the Viscosity of Race*. Minneapolis, MN: University of Minnesota Press.

Schneider, A. and Wright, C. (eds) (2006) *Contemporary Art and Anthropology*. London: Berg.

Trichur, R. (2000) Politics of Goan historiography. *Lusotopie*, 637–645.

Tsing, A. (2005) *Friction: An Ethnography of Global Connection*. Princeton, NJ: Princeton University Press.

Urry, J. (1990) *The Tourist Gaze: Leisure and Travel in Contemporary Societies*. London: Sage.

6   Seduction: Learning the Trade of Tourist Enticement

Noel B. Salazar

Few places in the world conjure up such rich images as the magnificent peaks, valleys and plains of Northern Tanzania. The highest mountains … the wildest lakes … the most abundant and varied wildlife – everything is here. Whether it's the contented roar of a big cat across the water at dusk, the timid face of an antelope calf seen through the rushes, or the sheer beauty of a thousand flamingos taking flight – the magic of this untamed earthly paradise will leave memories you will never forget…. Arusha, where all good things start (and finish). (Brochure from the Tanzania Tourist Board, 1999)

It is nearly eight o'clock in the morning. I start walking from Arusha's centre to the outskirts. As I am nearing my destination, at virtually every other intersection one or two fast-paced young Tanzanians are joining me. We are all headed towards one of the poorer neighbourhoods in the hills just north of the city. There, almost hidden between banana trees and lush vegetation, lays an inconspicuous two-storey building. The enlarged house is rudimentary and, aside from some basic facilities, there are only two rooms: a classroom and a room that functions simultaneously as office, library, computer room and second classroom. Outside the school, some students are enjoying a hearty breakfast of *uji* (millet porridge) and *chai* (tea), while others are just chatting or playing with their cell phones. Crammed inside the classroom, I count almost 100 heads. Seated on long wooden benches, everybody is focused on the automated slide show on the small computer screen in front. On every other slide, there is a colorful picture of a particular bird, followed by a second slide with its English name. Students compete with one another in correctly naming as many birds as possible. 'Southern black flycatcher … Jackson's hornbill … Redheaded lovebird … African emerald cuckoo. No, it's an African striped cuckoo!' Samwel, sitting next to me, proudly tells me that his friend Gurisha is able to distinguish over 500 different birds.

In 2007, I spent a year in northern Tanzania conducting research on tourism discourses and their underlying imaginaries (Salazar, 2010a). As part of the research, I regularly visited the Arusha Guide School (pseudonym). Strategically located nearby a number of national parks in northern Tanzania, Arusha functions as a 'safari capital'. Not surprisingly, the city attracts many migrants looking for jobs in tourism and hospitality. These newcomers quickly realise that they will not find any employment without having undergone some training. This is particularly true for tour guides, who generally are required to be skilled in fields as diverse as group dynamics, first aid, natural and cultural heritage interpretation, and imaginative storytelling (Salazar, 2006). Although not immediately visible when browsing the curriculum or attending class, in guiding schools there are types of learning going on other than the mere appropriation of specialised tourism vocabulary and English as a guiding language.

In this chapter, I explore how apprentice tour guides such as those at the Arusha Guide School are acquainted with foreign tourism imaginaries and associated discourses – what MacCannell (1992: 1) calls 'an ideological framing of history, nature and tradition' – and how they become skilled at strategically using them while guiding, often through trial and error. How are local guides taught to perceive their life-world through the eyes of foreigners? How do they learn to (re)produce tourism imaginaries? Or, to turn the question around, what role do guide training institutes and guides themselves play in the incessant circulation of tourism's foundational myths? I search for answers to these questions by analysing the various processes and mechanisms through which guides in northern Tanzania are 'seducated' – formally schooled and informally trained in the art of narrating and performing seducing tourism tales. As I will illustrate, the dynamics of seducation are heavily informed by asymmetrical power relations that structure the ways in which particular cultural forms are picked up and incorporated into how guides learn to see and represent the(ir) world.

As Seen on the Screen (and Elsewhere)

Tour guides operating in northern Tanzania have to build up a wide range of knowledge and skills. Bwana Baraka, the director of the Arusha Guide School, often compares a guide to a 'knowledge bank', a 'library' or an 'information bank', and stresses 'collecting info is a life-long job'. As he notes ironically, 'it's no longer enough to point to elephants'. In other words, guides need to learn how to tell and enact seductive tourism tales.

Tour guide interpretations largely feed off wider imaginaries, culturally shared and socially transmitted representational assemblages that interact with people's personal imaginings and are used as meaning-making devices, mediating how people act, cognise and value the world, and helping them to form identifications of Self and Other (cf. Strauss, 2006). The imaginaries underlying tourism are so predominant that without them there probably would be little tourism at all (Salazar, 2010a, 2012b; Salazar & Graburn, 2014). These images and discourses often propagate historically inherited stereotypes that are based on myths and fantasies related to nature, the noble savage, art, individual freedom and self-realisation, equality and paradise (Hennig, 2002; Said, 1994; Torgovnick, 1990).

Three types of myth frequently recur in tourism to developing countries: that of the unchanged, that of the unrestrained and that of the uncivilised (Echtner & Prasad, 2003). The imagery surrounding tourism to these countries is often about an ambivalent nostalgia for the past – ambivalent because returning to the past is not what people actually desire (Bissell, 2005). Such nostalgia tourism often taps into commoditised (neo)colonial imaginaries, evoking and mimicking the trope of first contact that was common in colonial travel narratives (Pratt, 2008). In general, discourses of the past – especially those related to Orientalism, colonialism and imperialism – seem to be extremely fertile ground for romantic tourism fantasies (Desmond, 1999; Edensor, 1998; Henderson & Weisgrau, 2007; Selwyn, 1996). Such tourism imaginaries become tangible and world-making when they are incarnated in institutions, from archaeological sites, museums and monuments to hotels, media and cultural productions (Hollinshead, 2007; Wynn, 2007).

Tourism imaginaries do not float around spontaneously and independently; rather, they need agency to 'travel', in space and time, from tourism-generating regions (which are also destination regions) to tourism-destination regions (which also generate fantasies) and back, in a dialectic way. Being part of much larger 'representational loops' (Sturma, 2002: 137), and empowered by global communication and media, tourism imaginaries are sent, circulated, transferred, received, accumulated, converted and stored around the world. While tourism imaginaries are by nature elusive, it is in practices and discourses that they become tangible.

Bruner (2005) devoted many years to tracking the spread of what he calls 'tourism narratives'. These narratives travel through a self-perpetuating 'touristic cycle', carried by people and organisations with very different stakes in tourism: marketers, service providers, government agencies, the media and tourists. According to Bruner, all narratives, appearing at different times (pre-tour, on-tour and post-tour) and places (at home and away), and in various modalities (oral, written, pictorial, symbolic or graphic), can be traced back to certain 'metanarratives', the 'largest conceptual frame within which tourism operates. They are not attached to any locality or to any particular tour, and they are usually taken for granted, not brought to consciousness' (Bruner, 2005: 21).

However, there is not one universal tourism discourse that sends undifferentiated messages to a homogenised global audience (Salazar, 2006). Because the logic of the global market prescribes diversification and the creation of multiple consumer identities, the language of tourism contains a wide number of registers, each one addressing a particular type of tourist with particular interests (Dann, 1996; Morgan & Pritchard, 1998). Tour guides step in this representational circle by refashioning general discourses as tourism tales, which are 'less encompassing in scope and more attached to particular regions' (Bruner, 2005: 22).

Because virtually all of the Arusha Guide School's teaching resources are foreign – primarily from Europe, the United States and South Africa – they actually greatly facilitate the students' exposure to globally circulating tourism imaginaries. Because wildlife tourism is the predominant form on mainland Tanzania (Salazar, 2009b), pedagogy necessarily stresses an emphasis on ecology and on mastering the widely popular environmental (eco-)discourse (Norton, 1996). Students learn that foreign tourists are most interested in big mammals and that this preference is the result of having seen (too) many spectacular wildlife documentaries and movies. In the words of teacher Frankie: 'Small children have watched *The Lion King*, so what do they want to see? Lions!' Consequently, students are taught to represent the Serengeti-Mara ecosystem as the world's greatest 'animal kingdom' and the Ngorongoro Crater as 'the place where Noah's ark came to rest' (a metaphor for the origin of species more than a biblical claim).

In the Arusha Guide School, many hours are devoted to explaining world heritage sites, biosphere reserves and conservation areas to students, as well as the importance these 'quality labels' have for tourists (Di Giovine, 2008). Keywords in tourism, such as authenticity and sustainability, are elucidated, too. 'Watu wanathink sustainable' (people think sustainable) is one of Frankie's mantras. As part of the graduation requirements, everybody has to compose a master information file, a long list of words including names of fauna, flora, attractions, people and tourism concepts. This is a very demanding task, forcing students to engage in many hours of reading and organising the materials (although lists composed by alumni are circulating too). The master list contains plenty of personalities from the colonial era: explorers, mountaineers, missionaries, scientists, writers, German and English administrators, and so on. The only Tanzanian personalities included are the country's Presidents, a couple of traditional chiefs and historical figures from Zanzibar. During the final exam, Bwana Baraka randomly picks out words from the list and asks the student to narrate a guiding commentary about them. While most collect about 300 keywords, the brightest alumni are able to produce lists of more than 1500.

Another ingenious drilling mechanism is the weekly wildlife video quiz, during which everybody receives a sheet with a summary of the video narrator's speech. The students' task is to fill in missing keywords in the blanks while watching the video. This makes students focus not only on the contents of the story but also on the way the tales are narrated – on the art of delivery. Storytelling is highly encouraged and commented upon in the classroom: 'A good opening sentence makes your clients more curious'; 'Legends are welcome in tour guiding'; 'It's a good story, *mzungu atalala!*' (the foreigner will fall asleep, meant ironically). In this way, students are made aware of the benefits of good interpretation. As Bwana Baraka puts it: 'Everywhere [in the world] there are zoos. You make the difference by explaining things.' As an added bonus, apprentice guides realise that telling stories can be used to mask ignorance: because tour guides are not researchers, but an instrumental cog in the reification of tourism imaginaries, the headmaster proposes an easy way out of difficult questions tourists might ask: 'This is a mystery. That's how nature is. Let's move on.'

I am often struck by the instructors' repeated (and uncritical) usage of popular tourism discourses. They know how important it is that guides mirror the imaginations tourists have already acquired about Tanzania before setting foot on its soil, the fantasies that tour operators or travel agencies have already sold to them. The school therefore provides its students with plenty of samples of promotional materials, powerful tools to indoctrinate student guides with foreign interpretations of their own natural and cultural heritage. Bwana Baraka emphasises that his students should learn 'to look at things through the eyes of a tourist'. One of the methods he uses to do this is to show photographs and ask where they were taken. At one time, for instance, he displays a picture taken inside Arusha's only Western-style fast-food restaurant. Most students think the picture is shot in New York, somewhere in Europe or in Dar es Salaam. Not one guesses it right. The principal then uses this example to stress the importance of developing a feel for places and things that are of interest to foreign tourists.

Learning the 'tourist way' clearly implies familiarising oneself with the home cultures of tourists. According to the principal, openness towards appropriating foreign cultural elements – a kind of strategic cosmopolitanism (Salazar, 2010b) – opens all doors: 'You stay Maasai or Chagga and you won't go anywhere.' Finally, a brash statement on tourism imaginaries: 'As I told you two weeks ago, there are people buying a ticket to Tanzania only because they want to see two things: a lion and a Maasai penis.... Especially American girls do this.' Sharing this type of information with the students, Bwana Baraka teaches them the widely circulating imaginary that Maasai men are well endowed, as well as speaking to the students' erotic dreams about Westerners.

'Meet the Local People'

On a regular basis, Bwana Baraka selects advanced students to guide tourists around Arusha or on other one-day excursions in the area. It is during these extended encounters with tourists that apprentices experience the 'magical' powers of guided tours (cf. Arnould & Price, 1993). Those students who are not selected can still pick up something from the in-class reports and evaluations after each trip. The story of Iddi illustrates how those who do have a chance to practise learn the hard way what tourism imaginaries entail. After his first safari with a group of Europeans, Iddi evaluates the trip in front of the whole class. In a rather agitated and slightly angry manner, he explains to his peers how the driver-guides of the tour company had skillfully manipulated the whole wildlife viewing experience. In order to make the five-day safari worthwhile, they made sure the tourists would not see too many animals on one given day. Through radio contact, driver-guides communicated with one another (in Swahili), exchanging the location of 'Big Five' species. This enabled them to carefully monitor and control the amount of wildlife shown to their clients during the trip. In such ways, tourism imaginaries are materialised and alter guiding practices in significant ways.

The learning process can even be more confronting when the imaginaries concern people. Alongside the amazing wildlife, the Maasai and the mysteries surrounding their culture are the flag-bearers of Tanzanian tourism (Salazar, 2009a). Because of the (colonial) imagery that circulates across the globe in countless coffee-table books, movies and snapshots, the undeveloped and time-frozen Maasai are one of the most (mis)represented African ethnic groups. The sight of a virile Maasai warrior, dressed in colourful red tartans and beaded jewellery, evokes the romantic image of a modern noble savage. Since the Maasai are often represented as an extension of wildlife (neglecting the fact that many Maasai are now educated and live in urban contexts), some tour guides have expanded the Big Five to the Big Six. Ally, who is Maasai on his mother's side of the family, experienced first-hand how tourism treats the Maasai. In front of the class, he negatively evaluates a short cultural tour that took place in a neighbouring village. The local Meru guides had explained to the mixed group of foreign tourists that the Maasai are the most primitive Tanzanians because they still wear no clothes: 'Today we [Meru] are more developed compared to the other tribes. We are more transitioned compared to the Maasai. The Maasai are more primitive compared to us. We adapted quicker.... The Maasai are the ones that wear blankets. The Meru don't wear blankets.' Such stereotyped comments draw on outdated ethnological accounts that were translated in colonial as well as post-colonial policies and reflect the general disrespect for Maasai people in Tanzania (Salazar, 2013).

One Maasai student, Eduardo, becomes furious when he hears these kinds of stories. He made his name in the Arusha Guide School the day he denounced the organisers of camel safaris because they introduce the camels by name to tourists but neither mention nor properly introduce the Maasai men who accompany the animals. The pattern of not treating Maasai as individuals is common practice among other ethnic groups in Tanzania. Eduardo used the occasion of his reporting to request formally to be called by his name in the school instead of being addressed always as 'Maasai'. However, even if tourism seems to impose monolithic meanings through the relentless circulation of its archetypical images and ideas, each representation of peoples and places is subject to multiple interpretations. What actually happens during the interaction between guides and tourists is nuanced and open-ended, allowing both sides to manipulate expectations and preconceived patterns creatively (cf. Skinner & Theodossopoulos, 2011).

Apprentice guide Joseph experienced first-hand how tour guiding is an interactive endeavour that can never be fully controlled. During a practice tour around Arusha's urban centre, he noticed some street children sniffing glue under the Uhuru Torch, a well known landmark commemorating the independence of the country. In order not to disturb the 'magic' of the tour, Joseph drew attention to a nearby shop instead of bringing the group to the monument and giving a detailed explanation, as is usually done. When one of the tourists spotted the kids and asked him about the problem of street children in Tanzania, Joseph was put on the spot and could no longer avoid the presence of the children. He skilfully combined his answer to the question with a more general commentary on the country's post-independence problems, using this as an opportunity to bring the monument back into his narrative.

Apart from merely reproducing tourism imaginaries, tour guide discourse sometimes works as a hidden transcript, expressing socioeconomic and political dissatisfaction without directly confronting or challenging the authorities (Schwenkel, 2006: 20). Learning that the interests (and imaginations or aspirations) of tourists are not necessarily the same as one's own, however, proves to be a more difficult lesson. On a visit to a Maasai village, Ernest took his group to the medicine man. This was the last part of the tour and it was already late. The medicine man started explaining his ritual practices but everybody was tired and bored. Ernest, who was himself fascinated by the topic, failed to notice the many implicit signs the tourists were giving, indicating they wanted to leave. Instead, he kept on asking the medicine man questions. The meagre tip he received from the tourists afterwards made him realise he had done something wrong. Another guide named Robert, who accompanied a group on a three-day cultural tourism trip, became very annoyed when not everybody showed interest in his long exposé regarding anthills. When all of a sudden the topic of female genital mutilation came up during a trip, Robert did not try to change the subject but instead started voicing his own opinion (thereby neglecting Bwana Baraka's mantra that 'a tour guide is neutral'). He defended the practice from a cultural perspective, an opinion unpopular with the American tourists. The highly emotional discussion that ensued showed the headmaster's wisdom, as it left the whole group of tourists very upset. During the evaluation of this practice trip at school, Robert acknowledged his mistake, allowing the other students to learn their lesson from his blunder as well.

The guide–tourist encounter, like all service contacts, is typically asymmetrical. By paying the guide for his or her work (and for access to certain areas), tourists expect quality service in return. However, there are many points in the interaction when shifts of role alignment occur and these same asymmetries are blurred or temporarily interrupted. Guides repeatedly rely on dualisms or binary us–them oppositions to position themselves interactionally *vis-à-vis* tourists and local people. Two different logics are at work simultaneously: a logic of differentiation that creates differences and divisions; and a logic of equivalence that subverts existing differences and divisions. As global marketing prescribes, guides often have no choice but to play the local, even if they are not necessarily natives of the sites where they work (e.g. almost all the guides in and around Arusha are Tanzanians, but many come from other regions and belong to different ethnic groups). In some instances, guides find creative ways to distance themselves from locals and align themselves on the side of the tourists.

The dominant global discourse, which tends to treat all Africans alike and, thus, conceptualise the guides as full members of local Tanzanian communities (Salazar, 2012a), can be subverted. The students from the Arusha Guide School quickly learn to distance themselves from local people encountered during a trip as a means of aligning themselves with the 'us tourists' side of the us–them binary. They achieve this, for instance, through the subtle use of demonstrative and personal pronouns, or temporal and spatial expressions (Katriel, 1994). An important function of such meta-language includes making judgements of or expressing attitudes towards others, which serves the purpose of drawing social boundaries between the self and the other, reinforcing similarities and differences respectively.

On the way to a village market nearby Arusha, for example, Erasto told his group of European tourists: 'We will be able to meet the local people at the marketplace. You can say *habari* (hello), so you can become popular suddenly, and they can respect you because you greet them in their language.' By carefully choosing personal pronouns, Erasto performatively resists stereotyping by not telling his clients he is very much a local, often frequenting the market they were about to visit to buy his groceries. Such acts of differentiating by indexing difference linguistically may be a per-formance of resistance or a subtle contestation even if, at the same time, it perpetuates stereotypes (cf. Feldman, 2007). Either way, it is through the strategic use of linguistic processes that local guides learn about stereotypes in general, of African locals and Western tourists, and find new avenues of self-expression. And although the nature of the engagement of tour guides may vary, their attempts to (re)produce tourism imaginaries are not straightforward matters of 'telling and showing' but entail 'complex negotiation between guides' self-positioning, that of their organization, the particular genre of tourism involved, the audience and the site itself' (MacDonald, 2006: 136).

Getting to the Source

Because becoming an accomplished guide is a never-ending process, novices need much instruction. The tourism master imaginaries are taken in and processed according to how the local scene can be presented and sold as 'paradise'. In Arusha, the guides benefit from the eco-hype, which allows them to interpret their surroundings in terms of an untouched, green Eden, where animals (and people such as the Maasai) live in harmony. The examples from northern Tanzania discussed in this chapter show that, while imaginaries and their associated discourses circulate through tourism schools and training programmes, there are many other channels of distri-bution. Depending on availability and personal interest, guides can rely on an entire gamut of information sources to structure their practices and nar-ratives. Guides often receive materials such as maps, guidebooks and travel dictionaries from tourists who leave them behind or mail them afterwards as a token of appreciation. Interestingly, this gift-giving (which is common in tourism to developing countries) is part of a qualified 'Otherness'. The tourists do see the tour guide as an 'Other', but one who aspires to become like 'them' and whom they can help. The guides, as intermediary figures, appreciate the gifts of the tourists probably more than the 'real' Others (e.g. because the guides can at least read in the foreign language).

Most of the sources used are not indigenous but foreign, either produced abroad or by expatriates living in the country. This lack of indigenisation of materials is an old problem in tourism education, but it also greatly facilitates the inflow of global tourism imaginaries and discourses. Some books even date to the colonial era. Yet, being acquainted with colonial views actually turns out to be an asset when working in tourism because natural and cultural heritage are often packaged, represented and sold in ways that are reminiscent of colonial times. In other words, precisely because the resources used are not local, guides are better able to learn about the culture(s) of international tourists and, eventually, the culture(s) of tourism.

Resources from a more recent date are usually not critical academic analyses but illustrated coffee-table books and popular literature such as *National Geographic* and audiovisual companions such as National Geographic Channel and home videos. Apart from oral history (legends, fairy-tales and beliefs), indigenous knowledge is almost completely absent in the training cycle of tour guides. Even if the guides in Arusha have fewer educational materials at their disposal, they learn quickly while practising, through trial and much error. Encyclopaedic knowledge, together with physical strength and seduction, prevail over elegance.

Younger guides in Arusha often try to bypass the lack of printed resources by resorting to the internet. While this is a much more affordable way to find information, what is obtained is not always reliable. Of course, the web has its own seductive power over the guides using it. It allows them to discover seductive imaginaries related to destinations across the globe as well as the place where they work and live. Not only can they look up travel information, but the internet also allows them to chat and exchange emails with (former) clients. For apprentice guides, the internet often adds to their confusion, as they sometimes find information (and imaginaries) going against what they were taught at school.

Unlike countries where the content of tour guide schooling may be controlled by the government, thereby ensuring that guides deliver a uniform, politically and ideologically correct commentary, the Tanzanian government seems at present to have little control over such matters. Moreover, my observations of training programmes in Arusha suggest that the planned curriculum is often very different from the one that is actually enacted. In other words, while schools and training institutes play an important role in the circulation of tourism imaginaries, one-way transmission of ideas is not possible. The issue is not about making the image conform to the Tanzanian world that tourists do not experience. There are strong financial incentives for protecting the image that tourism sells.

Conclusion

Through an ethnographically grounded analysis, this chapter has highlighted the processes by which seductive images and seductions as social relations move through very specific locales such as tour guiding schools and guided tours. Guiding clearly demands more than 'the superficial "processing" of a script or a memorized behavioral repertoire that might include smiling and friendly discourse' (Ness, 2003: 189). Through formal schooling and informal learning, apprentice guides become acquainted with seductive representations of their own culture and heritage that are deeply rooted in foreign conceptions of Otherness.

While schools and training institutes play an important role in the hermeneutic circle of tourism imaginaries, one-way transmission of ideas is not possible. Imaginaries mimetically feed the imaginings of tourists and guides alike but some images are more powerful, that is, more seductive. Whereas in the case of myths there are strong cultural incentives for leaving the contents unaltered, in the case of tourism imaginaries the motivations are largely financial. For tourism to propagate itself (and economically prosper), peoples and cultures better remain 'Othered'. After all, guides (and tour guide instructors) are different from 'teachers', in that they are primarily in the business of cultivating tourism imaginaries in a positive way rather than strictly educating tourists or transmitting 'objective' knowledge. Seductive Othering helps distinguish between home and away, known and unknown. The findings discussed in this chapter reveal that this logic applies both to tourists and to service providers.

The concept of 'seducation' that I introduce here has important analytical purchase to explain the long-term learning process in which tourists and guides are mutually seduced and educated. There are multiple but not equal meanings attached to seducation. The guides learn novel styles and forces of social relationships with other locals (status-building, economic differentiation and involving political or economic interests) and with foreigners (coolness, new desires, new behaviours and new forms of aspiration). Training courses and guiding experiences generate new or reformed practices of social intimacy and hierarchy that go beyond useful functional economic purposes to produce new social and cultural distinctions. Explicit teachings, informal stories and sometimes subconscious emulation interact in forming guiding skills.

This ethnographic study nicely illustrates how education, tourism imaginaries and the shifting relationships between self/other (or guide/tourist) act as mechanisms of seduction. An in-depth analysis of tour guide training and practice reveals how cultural production through tourism is extremely disciplining in how it serves to socialise and create subjects and subject positions. Recontextualisations of imaginaries serve to 'educate' the guides to become/to fit with the imaginaries set by travel agencies and tourism marketers. In other words, the power relations through which some elements of local culture 'stick' (in terms of being left within the guiding scripts) and the desires of the guides to live up to these images (even though they have conflicted feelings) are an essential part of the seduction process (cf. Picard, 2011). Discursive guiding techniques carry a lot of the argument concerning new modes of self-fashioning and self-commodification through the lure of powerful foreign representations of the Other in tourism (cf. Bunten, 2008).

In sum, tourism imaginaries and discourses come to guides through a variety of channels. No matter how many resources they have at their disposal, ultimately it is in the interaction with tourists that the imaginaries become tangible and are circulated; as with myths, they are perpetuated as well as subtly contested. The students of the Arusha Guide School are transformed in the process of becoming tour guides (e.g. by learning to control their personal reactions towards what they perceive to be negative imaginaries) but they also contribute occasionally to the transformation of tourism discourses (and, sometimes, tourists). Nevertheless, they all learn to think of tourists as 'clients', even as they address and treat them as 'guests' or even 'friends' (*rafiki*). Not only do they have to learn to look at their surroundings through the eyes of tourists, they also need to become aware that the imaginaries of *wazungu* ('white people') that circulate in local popular culture are as much stereotypes as the tourism imaginaries they are appropriating.

In fact, the Tanzanian guides are as seduced by foreign images of their country and its flora and fauna as the tourists are seduced by the exotic images that purport to be Tanzanian. Clearly, there are multiple seduc(a)tions at play in tourism encounters. Both tourists and guides willingly become complicit in their own seduction by tourism imaginaries. These imaginaries often shrewdly exaggerate the power of difference while neglecting and obfuscating the power of commonality. In his courses, Bwana Baraka always stresses the need for cross-cultural respect and mutual understanding. His long-term experience has undoubtedly taught him that changing widely spread preconceptions of the 'Other', either way, takes time and energy, and is not always desirable in tourism.

References

Arnould, E.J. and Price, L.L. (1993) River magic: Extraordinary experience and the extended service encounter. *Journal of Consumer Research* 20 (1), 24–45.

Bissell, W.C. (2005) Engaging colonial nostalgia. *Cultural Anthropology* 20 (2), 215–248.

Bruner, E.M. (2005) *Culture on Tour: Ethnographies of Travel*. Chicago, IL: University of Chicago Press.

Bunten, A.C. (2008) Sharing culture or selling out? Developing the commodified persona in the heritage industry. *American Ethnologist* 35 (3), 380–395.

Dann, G.M.S. (1996) *The Language of Tourism: A Sociolinguistic Perspective*. Wallingford: CABI.

Desmond, J. (1999) *Staging Tourism: Bodies on Display from Waikiki to Sea World*. Chicago, IL: University of Chicago Press.

Di Giovine, M.A. (2008) *The Heritage-Scape: UNESCO, World Heritage, and Tourism*. Lanham, MD: Lexington Books.

Echtner, C.M. and Prasad, P. (2003) The context of Third World tourism marketing. *Annals of Tourism Research* 30 (3), 660–682.

Edensor, T. (1998) *Tourists at the Taj: Performance and Meaning at a Symbolic Site*. London: Routledge.

Feldman, J. (2007) Constructing a shared Bible land: Jewish Israeli guiding performances for Protestant pilgrims. *American Ethnologist* 34 (2), 351–374.

Henderson, C.E. and Weisgrau, M.K. (eds) (2007) *Raj Rhapsodies: Tourism, Heritage and the Seduction of History*. Aldershot: Ashgate.

Hennig, C. (2002) Tourism: Enacting modern myths (trans. A. Brown). In G.M.S. Dann (ed.) *The Tourist as a Metaphor of the Social World* (pp. 169–187). Wallingford: CABI.

Hollinshead, K. (2007) 'Worldmaking' and the transformation of place and culture. In I. Ateljevic, A. Pritchard and N. Morgan (eds) *The Critical Turn in Tourism Studies: Innovative Research Methodologies* (pp. 165–193). Amsterdam: Elsevier.

Katriel, T. (1994) Performing the past: Presentational styles in settlement museum interpretation. *Israel Social Science Research* 9 (1/2), 1–16.

MacCannell, D. (1992) *Empty Meeting Grounds: The Tourist Papers*. London: Routledge.

MacDonald, S. (2006) Mediating heritage: Tour guides at the former Nazi party rally grounds, Nuremberg. *Tourist Studies* 6 (2), 119–138.

Morgan, N. and Pritchard, A. (1998) *Tourism Promotion and Power: Creating Images, Creating Identities*. Chichester: John Wiley.

Ness, S.A. (2003) *Where Asia Smiles: An Ethnography of Philippine Tourism*. Philadelphia, PA: University of Pennsylvania Press.

Norton, A. (1996) Experiencing nature: The reproduction of environmental discourse through safari tourism in East Africa. *Geoforum* 27 (3), 355–373.

Picard, D. (2011) *Tourism, Magic and Modernity: Cultivating the Human Garden*. New York: Berghahn Books.

Pratt, M.L. (2008) *Imperial Eyes: Travel Writing and Transculturation* (2nd edn). London: Routledge.

Said, E.W. (1994) *Orientalism* (rev. edn). New York: Vintage Books.

Salazar, N.B. (2006) Touristifying Tanzania: Global discourse, local guides. *Annals of Tourism Research* 33 (3), 833–852.

Salazar, N.B. (2009a) Imaged or imagined? Cultural representations and the 'tourismification' of peoples and places. *Cahiers d'Études Africaines* 49 (193–194), 49–71.

Salazar, N.B. (2009b) A troubled past, a challenging present, and a promising future?

Tanzania's tourism development in perspective. *Tourism Review International* 12 (3–4), 259–273.

Salazar, N.B. (2010a) *Envisioning Eden: Mobilizing Imaginaries in Tourism and Beyond*. Oxford: Berghahn.

Salazar, N.B. (2010b) Tourism and cosmopolitanism: A view from below. *International Journal of Tourism Anthropology* 1 (1), 55–69.

Salazar, N.B. (2012a) Community-based cultural tourism: Issues, threats and opportunities. *Journal of Sustainable Tourism* 20 (1), 9–22.

Salazar, N.B. (2012b) Tourism imaginaries: A conceptual approach. *Annals of Tourism Research* 39 (2), 863–882.

Salazar, N.B. (2013) Imagineering otherness: Anthropological legacies in contemporary tourism. *Anthropological Quarterly* 86 (3), 669–696.

Salazar, N.B. and Graburn, N.H.H. (eds) (2014) *Tourism Imaginaries: Anthropological Approaches*. Oxford: Berghahn.

Schwenkel, C. (2006) Recombinant history: Transnational practices of memory and knowledge production in contemporary Vietnam. *Cultural Anthropology* 21 (1), 3–30.

Selwyn, T. (ed.) (1996) *The Tourist Image: Myths and Myth Making in Tourism*. Chichester: John Wiley.

Skinner, J. and Theodossopoulos, D. (eds) (2011) *Great Expectations: Imagination and Anticipation in Tourism*. Oxford: Berghahn.

Strauss, C. (2006) The imaginary. *Anthropological Theory* 6 (3), 322–344.

Sturma, M. (2002) *South Sea Maidens: Western Fantasy and Sexual Politics in the South Pacific*. Westport, CT: Greenwood Press.

Tanzania Tourist Board (1999) *Karibu Tanzania*. Dar-es-Salaam: Tanzania Tourist Board.

Torgovnick, M. (1990) *Gone Primitive: Savage Intellects, Modern Lives*. Chicago, IL: University of Chicago Press.

Wynn, L.L. (2007) *Pyramids and Nightclubs: A Travel Ethnography of Arab and Western Imaginations of Egypt*. Austin, TX: University of Texas Press.

7 Bargaining Under Thatch Roofs: Tourism and the Allure of Poverty in Highland Bolivia

Clare A. Sammells

Introduction

If we accept the premise that poverty is a relationship between people, and not an absolute measure of wealth (Sahlins, 2003 [1974]: 37), then it should follow that social perceptions of poverty are fraught with social meanings. The discipline of anthropology has a long history of examining populations that are viewed as both economically marginalised and culturally distinct, and these perceived characteristics often blend together in ethnographic accounts. Nader's (1969) call to 'study up' – to conduct ethnography among populations that have political and economic power – continues to challenge the discipline for exactly that reason.

Among anthropologists, and more generally in Western societies, there is an implicit idea that poverty makes people more 'real', more culturally authentic and more theoretically interesting. The differences between anthropologists and the populations they examine, in terms of culture and class, are naturalised within the discipline. This emerges in part through narratives of cultural loss, where cultures are perceived as inherently diminished by access to, or participation in, the global economy (or even anthropological research itself). This set of assumptions has been productively questioned (Passaro, 1997; Wolf, 2001) but has not disappeared. They emerge from the history of the discipline; anthropologists typically were tasked with travelling to distant lands and returning with tales of different peoples and cultures within a context of colonialism and structural power dynamics (Trouillot, 1991).

In keeping with the disciplinary emphasis on poverty, anthropologists of tourism have tended to focus on the subset of tourism that involves citizens of industrialised countries (Europe, the United States, etc.) travelling to 'Third World' countries where locals are seen by visitors as culturally exotic.

Even anthropological research on domestic tourism tends to focus on visits of urban national citizens to populations that are ethnically, politically or economically marginalised.

Despite the differences between anthropologists and these kinds of tourists, they share an interest in the same populations (Crick, 1995). Anthropologists and tourists are clearly not the same, but they share a relationship of structural inequality with the objects of their interest. This inequality is partially based on class but is often presented primarily as cultural difference. Here I will focus on the type of tourism that seeks out indigenous cultural distinctiveness that is also marked by economic marginalisation.

'First World' tourists have the money, time and political power to travel around the world despite expensive airfares and the need for travel visas. In contrast, many of the most 'exotic' of the toured cannot afford long-distance travel, do not have formal jobs with paid vacation time and have difficulties acquiring passports and travel permissions. I am certainly not the first to remark on this. Recent work on slum tourism (Frenzel *et al.*, 2012) and Matthew Hill's work on mystic tourism in Peru (Hill, 2005) have also examined these inequalities.

Tourists are also well aware of these class differences, and thus categories of poverty and culture merge through their interactions with the toured. Many US vacationers play with concepts of class, inverting their own class identities through their touristic interactions with others (Gottlieb, 1982). Cultural distinctiveness is linked to poverty *within* the touristic encounter for both tourists and toured. Considering two ethnographic examples, I will consider how 'cultural authenticity' is dialectically constructed specifically through reference to markers of poverty within the context of touristic encounters between foreign tourists and Aymara residents of Tiwanaku, Bolivia.

Tourist Tiwanaku

Tiwanaku is located two hours by bus from the capital city of La Paz, in an Andean valley at 4200 metres above sea level. Tiwanaku is a pre-Incan archaeological site, a major urban centre until approximately 1100 AD, with artistic and cultural influence throughout the southern Andes (Janusek, 2008; Kolata, 1993). Long considered to be the most important archaeological site in Bolivia, it was named a World Heritage Site by the United Nations Organization for Education, Science and Culture (UNESCO) in 2000. I conducted two years of fieldwork there, from 2002 to 2004, in addition to shorter trips in 2007 and 2010.

Tiwanaku attracted over 80,000 visitors in 1999, over half of whom were Bolivians. Nevertheless, it is not generally marketed as a major global attraction to foreign tourists, nor presented as a primary attraction that would in itself motivate travel to Bolivia. Many foreigners decide to visit Tiwanaku once they are already in La Paz, and the site is often treated as a day trip from that city rather than a destination in its own right. Tiwanaku lacks the international recognition of other pre-Columbian Andean attractions such as Machu Picchu or the Nazca lines. Given its proximity to La Paz, very few visitors spend the night in the village of Tiwanaku, and time limitations usually prevent them from seeing the entire archaeological site. At the time of this research (2002–04) there was only one small hotel in the town; it was often empty or under-booked and survived through its restaurant clientele.

Bolivia itself is also not a major global tourist destination. In 2005, it received only 0.3% of the international tourists and 0.1% of the tourism receipts to the entire American continent (World Tourism Organization, 2006, 2011). Bolivia's marginal position in global tourism has important ramifications. This is not merely an example of tourism on a small scale, but rather represents a fundamentally different set of interactions between a national tourist economy and a global industry. Bolivia's marginality is presented as part of its appeal for tourists who wish to see what they perceive as the authentic indigenous cultures of the highlands and untouched ecological spaces in the Amazon.

Bolivian government and city-based tour agencies have actively promoted the tourist appeal of marginalised people and spaces through marketing campaigns. For example, the Bolivian Vice-Ministry of Tourism chose the tag-line 'lo autentico aún existe' – the authentic still exists – to focus its tourist marketing on indigenous people and natural Amazonian landscapes. The philosophy behind this campaign was made explicit in an article on Bolivian nation-branding co-authored by Ximena Alvarez Aguirre, who was the Bolivian Vice-Minister of Tourism in 2004–05. She writes:

> In terms of culture, the true identity of Bolivia is in its 'ancestral cultures', cultures that have been maintained without any alteration throughout time and that make Bolivia a unique place in comparison with its neighbouring countries.… In terms of marketing strategies … Bolivia has been utilizing a logo and the tag line 'lo autentico aún existe' – 'the authentic still exists' – which is coherent with the country's identity and conveys the main message that Bolivia wants to send to the world, namely that the country offers an authentic experience in terms of nature and culture. (Alvarez Aguirre & Renjel, 2007: 165, 167)

Many anthropologists, including myself, reject the claim that indigenous cultures anywhere have been 'maintained without any alteration throughout time'. No culture is unchanging, even those that have *not* had a centuries-long history of involvement with states and capitalist commodity chains, as indigenous Bolivians have (Abercrombie, 1998; Gootenberg, 2008; Topik, 2006). This conception of authentic culture appears to be undermined even by Alvarez herself. In her list of attractions that show the 'identity of Bolivia' there is no mention of indigenous groups at all (Alvarez Aguirre & Renjel, 2007). Instead, this list includes two types of attraction: natural attractions presented as almost free of humans; and colonial-era settlements.

Alvarez's claim of authenticity, however, is not analytical; as Bruner warns us, 'authenticity is a red herring, to be examined only when the tourists, the locals, or the producers themselves use the term' (Bruner, 2005: 5). The Vice-Ministry of Tourism was not producing ethnography but a blueprint for action. This was a plan to brand Bolivian populations and spaces in ways presumed to be appealing to the imaginations of foreign tourists. In this imaginary, Bolivia itself is timeless. Colonial spaces were built and inhabited by indigenous peoples, of course, but a dynamic historical continuity is not invoked. Instead, indigenous peoples 'from the past' sit in front of colonial churches 'from the past'. Natural landscapes remain untouched by human presence, despite the fact that indigenous peoples live in all of them. 'Modern' Bolivia is completely sidelined – the skyscrapers and universities (Centellas, 2008), anti-tuberculosis campaigns (Scott, 2009), vernacular architecture (Kohn, 2010), neoliberal reforms and resulting conflicts and rebellions (Gill, 2000; Kohl & Farthing, 2006; Shultz & Draper, 2008).

In the vision of Bolivia presented by the Vice-Ministry of Tourism, only the tourist is part of the contemporary world. Bolivia is in a past that is gazed upon by tourists. Indigenous peoples are living evidence that Bolivia has retained something that other nations have lost through the cultural and ecological ravages of industrial capitalism. In touristic narratives, the indigenous Aymara, such as those who live in Tiwanaku, are presented neither as a political force (which they are) nor as a 'problem' to be solved via assimilation (as national governments had, unfortunately, often viewed them in the past). Instead, indigenous populations are presented as part of the solution to the problems of environmental destruction, urban anomie and moral decline caused by the absence of their counterparts elsewhere in the world. The Aymara are portrayed as mystical and timeless populations engaging in unchanging and apolitical ritual and agricultural practice.

This timelessness has racial and class dimensions as well, given that, in the Andes, race and class are intimately linked (Albro, 2000; Gill, 1994;

Mangan, 2005; Orlove, 1998; Weismantel, 1988, 1997, 2001; Zulawski, 2000). 'Racial' categories are marked not only by phenotypic characteristics but also by cultural practices, such as residence, labour, clothing, language and speech patterns. Class forms an important part of this, so much so that to be 'authentically' indigenous in the highlands is to be a poor farmer. Scholars have debated the exact nature of race in the Andes. Orlove (1998) has argued race is better understood as a continuum. Weismantel (2001: xxxi) suggests that in particular interactions participants take on the form of a 'vicious binary', where one actor plays the role of 'indigenous' and the other of 'non-indigenous' in an inherently hierarchical encounter. She does not see these roles as fixed, but rather as emerging in specific social contexts. These two interpretations of Andean race and class are not mutually exclusive; instead, they describe two different scales of social interaction. At the level of society as a whole, racial and class categories fall on a continuum where individuals can move across porous boundaries. Within particular moments, however, these divisions are experienced in more starkly binary terms. I will return to this idea later, as this tension between a continuum and a 'vicious binary' also describes the boundaries between tourists and toured, 'hosts' and 'guests'.

Touristic discourses rely on 'picturesque' landscapes and culturally marked indigenous communities, but in highland Bolivia the indigenous picturesque is marked in ways that are locally understood as also marking poverty. According to census data, most Bolivian Aymara now live in cities, but the ideal type for indigenous culture remains rural (Sammells, 2012). These rural spaces are also among the poorest in the nation. While the Vice-Ministry of Tourism is intent upon marketing rural indigenous culture, many who live that life are trying to escape the poverty that comes with it. Many with whom I conducted ethnographic research in Tiwanaku invested the money they earned from tourism into sending their children to study in La Paz or elsewhere, so that they could become urban professionals. This desire was manifest in both small comments and important economic decisions. For example, one father once told me that he felt it was a waste that his child, who had recently graduated from high school (a notable accomplishment in Tiwanaku), was still at home on the farm. In many families, parents and older siblings made significant economic sacrifices so that younger children could finish their education and attend an urban college. Tourism valued the markers of poverty, but the poor themselves were pragmatic about improving their economic situation and that of their children.

Thatch Roofs on Display

I now turn to how these ideas play out at the local level, using two ethnographic examples. The first is a public meeting that took place just before an annual June solstice celebration, Tiwanaku's largest tourist event, in the early 21st century (for more on the solstice celebrations, see Sammells, 2012). As part of the preparations, a member of parliament came to Tiwanaku to meet with local people about providing services for the event. The parliamentarian, who was not indigenous or even from the highlands, was outspoken and, to the unfailingly polite Aymara, seemed abrasive. The audience – all Aymara, the women mostly dressed in large *pollera* skirts, the men in Western-style trousers and shirts, and with black hats, and thus all clearly marked through clothing as the indigenous rural poor – sat quietly in folding chairs in the conference room of the museum at the archaeological site as the parliamentarian told them, in no uncertain terms, that their town was not authentic enough. According to this official, Tiwanakeños needed to get rid of their metal roofs and use thatch. The streets of the town should be renamed, eliminating the names of patriotic Bolivian national heroes and replacing them with the names of pre-Columbian Inca kings (even though the Inca were also conquerors in the Aymara-controlled region of Tiwanaku). But at the same time, local cooks should learn to cook French fries and hamburgers for tourists. This food should be prepared using proper sanitation techniques (though these would require luxuries that almost no one had, such as hot running water). The village's weekly Sunday market should be reorganised and removed from the central plaza, so that the centre of town would be an open, empty public space rather than a crowded commercial one. The larger message was that Tiwanaku should model itself as an attraction after the example of the Peruvian city of Cuzco – a place that everyone in Tiwanaku, whether they had been there or not (and most had not), accepted as a successful tourist model.

This parliamentarian had a very clear idea about what should constitute authenticity in Tiwanaku. The town should display something important about the Bolivian nation – both its deep roots in the pre-Columbian past, evident in the archaeological site, and its ability to cater to the modern needs of urban Bolivian and foreign visitors. The town should combine markers of the indigenous – such as thatch roofs – with modernising civil organisation that ensured the provision of 'clean' (i.e. sanitary) food and 'clean' (i.e. empty) public spaces such as town squares, and permit the efficient flow of foot and vehicular traffic. This was an attempt simultaneously to domesticate and to commodify poverty – to regulate the lives of the poor, while using the markers of poverty to encourage money-making tourism that would supposedly lead to local economic development. This is a common tension in touristic endeavours (see Di Giovine, 2009).

The proposed thatch roofs were particularly interesting. While this parliamentarian saw them as authentic, for local Aymara, thatch roofs are generally understood as a sign of poverty. Thatch is a roofing material that requires no money but a great deal of labour. It is made from wild grasses, which are free to collect, but thatch roofs must be replaced every few years and are more likely to leak. When rural Aymara use them at all, they tend to do so only on first building their home. These first buildings are usually constructed early in a new couple's marriage, as they are getting established economically and need only a small amount of space. As their family expands, new buildings are added around a central interior courtyard, usually with purchased metal roofs that do not leak and require little maintenance. The first thatch-roof building tends to be repurposed several times, often ending as a storage space.

Many Tiwanakeños view metal roofs as a necessary part of most new constructions, and will not start a new building until they have the money to buy the roof. The roof is often the major construction expense. Adobe bricks are made locally; wealthier families can hire others to make these bricks but many families do this work themselves. The choice between roof types is not locally expressed in aesthetic terms, but practical ones.

For the parliamentarian and some others in the tourist industry, however, thatch indexes not poverty but 'culture'. If Tiwanaku were to have thatch roofs again (as it did in the 1920s, when most indigenous peoples in Bolivia lived in literal serfdom), then the town would fit into the touristic marketable past. When, exactly, 'the past' *is* is of course flexible. Most rural Aymara today reject the idea of using thatch roofs on their private homes for mere aesthetic appeal. It is only in the context of tourism that such markers can be recast as culturally authentic.

This is one example of the tensions that exist between those who hope to maintain markers of poverty as part of a picturesque (and profitable) tourist landscape and those who hope such markers of poverty will be eliminated by a (tourism-funded) development. After all, attracting tourism is about attracting money; many hope that money will benefit the poor who are also objects of the 'tourist gaze'.

Performances of Bargaining

My second example focuses on how this overlap between culture and class is evident in some tourists' interactions with the indigenous people they have come to see, in bargaining for souvenirs in highland Bolivian tourist markets. On the surface, this practice seems to be about tourists saving money, but this is not the primary importance of tourist bargaining. Instead, bargaining is a way for tourists to attempt to perform local cultural knowledge in a context where culture and poverty are viewed as intertwined. While such performances can never actually achieve the goal of making tourists 'local', it is nevertheless a meaningful project to the tourists who engage in it.

If the Vice-Ministry of Tourism's claim that Bolivia is where 'the authentic still exists' is at all true, then a quintessential place to find that 'authentic' is in outdoor indigenous marketplaces. Such spaces have attracted both tourist and scholarly attention (Buechler & Buechler, 1993; Buechler, 1997; Gordon, 2011; Larson, 1998 [1988]; Mangan, 2005; Seligmann, 1989, 2004; Weismantel, 2001). Both urban and rural marketplaces tend to be dominated by indigenous (or *chola*) women wearing the heavy *pollera* skirts associated with contemporary indigenous fashion. Market women in *polleras* appear often on postcards and tourist brochures representing the Bolivian picturesque. Younger women vendors often wear much cheaper, second-hand Western clothing, such as sweatpants and sweaters under aprons. This style of dress is locally recognised as the sign of deepest poverty, yet it rarely appears in tourist marketing.

Tiwanaku's tourist souvenir market fits neatly into this mould of authentic Andean marketplace. Most of the vendors are women wearing *polleras*, all vendors are bilingual in Aymara and Spanish and consider themselves to be Aymara. For foreigners, these women epitomise the indigenous Bolivia they wish to see. It is not coincidental that two vendors from this market were on the cover of a Lonely Planet guide to South America, animatedly playing soccer in their *polleras* (Gorry *et al.*, 2002; for further commentary see Sammells, 2009: 17–27). It is also not a coincidence that a development project that built kiosks for these souvenir vendors designed them with *totora* reed roofs placed over clear plastic, combining the practicality of modern building materials with a traditional-looking thatched exterior. *Totora* reeds were never used to thatch houses in Tiwanaku, as the town is not on the shores of Lake Titicaca; local *ichu* grass was used for this purpose. Regardless, this architectural style was meant to invoke traditional building methods in the eyes of visitors.

Let me preface my example of bargaining in this market by pointing out the inequalities inherent in this encounter. For most foreign tourists in Bolivia, saving less than US$1 rarely made a dent in their budgets. If it did, they wouldn't be there in the first place, given the cost of air transport and travel in general. Such sums *were* significant to vendors, for whom Bs1 (about €0.12) bought bread for the family's afternoon tea or a notebook for a school-aged child. Given that economic context, consider the following situation in Tiwanaku's tourist marketplace.

One day, a group of native English-speaking international exchange students, in their late teens to early 20s, arrived as tourists at the Tiwanaku marketplace. One of them started negotiating with a Tiwanakeña vendor for two shawls, which had been purchased by the vendor in La Paz for resale in this market. The vendor began at the reasonable price of Bs80, but the tourist begged and pleaded for a lower price. Another student from the group chimed in that they were from another city in Bolivia (this was where they were living) and that they wanted to take a souvenir of Tiwanaku back with them, something pretty, since the people here are so nice. Both tourists were saying all of this in non-native but fluent Spanish, in a sing-songy whine imitating a stereotypical Bolivian market woman's 'Mamita, no es así' ('Lady, it's not like that', that is, 'I can't afford to buy it for that price').

The vendor eventually, after much whining on the part of the two tourists, consented to accept Bs62 for both shawls, which was very close to what she had bought them for. She would not lower the price to Bs60 no matter how much they protested. The tourist then produced a Bs100 note and asked for change. At this the vendor started laughing; that was a lot of money! The tourist's friend then claimed that they needed the money for food, 'Without this we won't eat!' The vendor gave the change, and the tourist went to the very next stall and, in full view of the apparently un-surprised first vendor, began negotiations over some stone carvings. When another of the tourist group, standing a few stalls down, asked her what she had paid, the woman called across the marketplace in English, 'Bs62 for both shawls! Hurray! And she started at Bs80! But they're probably only worth Bs54 anyway.' She then saw me and another vendor watching and seemed somewhat abashed.

For these young women, who had spent literally thousands of dollars to come to Bolivia, I am going to presume that saving US$2 bargaining for tourist souvenirs was probably not motivated by saving enough money to eat. But I also don't want to criticise this young person – in part because I have also been guilty of some aggressive bargaining, in part because undoubtedly she was on a budget, and in part because this particular inter-action was not unique. Rather, I wish to examine the meaning of this kind of bargaining as a cultural practice.

Most foreign tourists in Bolivia were well aware that they were charged 'gringo prices' (the term 'gringo' in highland Bolivia refers to racially white foreigners, including Europeans and even white South Americans, rather than specifically to US citizens; it is often used in a descriptive rather than an insulting way). Market vendors often attempted to earn a little extra income from foreigners, who they perceived could afford to pay slightly more than locals, and who might also be ignorant of commonly accepted prices. Older or wealthier tourists sometimes explicitly talked about willingly paying gringo prices as an intentional practice, their own small act to lessen the discrepancies of global inequality by paying a bit more while on vacation, especially to those receiving the smallest part of tourist revenue. For other tourists, however – often young backpackers on longer trips – bargaining became an opportunity to prove that they knew accepted prices and spoke Spanish well enough to argue for them. Bargaining was primarily an attempt to perform local cultural knowledge, a performance for which local vendors were cast as the final judges of whether tourists had successfully learned local market practice. The triumph experienced by the young tourist above was centred on her ability to bargain successfully – thus the emphasis on knowing the shawls' 'real' prices and her friend's imitation of market vendors' speech patterns in Spanish. They were proving their knowledge of how the market worked, and their knowledge was validated by the price they paid. Successful bargaining 'proves' the tourist has deciphered the cultural rules of the game, and validates their local knowledge.

Being able and willing to bargain also suggests the camaraderie of poverty between a subset of tourists and local peoples. Younger tourists may genuinely feel that they are poor in relationship to older employed tourists from their own nations, but the idea that they share a level of poverty with rural Bolivians is illusory. Nevertheless, this suggests the existence of a tourist logic that foreigners can attempt to get closer to indigenous culture merely through the performance of poverty. As discussed above, this linking of culture and poverty is shared locally in tourist marketing contexts also. Indigenous people are central to the marketing of Bolivia: authentic and poor become two sides of the same tourist coin.

Of course, there is no inherent connection between tourists who stay in cheap hostels and engage in aggressive bargaining on the one hand, and 'being Aymara' on the other. Yet the triumph of our young tourist is not an economic one. By knowing how to bargain, she is attempting to perform a role that is less like that of a tourist and more like that of a local. Locals are not taken in by these performances, of course. Although the attempt cannot be entirely successful, tourist bargaining as a cultural performance has meanings far beyond how much money changes hands.

Conclusion

Tensions are manifest between markers of poverty that are idealised and taken out of context for commodification, and modernising practices that are simultaneously applied. The parliamentarian may have wished for thatch roofs and 'traditional' clothing, but also wished to 'clean up' tourist spaces by organising marketplaces, clearing roads of public transportation traffic, forcing food sanitation based on germ theory, and other practices. Meanwhile, many tourists come to places like Bolivia to see authentic culture, what in my darker moments I call 'gawking at poverty'. They pay large sums of money to do so, although little of it goes to the poor whom they come to see. Government officials, realising there is this tourist interest, want to maintain the picturesque aspects of poverty while at the same time bringing in money that would alleviate poverty through development projects and entrepreneurial business.

Tourists did not inevitably accept such invitations to recast poverty as culture. Many were keen observers of the realities of Bolivian poverty, often attributing it to excessive integration into the world economic system, or a failure to integrate sufficiently. Either of these interpretations is incompatible with the ahistoricity suggested by the tag-line 'The authentic still exists'. But touristic narratives are real even when they are not fully successful. In tourist Bolivia, indigenous people are cast as timeless, 'other', and disconnected from the worlds of tourists. Poverty is recast as cultural difference. This project of linking culture to poverty is incomplete, but poverty continues to be noticed – and sometimes performed – by tourists looking for the authentic.

All this forms part of the ongoing, dialectic process of creating touristic authenticity. The promise of tourist money may motivate locals to maintain or recreate culturally 'authentic' markers, but some tourists are active participants in attempting local performances of class. Regardless, these tourists' attempts to achieve authenticity through imitating local markers of poverty (such as bargaining) are doomed to failure. Tourists are inherently marked as people with the resources – money, state permissions and leisure time – to travel.

I earlier mentioned Weismantel's discussion of a 'vicious binary' that emerges in Andean contexts. While Andean ethnic categories are complex and fluid, within specific social encounters individuals adopt clear roles of 'indigenous' or 'non-indigenous'. We might suggest a similar 'vicious binary' that, in the tourist encounter, divides individuals into 'hosts' and 'guests' (following Smith, 1973). While tourists are never tourists all the time (they eventually go home), and toured peoples can become tourists (if only theoretically), these roles are solidified within particular social interactions. Like the question of race in the Andes, the boundaries between 'tourist' and 'toured' also encode a class relationship. Even where tourists and locals share the ability to travel, within particular encounters they adopt only one of these roles. This forces the tourist encounter to mimic a class division, where 'guests' are leisured and moneyed outsiders and 'hosts' are locals who provide services in exchange for money. This is a reversal of the usual hosts and guests role, where the offering of hospitality and gifts places hosts in the higher social position (Mauss, 1990 [1923]). In the context of tourism, however, the role of 'host' is a paid one, where social generosity (local information, assistance, meals and even friendship) is commodified.

In some contexts, such as Western Europe, these binaries may reverse themselves between encounters. People may take the roles of 'hosts' in one set of encounters and 'guests' in another. In Bolivia, however, few rural Andean 'hosts' are likely to travel to Europe or the United States as 'guests'. Bolivians are well aware of this inequality. I was constantly asked during my time in Bolivia, even by complete strangers on the bus, how much my airfare had cost. An honest answer confirmed to them that tourists were wealthy, as round-trip airfares between Chicago and La Paz routinely cost €750–850 or more. Given this knowledge, for most Bolivians the idea that North Atlantic tourists would be touring their nation on a hand-to-mouth budget seems unlikely, even though they recognise that some tourists are more affluent than others. For them, the binary between 'hosts' and 'guests' was not merely an artifact of a particular reversible tourist encounter but a reflection of larger inequalities.

I would argue that in this Bolivian context, tourist bargaining performances of an authenticity based on poverty are doomed to be 'infelicitous' (Trouillot, 2000). And yet, the fact that these performances can never truly be successful does not mean they do not have important meanings for those who attempt them. For the subset of tourists interested in seeking 'authentic' indigenous culture, participation is the ultimate experience. Tourists seek those kinds of experiences in different ways, but some feel that successful bargaining in an authentic indigenous market – one marked by thatch roofs – demonstrates that they have gone beyond merely gazing.

References

Abercrombie, T.A. (1998) *Pathways of Memory and Power: Ethnography and History Among an Andean People.* Madison, WI: University of Wisconsin Press.

Albro, R. (2000) The populist chola: Cultural mediation and the political imagination in Quillacollo, Bolivia. *Journal of Latin American Anthropology* 5 (2), 112–149.

Alvarez Aguirre, X. and Renjel, X.S. (2007) Country case insight – Bolivia. In K. Dinnie (ed.) *Nation Branding: Concepts, Issues, Practice* (pp. 165–169). Oxford: Butterworth-Heinemann.

Bruner, E.M. (2005) *Culture on Tour: Ethnographies of Travel.* Chicago, IL: University of Chicago Press.

Buechler, H. and Buechler, J-M. (1993) Networks domesticated: Work and household economies among producers and vendors in La Paz, Bolivia. *Anthropology of Work Review*, 13/14 (4/1), 3–5.

Buechler, J-M. (1997) The visible and vocal politics of female traders and small-scale producers in La Paz, Bolivia. In A. Miles and H. Buechler (eds) *Women and Economic Change: Andean Perspectives* (pp. 75–88). Arlington, VA: American Anthropological Association.

Centellas, K.M. (2008) For love of land and laboratory: Nation-building and bioscience in Bolivia. PhD dissertation, Department of Anthropology, University of Chicago.

Crick, M. (1995) The anthropologist as tourist: An identity in question. In M-F. Lanfant, J.B. Allcock and E.M. Bruner (eds) *International Tourism: Identity and Change* (pp. 205–223). London: Sage.

Di Giovine, M.A. (2009) Revitalization and counter-revitalization: Tourism, heritage, and the Lantern Festival as catalysts for regeneration in Hoi An, Viet Nam. *Journal of Policy Research in Tourism, Leisure and Events* 1 (3), 208–230.

Frenzel, F., Koens, K. and Steinbrink, M. (eds) (2012) *Slum Tourism: Poverty, Power and Ethics*. London: Routledge.

Gill, L. (1994) *Precarious Dependencies: Gender, Class, and Domestic Service in Bolivia*. New York: Columbia University Press.

Gill, L. (2000) *Teetering on the Rim: Global Restructuring, Daily Life, and the Armed Retreat of the Bolivian State*. New York: Columbia University Press.

Gootenberg, P. (2008) *Andean Cocaine: The Making of a Global Drug*. Chapel Hill, NC: University of North Carolina Press.

Gordon, K.E. (2011) What is important to me is my business, nothing more: Neoliberalism, ideology and the work of selling in highland Bolivia. *Anthropology of Work Review* 32 (1), 30–39.

Gorry, C., Adams, F., Boa, S., Boone, V., Dydynski, K., Hellander, P., Hubbard, C., Noble, J., Palmerlee, D. and Rachowiecki, R. (2002) *South America on a Shoestring* (8th edn). Melbourne: Lonely Planet.

Gottlieb, A. (1982) Americans' vacations. *Annals of Tourism Research* 9, 165–187.

Hill, M.D. (2005) New age in the Andes: Mystical tourism and cultural politics in Cusco, Peru. PhD dissertation, Emory University, Atlanta.

Janusek, J.W. (2008) *Ancient Tiwanaku*. Cambridge: Cambridge University Press.

Kohl, B. and Farthing, L. (2006) *Impasse in Bolivia: Neoliberal Hegemony and Popular Resistance*. London: Zed Books.

Kohn, A. (2010) Of bricks and blood: Constructing vernacular urban space and social lives in La Paz, Bolivia. PhD dissertation, Department of Anthropology, University of Chicago.

Kolata, A.L. (1993) *The Tiwanaku: Portrait of an Andean Civilization*. Cambridge: Blackwell.

Larson, B. (1998 [1988]) *Cochabamba, 1550–1900: Colonialism and Agrarian Transformation in Bolivia*. Durham, NC: Duke University Press.

Mangan, J.E. (2005) *Trading Roles: Gender, Ethnicity, and the Urban Economy in Colonial Potosí*. Durham, NC: Duke University Press.

Mauss, M. (1990 [1923]) *The Gift*. New York: W.W. Norton.

Nader, L. (1969) Up the anthropologist – Perspectives gained from studying up. In D. Hymes (ed.) *Reinventing Anthropology* (pp. 284–311). New York: Random House.

Orlove, B.S. (1998) Down to earth: Race and substance in the Andes. *Bulletin of Latin American Research* 17 (2), 207–222.

Passaro, J. (1997) You can't take the subway to the field! 'Village' epistemologies in the global village. In A. Gupta and J. Ferguson (eds) *Anthropological Locations: Boundaries and Grounds of a Field Science* (pp. 147–162). Berkeley, CA: University of California Press.

Sahlins, M. (1974 [2003]) *Stone Age Economics*. New York: Routledge.

Sammells, C.A. (2009) Touristic narratives and historical networks: Politics and authority in Tiwanaku, Bolivia. PhD dissertation, Department of Anthropology, University of Chicago.

Sammells, C.A. (2012) The city of the present in the city of the past: Solstice celebrations at Tiwanaku, Bolivia. In D. Fairchild Ruggles (ed.) *On Location: Heritage Cities and Sites* (pp. 115–130). New York: Springer.

Scott, S.K. (2009) The metrological mountain: 'Translating' tuberculosis in periurban Bolivia. PhD dissertation, Department of Anthropology, University of Chicago.

Seligmann, L.J. (1989) To be in between: The *Cholas* as market women. *Society for Comparative Study of Society and History*, 694–721.

Seligmann, L.J. (2004) *Peruvian Street Lives: Culture, Power, and Economy Among Market Women of Cuzco*. Urbana, IL: University of Illinois Press.

Shultz, J. and Draper, M.C. (eds) (2008) *Dignity and Defiance: Stories from Bolivia's Challenge to Globalization*. Berkeley, CA: University of California Press.

Smith, V. (ed.) (1973) *Hosts and Guests: The Anthropology of Tourism*. Philadelphia, PA: University of Pennsylvania Press.

Topik, S., Marichal, C. and Frank, Z. (2006) *From Silver to Cocaine: Latin American Commodity Chains and the Building of the World Economy, 1500–2000*. Durham, NC: Duke University Press.

Trouillot, M-R. (1991) Anthropology and the savage slot: The poetics and politics of otherness. In R.G. Fox (ed.) *Recapturing Anthropology: Working in the Present* (pp. 17–44.) Santa Fe, NM: School of American Research Press.

Trouillot, M-R. (2000) Abortive rituals: Historical apologies in the global era. *Interventions* 2 (2), 171–186.

Weismantel, M.J. (1988) *Food, Gender, and Poverty in the Ecuadorian Andes*. Philadelphia, PA: University of Pennsylvania Press.

Weismantel, M.J. (1997) Time, work-discipline, and beans: Indigenous self-determination in the northern Andes. In A. Miles and H. Buechler (eds) *Women and Economic Change: Andean Perspectives* (pp. 31–54). Arlington, VA: American Anthropological Association.

Weismantel, M.J. (2001) *Cholas and Pishtacos: Stories of race and sex in the Andes*. Chicago, IL: University of Chicago Press.

Wolf, E. (2001) *Pathways of Power: Building an Anthropology of the Modern World*. Berkeley, CA: University of California Press.

World Tourism Organization (2006) *Tourism Market Trends, 2006 Edition – Annex*. See http://www.unwto.org/facts (accessed August 2013).

World Tourism Organization (2011) *UNWTO Tourism Highlights, 2011 Edition*. See http://www.unwto.org/pub (accessed August 2013).

Zulawski, A. (2000) Hygiene and 'the Indian problem': Ethnicity and medicine in Bolivia, 1910–1920. *Latin American Research Review* 35 (2), 107–129.

Part 3
Travel, Other and Self-Revelation

8 Mediterranean Fields of Love: Embodied Encounters Between Male Tourism Workers and Female Tourists in a Coastal Town in Turkey

Sanne Scheltena

Introduction

Studies on the romantic and (hetero)sexual encounters between female tourists and local men tend to focus on categorising these relationships as either sex or romance tourism (Dahles, 1997; Dahles & Bras, 1999; Herold *et al.*, 2001; Jeffreys, 2003; Nyanzi *et al.*, 2005; Pruitt & LaFont, 1995; Sanchez Taylor, 2001, 2006). Romance tourism studies often tend to distinguish female from male sex tourists, while sex tourism studies often focus on binaries like rich–poor, north–south, exploiter–exploited, romance–prostitution and the question 'Do women do it too?' In these studies, the standpoint of Western domination and the impact upon the places visited inform the research questions. This chapter moves away from that discussion. I do not aim to categorise the relationships examined in this case study of female tourists in Turkey as either sex or romance tourism. Nor do I aim to redefine these terms. I want to go beyond this discussion by looking closely at the course of the encounter and the tourism experience of both partners. I approach the tourism experience as a physical and embodied encounter with other people and places (Crouch, 2000; Crouch & Desforges, 2003; Everett, 2009; Obrador Pons, 2003; Veijola & Jokinen, 1994; Veijola & Valtonen, 2007; Wearing & Wearing, 1996). Place is the stage on which tourism practices are performed, by tourists and tourism workers (Edensor, 2001). By describing how female tourists and Turkish tourism workers meet and how they respectively experience tourism I want to make the complexity of this encounter visible, and through this make a contribution to the debate about the encounters between female tourists and local men.

Tourism in Turkey has been growing since the 1960s. In coastal towns tourists come to relax at the beach and engage in different activities. Each town has its own population of tourists. The present research was conducted in a coastal town that is a popular destination for British, German, Dutch and Turkish tourists. Tourists in this town are mostly families, couples and groups of female tourists. Some tourists come for one or two weeks; others stay the whole summer in their villa or apartment. Tourism workers are mostly local men and a few male migrant workers from other places. In Turkey, tourism work is considered a man's job, as it is inappropriate for women to work in the public sphere (Tucker, 2007: 88). Besides that, Turkey is to some extent a conservative and patriarchal country, where heterosexuality is the norm. As a likely consequence, the majority of the relationships that derive from tourism encounters are between Turkish men and female tourists.

The fieldwork on which this chapter is based involved participant observation in a Turkish coastal town in the summer of 2009. I worked as a salesperson in a tour office and as a host/waiter in a beach restaurant. I did not work for the last four weeks at the end of the season; most of that time I spent among tourists at the beach, in restaurants and bars. I introduced myself as a student interested in tourism and writing about the 'encounters' between tourism workers and tourists. It was my choice not always to add the term 'sexual' to 'encounters', because I was interested in the whole encounter and I was afraid to collect only the stories of the people who were very much willing to talk about their sexual experiences and miss the stories of the people for whom sexuality is not a topic to talk about in public. Although I was rather open about my intentions, some people had their own ideas about my identity. Some rather saw me as an employee, a co-worker, an English/Dutch teacher, a single woman or a friend.

The informal conversations conducted during and after working were a great source of information. My basic Turkish language skills were a great advantage. I was able to speak with tourism workers in their own language, to talk with tourism workers who lacked knowledge of foreign languages and to listen in on conversations of tourism workers that were not meant for the ears of the tourists.

Participating gave me the opportunity to observe and meet many tourists and tourism workers. Besides that, it gave me insights into the divergent embodied practices and experiences of tourism by both tourists and tourism workers. I am a tall, brown-haired Dutch woman in her mid-30s. Although, due to Turkish gender rules, female tourism workers in Turkey are rather rare, it was not difficult to find jobs in tourism. My advantages were being available all summer, speaking four languages and having many years of experience working as a waitress, bartender and other service jobs. Being a woman in a Turkish tourism setting was sometimes difficult because some men did not accept a female co-worker as their equal or superior. They had strong opinions about equal wages, sharing tips and work like cleaning, which some of them thought was my job.

Being a (foreign) woman often made me the subject of seduction, experiences which gave me important insights into the patterns of the encounters between female tourists and the Turkish men. Working together with the tourism workers was not only sharing a work experience: it also gave me access to these men without always being the subject of seduction. Being a co-worker and being able to speak some Turkish made me an eye-witness and sometimes an accomplice in many of the encounters between (female) tourists and tourism workers.

In this chapter I will discuss two aspects of the encounter. First, I will show how an encounter between female tourists and Turkish tourism workers can become very intimate in a short period. I will do this by looking at the course of the service encounter and the strategies used to personalise it and enhance the sympathy between both partners. Second, I will describe the practices of both female tourists and tourism workers and show that tourists and tourism workers have divergent experiences of tourism. I argue that although both partners are in the same place and experience physical proximity, they lack empathy.

Personalising the Service Encounter

Encounters between female tourists and Turkish tourism workers usually occur at the workplace of the tourism worker. In Turkey, tourism is very customer oriented. This means that tourism workers make great efforts to please their customers. Tourists are always served at their table or chair: in restaurants, bars and nightclubs waiters walk around to serve them, and even on the beach tourists are served while lying on their sun beds. The encounters between tourism workers and tourists can be understood as person-to-person interactions between customer and service provider. In these, the service component is of great importance (Solomon *et al.*, 1985: 99). Tourism workers are service providers. These terms are mainly used in marketing research. The service encounter is evaluated in terms of the satisfaction of the customer with the service received. A determinant of this satisfaction is the degree to which it is congruent with the role expectations on one side and behaviour on the other side (Surprenant & Solomon, 1987: 87). A customer in a restaurant expects a waiter to behave in a certain way. A good waiter performs his role as waiter well. On the other side, the service provider has certain expectations of the performance of the customers or tourists. The course of a service encounter follows a fixed pattern, where both sides are following a script (Edensor, 2000, 2001; Leidner, 1999; Solomon *et al.*, 1985; Surprenant & Solomon, 1987). This is how the encounters between Turkish tourism workers and tourists initially start out.

Making the first contact and personalising this contact is of great importance to tourism workers (Czepiel, 1990: 16; Price *et al.*, 1995: 85; Surprenant & Solomon, 1987: 86; Wearing & Wearing, 1996: 241). In some service encounters, like in very expensive hotels, a formal attitude is required. In other encounters, an informal atmosphere is created. In the Turkish tourism realm, personalising the service encounter determines the relationship with the customer in the present and the future. Service providers who make the customer feel like an individual or even a special guest are successful in their job. Turkish tourism workers use a number of strategies to personalise the service encounter. During the first encounter, tourism workers are very friendly, smile and if possible speak the language of the tourist (Surprenant & Solomon, 1987: 88). Some Turkish tourism workers speak the basics of a dozen different languages. Before actually meeting the tourists, tourism workers observe their potential customers carefully in order to make a good guess of the best language in which to address them.

Eye contact and a friendly smile are other strategies that are used by the service providers (Surprenant & Solomon, 1987: 86; Sundaram & Webster, 2000: 381). Some Turkish tourism workers start talking only after they have made eye contact. A promoter who stood in front of a restaurant explained that once he has made eye contact he is able to talk almost any customer into entering his restaurant. Smiling is used in many service encounters. Smiling is more than a visual image: it is an embodied performance of hospitality, which lingers in facial expressions, gestures and voice (Veijola & Valtonen, 2007: 21).

During introductory conversations, many tourism workers use jokes, compliments and small-talk to break the ice and personalise the encounter (Surprenant & Solomon, 1987: 89). They ask questions like: what is your name, where are you from, is this your first time in Turkey, how long is your holiday, do you like Turkey and Turkish people or what places have you visited. This small-talk gives customers the feeling they are given individual attention. Tourism workers also use this information. For a tour office employee it is interesting to know whether it is the tourist's first visit to Turkey. Some tourism workers use the same small-talk to get to know a tourist better or to ask her out.

By introducing himself by name to his customers, a Turkish tourism worker often tries to make the encounter even more personal and friendly

(Surprenant & Solomon, 1987: 89). At the same time, he will get to know the names of his customers. The next time they meet he will be able to address them by name. Turkish tourism workers sometimes adopt English names or nicknames to make their names recognisable for tourists (see Dahles & Bras, 1999: 282). The personal nature of the encounter has the effect that friendly relationships and friendships occur (Czepiel, 1990) but it is nonetheless a commercial friendship in which the relationship is business as well as personal (Price & Arnould, 1999: 39). Tourism workers emphasise the latter aspect by saying things like 'my friend' to tourists.

The advantage for tourism workers is that many tourists are loyal to the person they are friends with or they think they know. Tourists like to return to the restaurant where they had a delicious meal or where they enjoyed the beautiful view, but they like even more to visit the restaurant where their friend works. During her holidays in this town Emma, a Dutch woman, tries to visit all her acquaintances at their workplace. We visited the workplace of a man named Bulut on different occasions, initially in the pizzeria where he was working and later in a luxury fish restaurant after he had changed jobs. Emma has known some of these men for many years. Shortly after arriving in this town she usually visits the places she knows; there she finds her friends or asks around where they are currently working.

Touch is another way to personalise the service encounter. Previous research has pointed out that close proxemics, the physical distance between service provider and customer, has a positive influence on the experience of the encounter (Price *et al.*, 1995: 87). Due to intentional ambiguity, touch is not always experienced as positive. Tourism workers use touch in their work to get attention and win the trust of the customer (Sundaram & Webster, 2000: 384). Ozan, a tour office employee, always shook hands or kissed his customers on the cheek. During the conversation he would make the distance between them smaller by putting his hand on the shoulder of the tourist. This way he could feel whether clients were open to him and he could direct them to his office. In bars and restaurants, touching customers has been noted to increase both their alcohol consumption (Kaufman & Mahony, 1999) and their tipping behaviour (Hornik, 1992: 454; Lynn *et al.*, 1998: 62). The income of Turkish tourism workers is very much dependent on how much they sell and especially on tips.

A tradition of close proxemics between tourism workers and tourists has another consequence. By kissing or touching, male tourism workers and female tourists experience physical closeness within a short period of time after meeting. It creates instantly an informal atmosphere, which gives openings for friendly, charming or seducing gestures. A waiter in a restaurant not only touched Emma on the shoulder but also touched her knee to find out whether she was interested in him. Emma moved away from him; he stood up and went back to his service role by asking what we wanted to drink. This way, the personalising service strategies which are not by definition meant to seduce female tourists are used for seducing purposes.

Hospitality as a Seducing Strategy

Encounters between Turkish men and tourists proceed according to the Turkish rules for hospitality. What is striking about these encounters is that they take place within the context of commercial tourism (Tucker, 2001: 879). Hospitality is expressed in friendliness, helpfulness, curiosity and invitations. Hospitality is also used in the romantic encounters between Turkish tourism workers and female tourists.

A good Turkish host should show his guests around. Visitors should see the most beautiful places in the surroundings, should visit the best restaurants or bars and should be introduced to the most delicious dishes of the Turkish cuisine. Hospitality is a good strategy for asking a female tourist out (see Dahles & Bras, 1999: 282). With this, the tourism worker meets the expectations of hospitality as well as the norms for being a good Turkish man. A good Turkish man should court a woman. During the introductory conversations he will have already found out what she likes to do, what she has done and what she hasn't done yet. With this knowledge he can suggest they go somewhere together. The tourism worker often remains ambiguous about this being a date or not, but actually it is a date.

Accepting hospitality is not without certain obligations (Tucker, 2001: 879). Out of respect it is very unusual to decline invitations to drink tea, to eat food, to see the environment or to visit family. For a tourist this is also a unique and adventurous experience. Through local knowledge and language the tourism worker can be her personal guide and give her a different experience than she would have as a tourist by herself. The advantage for the local man is that he has the power to decide where they go and sometimes he literally takes her by the hand. Depending on his expectations of this date and the developments during the night, he can take her to out to a public place or to a romantic place where they can be alone. Depending on both of their expectations, a romantic or sexual relationship can begin.

Sympathy as Basis for a Romance

Once conversations go beyond the introductory level, tourists may talk about their life at home. Those tourism workers who have never been outside Turkey often have a lot of questions: they ask about work, living, friends, family and holidays. In this way they get an impression of what life is like outside the Turkish borders (see Cohen, 1971: 224).

Turkish men tell the female tourists parts of their life history. With this he gives her a personal view of his life. These stories are often about tragic events. Among the topics is the history of the Turkish Republic. This seems a chauvinist topic, but for many Turkish people it is a romantic and tragic story. The moon in the red flag is being reflected in the blood of fallen soldiers. When the story is told the couple will most probably be in a place where they can see the moon. Another topic is the difficult times experienced in the army. Turkey has many hostile borders and all men are expected to do army service and if necessary to die for their country. Many young men have traumatic experiences of fighting and possibly losing comrades in battle. These stories make the men a little melancholic. They also talk about their difficult life. They talk about their difficult youth, the difficulties of working in tourism, loss of wealth, loneliness, death of best friends by motorcycle accidents and the lack of a true love in their life.

In return, the female tourists are asked to talk about some emotional topics. Some are asked about their bodily insecurities or their weight. Other questions are about reaching a certain age and being single or childless. Women around 30 appear are often very sensitive about such matters because they have also been thinking about these questions. Other questions are about sexuality, about ex-partners and sexual experience. This is for some Turkish men also a sensitive topic, because they usually lack sexual education and sometimes they have never touched a woman before. For more experienced men talking about sexuality is a way to find out whether a female tourist is willing and interested in him or to get in the mood.

By talking about tragic life histories and other emotional topics, a special bond may be created. He likes that she talks so openly with him, because Turkish women are not so open. And she feels feminine and good through this male attention and experiences the intimate atmosphere as very romantic. Sympathy is growing between them and is working a sexual attraction. In a short time they have become emotionally very close, which makes it only a small step to become sexually close. Sex indicates the beginning of this relationship.

Tourist Experience Versus Tourism Worker Experience

At first sight these encounters seem romantic and unproblematic. But by looking closely at the physical and embodied experiences of tourism I will argue that two such people who meet in the same space and have physical proximity go through very divergent experiences of tourism.

In the tourist experience there is not only an encounter between people: there is also an encounter with place and space. These terms are used in social geography. Place can be a beach, a city, a campsite, a river, a hotel, a restaurant or a historical site. Space is practised in place; for instance, the street, defined by urban planning, is the place, which becomes transformed into space by the people who use it (de Certeau, 1988, in Wearing & Wearing, 1996: 234). Encounters with place are defined by what people do. Doing tourism is a subjective and embodied experience (Crouch, 2000: 64; Crouch et al., 2001: 254). In the tourist experience the body is central (Franklin, 2003: 213; Veijola & Jokinen, 1994). To experience, to do, to feel, to touch and to see are all intrinsic physical experiences (Cloke & Perkins, 1998). We could say that the interactions with place and people give meaning to a tourist experience.

In the context of the present research, tourists visit this coastal town primarily to experience relaxation and enjoyment. Sun, sea and beach are an important motivation to visit the Mediterranean coast (Franklin, 2003: 137; Thomas, 2005: 574). Tourists often contrast the sunny Turkish weather to the rainy north European climate. Simone, a Dutch woman, said she always chooses a sunny holiday destination, otherwise it would not be a good and relaxing holiday for her. The beach is the place where tourists get the feeling they can let go of their daily life. They do that by taking off their clothes and dressing in beachwear. At the beach they can relax by sunbathing, sleeping, swimming or reading. Most of these activities are related to being on holiday. For many tourists, the holiday is a period of relaxation and play, which marks a release from work and duty (Edensor, 2000: 325). Time is also experienced differently. Tourists can let go of the time. Although restricted by the duration of the holiday, time seems endless.

Money is for tourists a restriction they also want to let go of. Most tourists in this coastal town are middle-class people, who save money for this holiday. They don't want to worry about money all the time. They eat out every night and treat other people to drinks. Sometimes in small groups all individuals put money in a wallet that one person keeps. This way there will not be any fighting over who ate what and who paid what.

Many tourists also wish to experience adventure. Travelling to other countries is already an adventure in itself (Thomas, 2005: 574). A day or a few days of relaxation on the beach are alternated with days of 'doing something'. In this coastal town there are a number of activities tourists can undertake. They can do boat trips, diving, swimming with dolphins, windsurfing, kite-surfing, horse riding, shopping and jeep safaris. The jeep safari is an activity that takes tourist out all day. They see the rural countryside, cross a river with a fast current, walk in the second longest gorge in Europe, eat at a river restaurant, do rafting and take a mud bath in the river; the day typically ends on the beach, where, thirsty, hungry and sunburned, tourists cool off in the sea. To enjoy the adventures, tourists need a degree of familiarity (Franklin, 2003: 10; Cohen & Avieli, 2004: 758). Although this trip is organised from minute to minute it gives the tourists an adventurous feeling.

Another example of a daring tourist experience is eating food. Food is not an external bodily experience like doing a tour. By eating the food it gains access to the tourist body, which enhances the risk and feeling of adventure (Cohen & Avieli, 2004: 758–759). Adventurous tourists like tasting and eating local dishes. Eating Turkish food is a way of getting in touch with the place. This feeling is reinforced by local music. Some restaurants create a romantic and authentic atmosphere by playing live music. The musicians play Turkish traditional or local songs. These are songs that are usually sung in Turkish bars, where mostly Turkish men drink *rakı* and eat *mezze*, Turkish appetisers. *Rakı*, the strong alcoholic drink that tastes like anise, is seen by most Turkish as masculine and risky to drink. Turkish history teaches that one who drinks a lot of *rakı* will become crazy.

'Tourists travel in quest of novelty and strangeness, but most need a degree of familiarity to enjoy their experience' (Cohen & Avieli, 2004: 758). In order to enjoy this experience, most tourists also need a degree of familiarity with the food they eat. Popular Turkish dishes include grilled meat, kebab, *pide*, which resembles pizza, and *gözleme*, which is a sort of pancake. All these dishes are variations on the safe food tourists know from home. One English couple told me: 'We really love Turkish food, especially all the meat dishes.' Besides the traditional food, most restaurants offer familiar British food like chips, burgers, sandwiches and desserts like pancakes with lemon and sugar. British tourists often find the Turkish breakfast of tea, white bread, tomatoes, cucumber, honey, jam, white cheese and olives too light. They prefer a full English breakfast, including toast, bacon, beans, sausage and eggs. Therefore many restaurants have this on their menu. Eating English food gives a feeling of Britishness (Andrews, 2005: 252). This way tourists can feel at home away from home, an expression that is often used in advertisement by Turkish hotels and restaurants.

Because tourists are temporary in a new place they are freed from the rules and social control they normally experience. They can behave as, and even become, another person (Meisch, 1995: 454; Thomas, 2005: 575). 'This might be the opportunity for the tourist to indulge in fantasies and explore a new aspect of herself by engaging in behaviour that she would never allow herself at home' (Pruitt & LaFont, 1995: 426). Maria, a Dutch woman, said that on holiday she can be whoever she wants to be. She feels 'blanco' to create a new identity. To illustrate this she said that she even had clothes that she wore only on holiday.

Adventure is also experienced by tourists through drinking alcohol, dancing and sexual encounters (Edensor, 2001: 77; Franklin, 2003: 255; Pritchard & Morgan, 2006: 766). For many female tourists the possibility of a romantic encounter adds to a fun and adventurous holiday. Women who were warned by their family and friends about the charming Turkish men had a tendency to fall in love. It feels risky and safe at the same time. What they can't do at home they can do on holiday. And the stories of what happened in Turkey often stay in Turkey. Two Dutch sisters-in-law told me not to be each other's babysitter. While their husbands were at home they enjoyed the male attention a lot.

These romantic encounters between female tourists and Turkish tourism workers take place within a familiar context. The women often describe their new boyfriend as modern, because he speaks English, is a student or wants to study, likes traveling and wants to see Europe, is Muslim but not a fanatic. This is probably why some female tourists approach this relationship as they would a partner at home. The romantic encounter is intense and becomes intimate very fast. Female tourists often told me that such an encounter was a special or unique experience and it felt like true love.

Relaxation and a feeling of adventure are typical tourist experiences. Tourists have these experiences at the beach, in restaurants, bars or nightclubs or during a tour. These are the same places where the Turkish tourism workers work. The tours, the food, the relaxation, the enjoyment are all facilitated by tourism workers. These tourism workers have different experiences. Firstly, they have to work very hard, under insecure circumstances. Working in tourism in the town where the research was undertaken is a seasonal job (as elsewhere). In the summer months there is a lot of work; in the winter there is no work and therefore no income. The income of a tourism worker is typcially €200–600 a month. Some work on the basis of commission while others have a steady income. Considering the high cost of living (especially food and drinks) this is hardly sufficient (Kusluvan & Kusluvan, 2000: 261). That is why many tourism workers live with their parents, families or at the workplace.

The work is hard because tourism workers are service providers and their income depends on the satisfaction of the customers. The job comes with emotional stress, which can weigh heavily on the workers (Price *et al.*, 1995: 90). In addition, most are expected to work long days, from early morning to midnight or from the afternoon till the early morning. They do what their boss tells them to do. Some workers do two or three different jobs in one season for the same employer. One day they are drivers, the next day they can be waiters. Every day they expect their work to change, but at the same time every day feels like repeating the day before. Their presence is required even when there are no customers. Breaks and meals are at irregular times, if at all. Most tourism workers lose some kilograms of weight during the tourist season. Besides that, Turkish tourism workers have very insecure employment. They have no contract and can be fired instantly. For most, it is hard to find another job during the season. It needs little explanation why being fired is called being retired by the Turkish tourism workers.

Furthermore, tourism workers experience hierarchy and rivalry at the workplace. Every worker plays a part in the whole performance of tourism. In a restaurant, for example, there is a promoter who talks customers into entering the restaurant, a manager who sits and gives orders, waiters who take the orders of the customers, boys to help serve the food and drinks and do cleaning and dish-washing, cooks and a cashier who is responsible for all procedures with money. The lower in hierarchy the heavier the work is. When a tourism worker has more experience in working in tourism he can climb up the hierarchy. By that time he has learned how to negotiate good circumstances for himself. Language skills make an employee more valuable for an employer and are often used in the job negotiations.

Rivalry and competition are not only between organisations but also between co-workers. Tourism workers struggling for an income are not always collegial. It is not easy to find friends among tourism workers (Kusluvan & Kusluvan, 2000: 261). They are often jealous, gossip, fight and mislead each other (Tucker, 2003: 103). Ozan, a tour office employee, saw his colleagues as competitors, who were not to be trusted, with whom he shared as little information as possible and with whom he fought for customers. This might be why some tourism workers said that they felt more sincerity and friendship with tourists than with their co-workers and that they liked spending time with tourists. Besides that they also wanted to enjoy life, like they saw the tourists do all the time.

Encounters Between Two People With Divergent Experiences of the Same Place

Encounters between service providers and customers, tourism workers and tourists are characterised by the dichotomy of work and holiday. While tourists are enjoying a well deserved holiday, tourism workers make this possible. Tourists don't pay much attention to the working conditions and experiences, because they have a completely different bodily experience (Veijola & Valtonen, 2007). Even for me, after working in tourism and being served again, it took some effort to stay aware of it. In the encounter between female tourists and Turkish tourism workers these divergent experiences come together. There are many small and large incidents between tourists and tourism workers that show this.

Tourists often experience the workplace of tourism workers as if it is the best and most beautiful place to be. They even imagine working there and sometimes congratulate the tourism worker for having a great job. One customer, after the weekly beach party, commented on the nice life on the beach the owner of the bar must have. 'Yes', said the owner, 'working day and night.' The tourist was a bit envious because the owner was staying in the place that he considered paradise.

One evening, after having dinner at the restaurant where Bulut worked, Emma asked him to have a drink with us in a bar. He arrived straight after he finished working and still had his waiter's suit on. He stayed very formal and smiled a lot. She thought of him as a friend; however, that evening he was visibly uncomfortable with this position. He continued his waiter performance. He came because she asked him to come.

Alice, a young English woman, slept long in the morning; in the afternoon she went to the beach; at night she got dressed and went to the bar where her boyfriend worked. She waited for him to finish working and then they went out to some nightclubs. She was complaining that she was bored waiting for him every evening. He said she was lazy, which upset her because he apparently didn't understand that at home she works hard and her life is not a lazy holiday all the time. The following nights they went out later. That he had gone to work when she woke up was a reason for her to feel bored again. What she didn't realise was that he was working long days and getting only two or three hours of sleep each night.

Sara, a German woman, fell in love with Osman, a restaurant manager. After one week Osman asked her if her feelings for him were sincere and he invited her to share their lives and start a business together in Turkey. Sara told him she would like to come back to Turkey, to spend more time with him and find out if their relationship could work. She also explained that she would not instantly give up her job, her house and leave her two teenage children. He became angry. Coming so close to realising his dreams led him to overlook her life in Germany. Sara, who was in love, thought she had met a happy and successful manager. What she didn't understand was that, at the time they met, he was about to lose his job, his Turkish wife wanted to divorce him, his son had recently come back traumatised from the army and his youngest daughter was ill with the stress over the looming divorce.

These examples show that two people who find themselves in the same place have very different experiences. The encounters between tourists and tourism workers are a convergence of divergent tourism experiences in the same place. Even when they become physically and emotionally close there seems to be a lack of empathy.

Conclusion

Tourists experience relaxation and a feeling of adventure while being away from home. Holiday is like a temporal liberation from daily life, local norms and obligations, and tourists can present themselves differently from how they do at home (Meisch, 1995: 454; Thomas, 2005: 575). As Maria said: 'On holiday I can be who I want to be.' Away from home she feels 'blanco' and creates her identity through activities and encounters with others. Most tourists want to enjoy their holiday and have fun. A holiday romance is one way for them to have fun and enjoy the male attention they sometimes feel they lack from the men in their home country. Although the motivations of these women vary from wanting a sexual experience, feeling feminine through receiving compliments to searching for a partner for life, the question is whether they want to feel free from local norms temporarily or seriously want to break away from it by engaging in a romantic relationship which in the long run could change their lives.

Experiencing liberation from local norms is not only a tourist experience. In the literature on the sexual encounters between tourists and locals little attention has been paid to this. Tourism is a 'free zone' for tourists as well as tourism workers (Tucker, 2001: 882), where the prevailing norms differ from those 'outside'. Most tourism workers, besides working, also want to enjoy life. This is partly a reaction to the tough working conditions, the tourist enjoyment they are confronted with every workday and local Turkish norms. Expressions like 'to make fun' or 'to enjoy with you' can be understood as an intention to have sex or start a romantic relationship. Although engaging in sexual relationships seems normal within tourism, sexuality between unmarried couples in Turkey is taboo. Young waiters on the beach sometimes don't know how to behave, because they have never seen (half) naked women before. Older and more experienced men say that their numerous sexual encounters are part of their life in tourism.

In this chapter I have discussed two aspects of the encounter between female tourists and Turkish tourism workers. Firstly, I have shown how two strangers meet and become very close in a short period. Secondly, I have shown that the *two* people in this *one* encounter have divergent experiences. It is in the encounter that two persons and their experiences come together.

A tourism experience includes the experiences of all actors. That is why I studied the experiences of both tourists and tourism workers (Tucker,

2003; Veijola & Valtonen, 2007). By describing both sides I have revealed a work–holiday dichotomy, not only the between the experience of daily life and the holiday but also in the encounter between two people with divergent experiences. While the tourist is enjoying the holiday, the tourism worker makes this possible by working. Although this difference seems self-evident, it is not something to take for granted.

To understand the encounters between local men and female tourists it is necessary to take a close look at how these people meet and how they both experience tourism. Any romance between Turkish tourism workers and female tourists develops during the service encounter. By personalising the encounter, the service provider is breaking the ice and winning the trust of the customer. With these strategies the service provider intends to bring the service encounter to a personal level. The same strategies tourism workers use to personalise the encounter can also be used to go further and to get to know each other better. For asking the female tourist out, tourism workers use Turkish hospitality. In this way they can stay ambiguous about their intentions and anticipate what might happen during the date. By asking about and telling parts of life histories and other emotional stories, sympathy between them is encouraged and the couple become emotionally very close. From there it is only a small step to become physically and sexually close. This usually all happens on the first or second day after they meet.

Female tourists are very much taken by the attention they receive from the Turkish tourism workers. Women who visit Turkey for the first time are often surprised by all the male attention they receive. They are being served like queens, given compliments, asked lots of personal questions and being touched. This attention makes them feel very feminine, a feeling they often lack in their encounters with men in their own country, where there seems to be a 'courtship crisis' (Dafoe Whitehead, 2003: 186). Maria, a single Dutch woman, said that: 'Turkish men are real men'. They are masculine, charming and make her feel like a feminine woman. While talking with her female friends about holidaying in Turkey, she often refers to how much she enjoyed the male attention she received. This attraction is somewhat paradoxical because these independent women fall for masculine men and they most probably have different ideas about gender norms.

Romantic and sexual encounters between female tourists and local men have been studied extensively. These studies tend to focus on categorising these relationships as sex or romance tourism. Moving away from this discussion resulted in a deep understanding of the tourism experience and the course of romantic encounters in tourism. This chapter shows that the relationships between local men and female tourists are very complex. Initially, it seems like an unproblematic encounter between two people who feel sympathy for each other. But when two people meet in the same place and one of them is working and the other one is not working, they have divergent experiences. It proves not easy to know what the experiences of the other are. With this I want emphasise that although they feel emotionally and physically very close, there is a lack of empathy. To understand tourism encounters and relationships, a very detailed look at what goes on between both partners is meaningful.

The complexity of tourism encounters in the Mediterranean fields of love becomes very visible when studying how female tourists and tourism workers negotiate local and global power (Scheltena, 2011). Female tourists often have more economic power than their Turkish boyfriends. It would be easy, but inequitable, to argue that the power positions are asymmetrical in favour of the female tourist. As I have shown, Turkish tourism workers use hospitality as a seducing strategy, but they also use it to negotiate their power position. One way of doing that is by organising the date. The tourism worker will decide on where they go and what they eat. In this way, his economic power can grow. To impress his potential girlfriend he will choose a nice restaurant where a friend happens to work. He will order their drinks and food in Turkish. The female tourist feels adventurous by relying on him as her guide and translator. And she also feels very feminine in the company of this masculine man. At the end of the dinner, when he goes to his friend to pay, not only does he live up to Turkish masculine norms but his economic power grows, even though he has less money to spend than her. He can make a good impression on her and he is in control. Although the power positions are asymmetrical, they are not static. For both female tourists and Turkish tourism workers there are various ways to negotiate their power positions.

References

Andrews, H. (2005) Feeling at home: Embodying Britishness in a Spanish charter. *Tourist Studies* 5 (3), 247–266.

Cloke, P. and Perkins, H.C. (1998) Cracking the canyon with the awesome foursome: Representations of adventure tourism in New Zealand. *Environment and Planning D: Society and Space* 16 (2), 185–218.

Cohen, E. (1971) Arab boys and tourist girls in a mixed Jewish community. *International Journal of Comparative Sociology* 12, 217–233.

Cohen, E. and Avieli, N. (2004) Food in tourism: Attraction and impediment. *Annals of Tourism Research* 31 (4), 755–778.

Crouch, D. (2000) Places around us: Embodied lay geographies in leisure tourism. *Leisure Studies* 19, 63–76.

Crouch, D. and Desforges, L. (2003) The sensuous in the tourist encounter. Introduction: The power of the body in tourist studies. *Tourist Studies* 3 (1), 5–22.

Crouch, D., Aronsson, L. and Wahlström, L. (2001) Tourist encounters. *Tourist Studies* 1, 253–270.

Czepiel, J.A. (1990) Service encounters and service relationships: Implications for research. *Journal of Business Research* 20 (1), 13–21.

Dafoe Whitehead, B. (2003) *Why There Are No Good Men Left: The Romantic Plight of the New Single Woman*. New York: Broadway

Dahles, H. (1997) The new gigolo: Globalization, tourism and changing gender identities. *Focaa: Tijdschrift voor Antropologie* 30/31, 121–137.

Dahles, H. and Bras, K. (1999) Entrepreneurs in romance: Tourism in Indonesia. *Annals of Tourism Research* 26 (2), 267–293.

Edensor, T. (2000) Performing tourism: Tourists as performers. *Annals of Tourism Research* 27 (2), 322–344.

Edensor, T. (2001) Performing tourism, staging tourism: Reproducing tourist space and practice. *Tourist Studies* 1, 59–81.

Everett, S. (2009) Beyond the visual gaze? The pursuit of an embodied experience through food tourism. *Tourist Studies* 8 (3), 337–358.

Franklin, A. (2003) *Tourism: An Introduction*. London: Sage.

Herold, E., Garcia, R. and DeMoya, T. (2001) Female tourists and beach boys: Romance or sex tourism? *Annals of Tourism Research* 28 (4), 978–997.

Hornik, J. (1992) Tactile stimulation and consumer response. *Journal of Consumer Research* 19 (3), 449–458.

Jeffreys, S. (2003) Sex tourism: Do women do it too? *Leisure Studies* 22, 223–238.

Kaufman, D. and Mahony, J.M. (1999) The effect of waitresses' touch on alcohol consumption in dyads. *Journal of Social Psychology* 139 (3), 261–267.

Kusluvan, S. and Kusluvan, Z. (2000) Perceptions and attitudes of undergraduate tourism students towards working in the tourism industry in Turkey. *Tourism Management* 21, 251–269.

Leidner, R. (1999) Emotional labor in service work. *Annals of the American Academy of Political and Social Science* 561, 81–95.

Lynn, M., Le, J.M. and Sherwyn, D. (1998) Reach out and touch your customer. *Cornell HRA Quarterly* 39, 60–65.

Meisch, L.A. (1995) Gringas and otavalenos: Changing tourist relations. *Annals of Tourism Research* 22 (2), 441–462.

Nyanzi, S., Rosenberg-Jallow, O., Bah, O. and Nyanzi, S. (2005) Bumsters, big black organs and old white gold: Embodied racial myths in sexual relationships of Gambian beach boys. *Culture, Health and Sexuality* 7 (6), 577–569.

Obradar Pons, P. (2003) Being on holiday: Tourist dwelling, bodies and place. *Tourist Studies* 3 (1), 47–66.

Price, L.L. and Arnould, E.J. (1999) Commercial friendships: Service provider–client relationships in context. *Journal of Marketing* 63 (4), 38–56.

Price, L.L., Arnould, E.J. and Tierney, P. (1995) Going to extremes: Managing service encounters and assessing provider performance. *Journal of Marketing* 59 (2), 83–97.

Pritchard, A. and Morgan, N. (2006) Hotel Babylon? Exploring hotels as liminal sites of transition and transgression. *Tourism Management* 27, 762–772.

Pruitt, D. and LaFont, S. (1995) For love and money: Romance tourism in Jamaica. *Annals of Tourism Research* 22 (2), 422–440.

Sanchez Talyor, J. (2001) Dollars are a girl's best friend? Female tourists' sexual behaviour in the Caribbean. *Sociology* 35 (3), 749–764.

Sanchez Talyor, J. (2006) Female sex tourism: A contradiction in terms? *Feminist Review* 83, 42–59.

Scheltena, S. (2011) Een wereld van verschil. Belichaamde ontmoetingen tussen Turkse toerisme-arbeiders en vrouwelijke toeristen. Unpublished thesis, University of Amsterdam.

Solomon, M.R., Surprenant, C., Czepiel, J.A. and Gutman, E.G. (1985) A role theory perspective on dyadic interactions: The service encounter. *Journal of Marketing* 49 (1), 99–111.

Sundaram, D.S. and Webster, C. (2000) The role of non-verbal communication in service encounters. *Journal of Services Marketing* 14 (5), 378–391.

Surprenant, C.F. and Solomon, M. (1987) Predictability and personalization in the service encounter. *Journal of Marketing* 51(2): 86–96.

Thomas, M. (2005) 'What happens in Tenerife stays in Tenerife': Understanding women's sexual behaviour on holiday. *Culture, Health and Sexuality* 7 (6), 571–584.

Tucker, H. (2001) Tourists and troglodytes: Negotiating for sustainability. *Annals of Tourism Research* 28 (4), 868–891.

Tucker, H. (2003) *Living with Tourism. Negotiating Identities in a Turkish Village*. London: Routledge.

Tucker, H. (2007) Undoing shame: Tourism and women's work in Turkey. *Journal of Tourism and Cultural Change* 5 (2), 87–105.

Veijola, S. and Jokinen, E. (1994) The body in tourism. *Theory, Culture and Society* 11, 125–151.

Veijola, S. and Valtonen, A. (2007) The body in tourism industry. In A. Pritchard, N. Morgan, I. Ateljevic and C. Harris (eds) *Tourism and Gender: Embodiment, Sensuality and Experience*. Wallingford: CABI (e-book).

Wearing, B. and Wearing, S. (1996) Refocussing the tourist experience: The flâneur and the choraster. *Leisure Studies* 15, 229–243.

9 Wild Inside: Uncanny Encounters in European Traveller Fantasies of Africa

Marcela Knapp and Frauke Wiegand

Trying to Understand Your Culture, as if your culture is a thing hidden beneath your skin, and what you are, what you present is not authentic. Often he has felt such a force from them to separate and break him apart – to move away the ordinary things that make him human – and then they zero in on the exotic, the things that make him separate from them. Then they are free to like him – he is no longer a threat. They can say, 'Oh I envy you having such a strong culture,' or, 'We, in the West, we aren't grounded like you…. Such good energy…. This is so real.'
Da-ra-ra-ra.
Ai!
(Wainaina, 2006: 225)

Introduction

Africa has long served as both an idea and a space of projection for European fantasies. The writer Binyavanga Wainaina (2005) suggests that in European texts 'Africa [usually] is to be pitied, worshipped or dominated'. The analysis of novels and reportage, to which Wainaina refers here, as well as of travel accounts *about* trips through Africa, shows that European imaginations of the continent usually oscillate between wilderness, nature and romance on the one hand and chaos and abyss on the other. The myth of a romantic and authentic Africa is most present in tourism discourses and is actively used by travel agencies – as well as a wide range of popular media – for advertising purportedly untouched nature and unique wildlife. This narrative of an ahistorical and unspoilt, colourful and welcoming Africa (Bruner, 1991; Tucker & Hall, 2008), which promises transforming experiences, starkly contrasts with discourses from the news media about the persistent political and humanitarian strife of the continent. The apparent opposing images of an untouched continent are, however, no less innocent than discourses about war, hunger and diseases. This motivated our research into the experiences of tourists travelling in Africa. Their accounts reveal a very serious, excited, dedicated and, in a way, 'seduced' type of traveller.

In this work, following Johannes Fabian's account of the anthropologist's encounter with and writing on the Other (Fabian, 2002 [1983]), we scrutinise the verbal performances by travellers made in the course of interviews and in published travelogues. The chapter discusses the role that tourism to Africa plays in European formations of an aspirational cosmopolitan identity. It examines narrations of travel experiences as a way of presenting the Self[1] in relation, on the one hand, to the imagined space 'Africa' and, on the other, within an imagined community of European 'connoisseurs'. These tourist accounts can be read against the background of contemporary postcolonial power relations, and are connected to popular mediations of imagining 'Africa'. 'It is in the nature of the struggle to understand what Africa is and her place among other cultural spaces in history that it excites a lot of passion and sometimes regret', writes Okwui Enwezor. 'We choose which Africa suits our intentions, or, as it were, inventions' (Enwezor, 2006: 11). Tourists, no matter the African destination, all invoke particular collective understandings of 'Africa' and 'Africanness', often despite – and without giving consideration to – the variety of actually existing cultural, religious and geopolitical differences. The imaginary of Africa we tackle here is the 'Africa' as intended, invented and negotiated in the tourist narration.

The material used in this work is taken from a 2006 study on the performative qualities of travel narration and travel photography, and the different inventions and ideas of 'Africa' therein. It is a compound of individual interviews, private diaries, travel weblogs and even a radio broadcast, where interested listeners could phone in to ask two experienced travellers about touring Africa.[2] Looking at the different stories and answers revealed that a large part of the narrative is dedicated to drawing comparisons between the travelling self and the encountered other – both the other tourist and the local African Other.[3] The positions embodied by the tourists are composed of diverging strategies of differentiation and alterisation, relating the self to the experienced tourist event and different audiences back home. There is plenty of literary, ethnographic, cultural analytical and social psychological work on the genre and form of the travelogue and its negotiation of differences and narrations of alterity, the production of Otherness and the performance of the Self. It is here where stubborn myths of 'belated travellers' (Behdad, 1994) are depicted and their persistence criticised. It is only on rare occasions, though, that possible reasons for the persistence of, for example, 'colonial mentalities' (Hook, 2008: 270; see also McClintock, 1995) are analysed on both the affective and the discursive level. In what follows we trace the patterns in travelogue performances along their underlying and at times openly articulated negotiations of ambivalent moralities impacting on the traveller.

The retelling of experiences is a crucial stage within touristic practice as it displays the process in which the tourist incorporates the travel into her or his life biography. 'It is in the performance of an expression', write Bruner and Turner (1986: 11), 'that we re-experience, re-live, re-create, re-tell, re-construct and re-fashion our culture'. Central to the performance of the travelogue is its semi-fictional character, seducing the tourists to reinvent themselves by providing a stage for presenting character-forming stories of challenge, freaky encounter and adventure, in which the traveller appropriates the lived experiences in interaction with an audience. After the trip, travellers relive the sensual experience and share it with others by narrating it. Regina Bendix argues for the deep connection between tourism and narration, and the importance of 'narratable memories' to tourism's evolution as a modern industry:

> The most powerful evidence of the search for the singular, unique, and authentic within tourist experience, however, is narration. Goethe's enlarging of the soul – the physical thrill experienced in anything from a first sighting of an ancient tomb to rappelling into the depths during a first cave exploration – lasts but a moment. The process of narrating the experience *recovers* the moment, if not its experiential singularity, and allows for its communicative restaging and its ever new mental savoring. (Bendix, 2002: 473)

It is within the narration that we can follow the tourist's conscious or unconscious negotiations of different moral discourses. The travel performance for an audience 'back home' cannot be separated from identity formations and in this process is connected to social imaginaries (Salazar, 2012), shared understandings manifested in collective representations of sites and their 'moral economy' (MacCannell, 1999 [1976]) as well as moral discourses in society. The existence of colonial and expansionist imaginaries in present-day performances reveals the deep cultural impact of colonial times and mind-sets, notably on contemporary travel within the postcolonial global south. This colonial paradigm, as we shall call it, is distinguishable by the implicit and explicit construction of the European Self and African Other. Its influence is furthermore increasingly expressed by travellers' reflections on their own (un)colonial behaviour.

The study revealed that while the colonial paradigm impacts one layer of meaning, a second layer of meaning can also be distinguished, which points to the construction of a cosmopolitan identity through the tourist performance. This identity is characterised by its rhetoric of knowing (about) the world – especially those parts that are most different and far away from home – which is an experience differentiating travellers from their fellow Europeans who have not had the opportunity or desire to travel to the site of the Other. All travel performances negotiate the traveller's position in relation to a semiotic space which is made manifest in the concrete location visited. 'Africa' becomes a site of projection, an invented quality for different sentiments and characteristics. It enters the performance as that shifting signifier described above by Enwezor. The performances are characterised by different levels of involvement in a moral discourse on colonial continuities, a negotiation between the memory of a cruel colonial past that is symbolically reaching into the present and a postcolonial present imagined as offering equal participation for everyone. The travel narration displays workings on the self as effected by what Jarett Zigon, drawing on Foucault, calls 'moral problematics' or 'moral breakdowns' (Zigon, 2009: 261). Those are instances of conflicting moral positions within a single traveller and her or his conscious oscillation between different moralities. Travellers are confronted with two opposing public discourses about their 'peculiar identity position' (Gillespie, 2007) that they constantly negotiate: their image as ignorant voyeurs and their aspiration to be involved cosmopolitan connoisseurs (Hannerz, 1996). This makes the post-travel performance a particularly poignant stage in the identification processes, characterised by the subject's distancing from the 'typical tourist', who is popularly presented as ignorant, intolerant, uninformed and egoistic.

In addition, there is an increasing awareness of continuities of Orientalist and colonialist travel in contemporary travel practice: tourists do not want to behave like or be perceived as 'colonialists'. Due to the emergence of a discourse about the history and memory of colonialism, this discourse also consciously and unconsciously affects tourists' perceptions of the encountered Other, the Other's perception of the Western tourist and, again, their mutual knowledge of these popular representations.

Moral Discourses in Tourist Performances

In the following paragraphs we will trace the different patterns of performance by tourists to Africa and show how the production of a cosmopolitan, geographically non-localisable identity is deeply rooted in local and cultural traditions. Different moral discourses affect travellers, who situate their narratives accordingly, both to evaluate others' practices and to justify their own (right) way of travelling. Travellers will favour one moral frame over another, but generally all these discourses can usually be detected in a more or less dominant position within a single narration. Individual travel is thus legitimated by reference to distinctive states of mind and positions: travel is presented as a challenge (a physical task), a relief (as absolving the Self from responsibility), a cultural immersion (leading to knowledge through experience), or an 'objective' reflection on both the present and the past (through embodied observation). The narrations are framed by different historically informed discourses, namely, discourses on *civilisation*, *authenticity* and *interculturality* (organised along the binaries of civilisation/ culture versus nature, or authentic versus inauthentic culture), as well as a discourse on *objectivity* and *postcolonial responsibility*.

Narratives of individual challenge

The first narrative pattern to be discussed emphasises physical and psychical challenge. Africa's nature, which includes its people and societies, is conceptualised as a challenge to the constitution of the individual tourist body – a challenge, it should be noted, which is sought out in order to be mastered. This narrative transgresses previous life experiences and focuses on the personal growth gained from facing this challenge. The pattern conceptualises Africa from within a civilisational discourse, regarding 'Africa' as pure wilderness set against 'European' civilisation. Africa here becomes an adjective describing Europe's 'Other'. The following words of Peter, an experienced, middle-aged, male Africa traveller exemplify this polarity, by equating 'civilisation' with infrastructure and 'challenging wilderness' with lack of infrastructure. When asked about his expectations before his last trip through Kenya, Tanzania and Zanzibar, he answered:

> We expected to find a simple-structured country, as little infrastructure as possible, so that travelling involves a personal challenge, having to think about how to reach where, having to apply one's organisational talents in order to move on. In South Africa, for example, travelling is easy; there are tar-roads everywhere and petrol-stations. Travelling there needs no skill at all!

What is striking and also points to the institutionalised moral framework is that Europe is not directly mentioned, but exists only as a reference in the background. The tourist appeals to the audience's collective imagination of 'Africa' as 'simple-structured' and challenging, but excludes South Africa. South Africa is placed on one pole, opposite to the 'real' Africa. The German narrator identifies with South Africa and discards it as uninteresting. Apparently, the challenge is located on the other side of the binary – another Africa. Successfully meeting the challenge of Africa's Otherness allows the traveller to transgress his previously limited self and this transgression becomes manifest in the post-travel narration. Due to the localisation of the challenge on a non-European, particularly East African, territory, this foregrounds (and legitimates) the travel as a necessity, which simultaneously allows for setting oneself apart from those who remain at home. Travel to Africa becomes a point of distinction for the traveller.

The narration furthermore recalls the image of 'lonesome heroism' (see Fabian, 2002 [1983]: 58) in travelling through 'wild' and still partly untamed Africa and can be traced in the narrations of the first European travellers to Africa. The narrative style of an adventure story (see Pratt, 1992: 75, 86f) often underlines the sought-after challenge, on the one hand, and the affirmation and confirmation of the self, on the other hand. The foreign 'land' becomes a space of self-discovery and self-development, a stage on which the conquest of the exterior Other in the shape of nature is paralleled by the conquest of the 'civilised', and therefore softened, self.

In addition, what becomes obvious in this pattern is the aspect of power. It is a question of *mastering* the Other, which means taming it and making it subject to the self, which is an inherently colonial practice. It is also an act of colonial desire, the wish to 'become Other'. However, the colonial discourse is removed from consciousness and neither negotiated nor acknowledged.

Narratives of cultural immersion

The discourse on *civilisation* is taken up again in another type of tourist narrative, in which the degree of *cultural* Otherness in the visited African destination is negotiated. This performative mode of 'culture decoding' plays on the empathic understanding of the Other. Cultural immersion exists in a search for cultural 'authenticity', which is considered to be in opposition to 'inauthentic' European culture. In the following quote, Kristina, a middle-aged woman interviewed on a radio programme, compares the different grades of authentic gratification achieved by travelling in either eastern or southern Africa:

> There [in Namibia] you even get German bakeries; well, this is really rather like home. There's not much culture there ... with regard to what you can learn from Africa.... [Namibia is] not the perfect place to get to know Africa.

Culture, here, is imagined as something strictly different (from Germany), distinct, pure and, furthermore, consumable and tangible. In line with many other discourses by tourists, it strongly draws from a discourse concerning authenticity. The idea of cultural authenticity starts from the premise of distinct, separate and especially static cultural entities that are liable to be destroyed through cultural contact, particularly with imperial cultures. This 'truth' is not questioned within this narrative mode; it is, rather, the proclaimed aim of travel to bodily experience and encounter this Otherness where it is 'still' present, for example in the 'more African' parts of Namibia. The renewed distinction between Self and Other, 'real' Africa and Europe, marks the space of Africa anew as an arena for singular experiences, apart from any experience one can encounter within Europe. What counts as the right way to travel is not only the distinction between 'authentic' and 'inauthentic' cultures, but the experience of immersion into the foreign, that is, the most different and authentic culture. Kristina continues:

> to experience culture a bit more, well, this might be a little unfair, but … you need to go to the right places…, the Herero [a language/cultural group in Namibia], for example. I am sure there's lots to learn, their language and religion; one can learn a lot from them.

While the adventurous traveller experiences the limits and possibilities of the narrator's physical body, the cultural decoder experiences the Other in a cultural dimension. 'Successful' travel is determined by a gain in 'other' knowledges. The quote illustrates an evaluation of 'right' and 'wrong' tourist behaviour, which is measured according to the degree of immersion in the Other culture. The cultural immersionist narrative is a mark of distinction not only from any experience on European ground, but it also differentiates this travel experience from those who are 'only' tourists. 'Real travelling' is marked by an imagined transgression not of physical self but of cultural boundaries and familiar knowledge. This is not to say that travelling cannot or should not involve actual learning but it seems important to highlight that learning about sameness or shared circumstances – ranging from German bread to imported beer, Coca-Cola and hip-hop wear to made-in-China fabrics and Maggi stock cubes (all items referred to in other travelogues) – is either ignored or not considered learning.

The performance of the travelogue witnesses a balancing act between a public discourse on cultural tourism (e.g. the importance of intercultural sensitivity and an interest in other ways of life, which deserve to be preserved) and individually embodied dispositions, at times also expressed as vindication. For example, the statement 'well, this might be a little unfair' shows that Kristina is at least partly aware that she judges both Namibian culture and tourists who presumably do *not* travel 'to the right places'. She might also be playing on an anticipated discourse of modesty, trying not to be arrogant. Nevertheless, she feels assured and entitled to her statement, illustrated by the 'but' which immediately follows. She posits herself as an agent able to transgress cultural limitations and eventually cultural fixation. Unlike those whom she visits, and from whom she expects authenticity, she is unbound by cultural boundaries.

Turning back to the narrator in Wainaina's short story reveals interesting connections to coping with realms of Otherness in tourism. Matano, driving tourists around in his taxi, concludes 'Then they are free to like him – he is no longer a threat'. He is highlighting here the fact that the act of *othering* the visited culture and marking the territory of their white fantasy gives a certain comfort and security. This recalls Frantz Fanon's words: 'Confronted with this alterity, the white man needs to defend himself, i.e., to characterize "the Other", who will become the mainstay of his preoccupations and his desires' (Fanon, 2008 [1952]: 147).

While we are sometimes quick to treat the Other as a threat and find solace in the known and familiar, the situation seems more complex. It gives us a glimpse into the ambivalent discourses the traveller is facing and her difficulty in reconciling experiences with individual longing and different moral discourses. The cultural imaginary of the 'exotic African' is a safe (though morally forbidden) fantasy, in that it consigns the individual to a position easier to handle. The self-imposed desire and longing for the other becomes a weapon against an unexpected intrusion from the Other. This can be regarded as an act of operationalising the uncanny, not by making it homely and familiar, but by marking it as even more clearly exterior to the Self. Reflecting on Stuart Hall's reading of Fanon and the sexualised nature of racism, Derek Hook concludes that the 'paradox at hand is that the presence of desire in the white onlooker often takes precisely the form of the violent repudiation of desire' (Hook, 2012: 135) or, we could add, the equalisation of curious desire with intercultural interest. In the case of the cultural immersionist mode, desiring the most different is both valued as 'natural' and therefore enriching, while simultaneously being condemned in a discourse on postcolonial responsibility.

While not easy to achieve, cultural understanding seems possible if the traveller only makes an effort, as the following statement by Gloria, a young woman volunteering in urban Zambia, shows:

> Once he [an old man] understood that I was indeed about to learn Citonga [a local language], but that I was sorry to not yet be able to have a proper conversation, he started to shake his head in astonishment and, while loudly exclaiming his astonishment, he went his way.

This quote includes the idea of familiarity and cultural immersion, on the one hand, and, on the other hand, conveys a sense of exclusivity, making the individual traveller an exceptional figure. In abstraction, this kind of experience and the narrated performance draw on discourses concerning interculturalism and intercultural competence, which today strongly appeal to the European 'do-gooder' consciousness, and the tourist's behaviour and attitude, which are prominently featured in both institutional and public discourses. In doing so, the traveller performs a sort of conspiracy against her society of origin, in that she imagines herself as being closer to the foreign culture than her culture of origin. Interestingly, the threatening similarity between local Zambian and eager travelling German is tamed by the achievement of the latter in actively overcoming the gap between cultural Other and Other self. The cultural insider's narration is closely linked to structures and philosophies of contemporary German development policy. She travels to collect – or narrates to demonstrate – intercultural competence that can be actively used for the purpose of producing knowledge and learning skills *from* the Other, which are lucrative commodities.

While performing cultural 'equality', this pattern also masks social and cultural hierarchies. The hierarchies are rather implicit. Here we have static cultures, unable to change – or, if they do change, losing their status as 'valid' sights. And there we have the flexible traveller able to transgress cultural belonging. However, this pattern does not allow for these questions to arise. It is part of the moral frame to perform equality while nevertheless expecting and proclaiming unchangeable rooted difference.

Objectivity and observational distance

Striving for 'experientially objectified' knowledge is guiding another popular tourist narration, in which travellers differentiate themselves from the value of cultural immersion by clearly indicating their culturally and socially distinct position against the Other. From an imagined observational distance, the travel narration is a classical negotiation of the difference between Self and Other, rooted in a discourse on *objectivity*, which is informed by a cognitive rationality. The following quote is illustrative of its peculiarities and is taken from a couple's web travelogue about their two-year Africa trip. Here they recall entering the town Zinder in Niger:

> We are assaulted from all sides. We are confronted with an aggression to earn money with us which we haven't experienced since Morocco. Our objection, that we have nothing to exchange and that we are merely 'real' tourists in transit, and that we do not want to sell our car, is buried in the commotion. Everybody that turns up here with a car has a business to carry out. It is past the possibilities of the imagination of these people that there is someone driving through the countryside just for fun.

This narration apparently merely describes a situation, a description many travellers will be familiar with. But the last sentence of the quote discloses the evaluative dimension of such a description. Here, the distinction between Self and Other is clearly expressed, and with it the different (imagined) moral frameworks that clash in this situation. However, the boundaries between Self and Other are not questioned, unlike the pattern of the culture-decoder, where the experience of the Other is temporarily allowed to intrude into the traveller's horizon of being.

The knowledge produced appeals to a rational and 'objectifiable' understanding, in contrast to the emotional understanding of the moral discourse of *interculturality*. This pattern relies on the colonial paradigm, following in the footsteps of the 19th-century scientific mission, which reigns under the cover of 'objectivity' and 'expertise' (Fabian, 2002 [1983]; Pratt, 1992: 30ff). Observation in the African travel context actively looks for and constructs the human Other by claiming to prove its differentness. The travelogue becomes a recipe for how to deal with certain threatening situations; the coping strategy suggested is one of compensating the foreign by juxtaposing it with the known; the safe frame of the known and homely is installed by recalling and assuring oneself of the accuracy of one's own parameters of thinking and reacting in the situation. Being perceived and treated like 'real tourists' here suddenly becomes the missing liberating link, while it is feared and perceived as embarrassing in other situations. Just a few lines earlier on their blog, the couple describes the comforting feeling of being completely absorbed in the local daily routine and the pleasure of hiding, walking unseen, letting go of anticipating typical tourist confrontations and 'not being perceived as a walking wallet'. The threat of being overpowered by local everyday business is met with the claim not to belong, to be different. This balancing pattern, of daring proximity to the Other and at the same time ensuring sufficient distance to avoid its intrusion – the feeling of being in place and out of place at the same time – can be traced back to the ambivalence of the colonial encounter, and law, order and everyday private life in the colonies.

The narrative pattern of 'objectivity' is also not free from power relations, although again occluded from view, or actively talked and argued 'out of the way'. An acknowledgement of power inequalities between observer and observed would make the travel narrative, which is the prize of travel, in a postcolonial world impossible or at least lead to the conflicts within the individual discussed in this chapter. The socially accepted narrative posits that the postcolonial world is committed to equality, having left colonial structures of dominance and subjection behind. The struggle to keep up with this narrative emerges when the locals' unforeseeable perception of the tourist is met by the latter.

Remembering colonial heritage

Conscious negotiations of morally contradicting and ambiguous moments in the evaluation of the tourist encounter are rare in the travel narrations. We understand a moral dilemma in tourism as the negotiation of the individual between social, cultural and historical responsibility (which includes inequality at a plurality of levels) and the idea of a travelling subject who performs the travel as a means of transgressing the social, cultural and personal context and involvement. It is here where ethics step in. Moral dilemmas do surge forth at times and the following example, which continues the observing pattern of cognitive reflection, is very telling in its denial of colonial responsibility. More specifically, the colonial history is relativised by taking in the (ideal?) perspective of the local people claiming the positive sides of German colonialism in Tanzania. Here's what Peter in an interview about his latest trip to Tanzania said when asked whether he thinks that, as a tourist, one slips into another role or rather gets closer to oneself:

> There's both. You do slip, well, you do of course play some kind of role, so, it's not the question if you want to slip into another role, but ... the surrounding, the people, the surrounding, it dictates you a bit, in which role to act, there's simply ... you ['one'] have to admit ... black–white. A black person simply has a certain feeling towards a white person and the Tanzanians towards the Germans, they have actually ... a certain gratitude, a certain kindness, openness, and are thankful that there was once built a railway, that is still there ... otherwise ... without ... they alone would not have one. Well it's for that; Germany simply did not have the possibility to do wrong to the Tanzanians, or to exploit the country. England did that job later, and because of this Germany just gets on well in this country. The people are friendly, but you are always looked upon as if you were standing on another ... level, although, this is not quite my impression, or my, that I would say, I want to walk around as their king, no, not like that, but you are really a bit manoeuvred into this position, so that you have to make sure, that you put on a natural affectation ... to go back to normal.

This sequence starts with a description of, and reflection on, the relation between black and white people in Tanzania, particularly the relation between (white) Germans and (black) Tanzanians. The negative evaluation of colonial history in public discourse as well as its relation to the tourist economy is acknowledged. The interviewee shows awareness of the public's rejection of colonialism and its related hierarchy of power. While he does not fully reject this evaluation, he searches for instances with which he can nonetheless 'justify' colonialism and its aftermath, and therefore his role as successor of German colonialists. The first legitimation of his role as innocent traveller is the particularity of German colonialism, which he opposes to English colonialism and values as 'good' or 'soft' colonialism. He apparently chooses to ignore the brutal colonial reality in the then German colonies. In the second legitimation he basically hands over responsibility to the victims of colonialism, namely the Tanzanians, who free the traveller from his negative role as successor to the colonialists by backing up his judgement of German colonialism as 'good': if the Other discharges the traveller from his responsibility, it is not the traveller's responsibility to reject this.

The quote reveals at least two points where ethics play a role, circulating around two questions which are very likely driving other narrations as well – if only unconsciously. How can the situation – being a German tourist, successor of former colonialists – be legitimised? And what is the right way to behave in a situation where a gap in social and economic power becomes apparent? As pointed out above, the first question is answered with the authority of fact, since the situation is described in a matter-of-fact tone. The power relations and the 'feelings' which black people have towards white people are taken as a fact applying to the whole country. The present is described as a logical consequence of the past. However, his last statement points towards a dynamism and flexibility within moral discourses. To 'go back to normal' is voiced in order to de-escalate the awkward situation. The speaker is aware of a discursively illegitimate role, namely the colonialist's role, but he apologises by pointing to his non-intentionality and powerlessness within the situation, as well as to his good-will. What reveals itself here is what we might call a conflict of missing sentiment: the gratitude of the Tanzanians should normally find its completion in some sentiment connected to the past shared with the German travellers. This could be a relief, either because the cruel and humiliating colonial rule did at least some good, or because one is welcomed as a tourist and not banished as a successor of colonialists.

The statement is guided by the traveller's knowledge about a colonial past that is acknowledged to be crucial and involves consequences in the present. Yet it is simultaneously defended; a reaction to previous, probably internalised, public accusations. His learned code of conduct in such a situation is to act humble and avoid being like others who apparently behave in a patronising way ('as their king'). In addition, the past he is aware of seems to determine his role as a tourist or, rather, his role as a German tourist. It is a mediation between his own 'innocent' position and a non-innocent past, from which he, however, tries to filter out a positive possibility for identification in order to avoid questioning his tourist experience in general. In addition, the stated opinion of the Other ('Tanzanians ... are thankful ... [for the] railway') is appropriated and used in order not to have to seriously question the role of the traveller. Towards the end of the quotation, the interviewee constantly uses the German 'neutral' pronoun *man* – here translated with 'you' or 'one', which invokes a sense of behaviour commonly accepted by responsible travellers.[4] He claims support from an anonymous collective with which he identifies and which becomes the legitimising ground for his behaviour.

This utterance is thus a negotiation between the tourist ethos of a 'right' way to travel and a colonial discourse, which challenges his responsibility and which is perceived by the tourist as crucial in the sense that he is aware of moral wrong. The 'moral breakdown' is solved by putting a positive spin on the colonial discourse and taking on a moral discourse position by generalising one's own behaviour as proper. Basically, this negotiation culminates in a rejection of responsibility for the historical context.

Responsibility out of reach

In contrast, the last kind of tourist narration we discuss lays claim to a 'mystic' experience with the magic of 'pure nature' that frees the Self from any historically or socially discursive locatedness and therefore responsibility. The desire for a non-earthly experience, embodied by the realm of exotic Otherness, is projected onto a welcoming space with room for ecstasy and mysticism. Statements like the following by the young volunteer in Zambia were frequent. For the volunteer, the entity of 'Africa' is seen as something to be achieved only in particular embodied experiences (*Erlebnis*) (note the use of 'Africa' and 'Zambia'):

> The sense of endless freedom was floating through my body. I got an idea of what it meant to be in Africa.... The stars were immensely fascinating. The night and its clear sky had always made an impact on me, but here in Zambia, more bright and untouched than anywhere else does the sky mediate a feeling of purity and security.

Travel to Africa is communicated here as the self-discovery of inner climaxes. This subjective 'mystic mode' seeks to reveal the real inner self through the travel experience and the encounter with the 'pure' Other. In contrast with the adventurous experience of self, the mystic travel performance seeks union with nature, rather than needing to conquer it. This encounter absorbs the foreign as Self while aiming at the emotional experience of a total embodiment which evokes a state beyond moral discourses and constraints of the society of origin. This 'mystic' state would be conforming more to the inner desires suppressed in everyday life, justified by 'the properly modern ethics of "following the drive"' (Zizek, 1997). Travelogues often refer to a 'feeling' or a 'sense of Africa'. This treats the projected imaginative quality of the experience *as* 'African', and is not a reference to any single destination *in* Africa. The mystic performance in its purest form is the mode of the 'I', the first-person singular. Human encounters are less important than the individualistic, personal travel to the absolute inner self, which has been spoilt and poisoned by Western society. This is the search for some kind of purification in Africa.

Both immersionist narrations converge in what Pratt calls the 'sentimental mode' (Pratt, 1992: 74ff). The mystic narrative particularly stages a 'sentimental protagonist' who is, in Pratt's words, 'constructed as a non-interventionist European presence' (Pratt, 1992: 78). Being non-interventionist is thereby similar to intercultural competence, which is regarded as being part of 'correct' and justified tourist behaviour. It is also beyond the scope of ethics as such, in that the tourist here does not have to justify her presence and intrusion, acting beyond sociocultural involvement and historical or economic responsibility. This discourse of the romantic gaze is morally justified by tour operators, who promise relief from everyday responsibilities and worries, and is supported by upper-middle-class urban lifestyles incorporating aspects of non-Western health practices. In the narration, the act of articulating the unspeakable event, the anticipation of a needed quality filling an empty spot in the Western Self, meets the shared discourses about the projected space. This space-in-between is what makes the desire livable and keeps it alive as desire. At stake are, literally, cosmopolitan sentiments as the urge to feel as a citizen (*polites*) of the universe (*cosmos*), which precedes and goes beyond the social experience of being in Europe or elsewhere in the world.

Reconciling Moral Orders

What unifies the individual performances is the narration of an experience that is imagined as unique, and which stresses the traveller's experience as transgressing the European frame of experience. In their exceptionalism, the experiences nevertheless connect with a body of collective knowledge shared by the present audience in order to be decoded and valued as unique. The cosmopolitan itinerary is therefore as much connected to a certain consensus on the things to do, see and know, a 'moral order of sightseeing' (MacCannell, 1999 [1976]: 39f), as every other tourist identity, independent of the location visited. Achieving a certain cosmopolitan image is bound to a public moral discourse, which is challenged or confirmed by the individual tourist performance. The tourist performance engages with this public discourse and takes a position in relation to it.

Within African travel, and presumably all travel where the relationship between traveller and visited builds on an unequal socioeconomic status, the moral stability of the tourist consciousness is provided by an increasing consensus over 'right' and 'wrong' ways to travel. The discursively influenced narrations claim a different take on the morality of travelling. Yet, while an awareness of colonialism and the moral difficulty of travelling to postcolonial Africa is apparent in tourists' accounts, the narrations seem to justify a proper, non-colonial way of travelling. The travelogues therefore take the form of a mediation between the colonial and cosmopolitan discourses and finally enable a positive identification with the latter. The structures of desire are located between conflicting discourses (Hook, 2008: 271).

The attraction of the exotic Other remains the most overtly enacted seducing narrative in travel media, feeding into that mix of fascination and fear in encounters with Africa. The moral ideal of a good cosmopolitan and responsible traveller leads to the repression of *othering* fantasies. Recalling Freud, repression forms 'that necessary condition for enabling a primitive feeling to recur in the shape of an uncanny effect' (Freud, 1955 [1919]: 241). The negotiation of 'uncanny encounters' seems to contradict different moral discourses about how to travel in the most correct or most distinguished way. The still present colonial fantasies haunt the traveller's imagination. Returning as desire or threat, colonialism's aftermath is being collectively repressed and kept in an allochronic discourse (Fabian, 2002 [1983]). Following Freud further, the 'class [of the uncanny] which proceeds from repressed complexes is more irrefragable' than the one of 'surmounted' forms (Freud, 1955 [1919]: 250). Colonial mentalities are being repressed in public discourse but at the same time communicated as surmounted, which gives them their persistent influence on the traveller's identity position, and therefore only slowly lead to acts of emancipation.

Conclusion

Tourism's embodied presence and activity is guided by mental images that preform, though do not determine, its activities. The travel narration and performance make cultural narratives part of individual memory, while at the same time interacting with and transgressing cultural myths (Larsen, 2010: 321). Our analysis exposes the 'patterns of exclusivity' which seem to be unaware of their performed and preformed 'colonial' character. In instances, however, when the colonial discourse is leading to moral break-downs within the tourist, it is rejected or mitigated in order to defend and protect the cosmopolitan identity aspired to. Travel to Africa is enacted as a means of freeing oneself from ties as well as of imagining freedom from social hierarchies. This, notwithstanding, does not mean that social hierar-chies are not continuously re-performed while travelling. The divergence between self-perception as a free-floating entity living up to the real inner suppressed desires and a real context of global power relations (in which colonial continuities play a significant role) points towards an unresolved tension in tourism. This tension, moreover, is rarely made evident as part of the travel experience. Tourism as a cultural phenomenon has brought forward a moral framework that allows travellers to ignore the tension and thereby to enable their enhanced position as citizens of the world.

The travellers' performances as subjectivities beyond European situatedness bring to view their identity construction as an unlocalis-able, global cosmopolitan. In the travelogue performance, cosmopolitan identity is imagined and called upon as a socially accepted and morally sanitised position, one opposed to colonialist's ambitions for domination, oppression and power. Due to the ambiguity of the tourist's identity in public discourse, this complex process of identification is guided by the urge to distinguish oneself from 'wrong' ways to travel to and in Africa, from historical responsibility and from fellow Europeans. Though a colonial rationality strongly affects cosmopolitan discourse, the tourist's perfor-mance appropriates, to varying degrees, cosmopolitan values as an escape from historical, social, economic or cultural locality and responsibility. As has been shown, different discourses of interculturality, civilisation, objec-tivity and postcolonial responsibility are impacting on the travel narration. Each performance, however, is played on the surface of social Otherness, which becomes manifest in the image of Africa, whether as a challenge, as a source for origin and authenticity or as social difference. Although cosmo-politan identity claims a non-situated epistemology, the cultural patterns it reverts to are particular and situated, in that they access a colonial imaginary of Africa as the European Other. The making of cosmopolitan identity therefore universalises the (neo/post)-colonialist's perspective anew instead of decentring it. It is through such 'moral breakdowns' and ethics worked out on the self in post-touristic performances that we get an idea of the traveller's awareness for conflicting and contradicting moral discourses around being a tourist. Zooming in on some of the quotes shows that most tourists cannot totally ignore these and other tensions and do not feel 'homely' with everything they report. In most travel narrations we find moments of hesitance, ambivalent feelings of embarrassment and order, that all give access to the complex field of negotiating different moral discourses. There's a 'therapeutic' quality to these narrations, tying in with Lacan's maxim of psychoanalytic ethics, namely not to give way to one's desire, on the one hand, and, on the other, going through that same desire (as lived in the touristic experience) and articulating it publicly (for a discussion see Zizek, 1997). Here are (at least) three layers of ethics at work: firstly, the ideal of an individualistic, self-fulfilling way of life in which boundaries are tested and inner desires met; secondly, the ethical realm of socio-historical awareness of entangled colonial pasts and the need to tackle them responsibly; and thirdly, the highly valued moral predicament of the cosmopolitan traveller replacing the state of inequality. The tourists' negotiations display the confrontation of travelling in Other spaces, becoming aware of the ambivalence of discourses and seeking to reconcile them.

Notes

(1) On the performative character of tourism see, for example, the work of Edward M. Bruner (1991), David Crouch (2002), Tim Edensor (2001) and Jonas Larsen (2005; also Larsend & Haldrup, 2010).
(2) All quotes are translated from German by the authors. All names are fictitious.
(3) Other/Otherness is written in capital letters when referring to the construction and reproduction of a social Other, which can be distinguished from individual others. The same applies to the construction/reproduction of a Self referring to an identitary group, while self refers to the individual traveller.
(4) Dervin (2011) makes similar observations on the third-person singular neutral pronoun (in French).

References

Behdad, A. (1994) *Belated Travelers: Orientalism in the Age of Colonial Dissolution*. Durham, NC: Duke University Press.
Bendix, R. (2002) Capitalizing on memories past, present, and future: Observations on the intertwining of tourism and narration. *Anthropological Theory* 2 (4), 469–487.
Bruner, E.M. (1991) Transformation of self in tourism. *Annals of Tourism Research* 18, 238–250.
Bruner, E.M. and Turner, V.W. (1986) *The Anthropology of Experience*. Champaign, IL: University of Illinois Press.
Crouch, D. (2002) Surrounded by place: Embodied encounters. In S. Coleman and M. Crang (eds) *Tourism: Between Place and Performance* (pp. 207–219). Oxford: Berghan.
Dervin, F. (2011) The repression of us- and we-hoods in European exchange students' narratives about their experiences in Finland. *Journal of Comparative Research in Anthropology and Sociology* 2 (1), 79–94.
Edensor, T. (2001) Performing tourism, staging tourism: (Re)producing tourist space and practice. *Tourist Studies* 1 (1), 59–81.

Enwezor, O. (2006) *Snap Judgements: New Positions in Contemporary African Photography*. München: Steidl.

Fabian, J. (2002 [1983]) *Time and the Other: How Anthropology Makes Its Object*. New York: Columbia University Press.

Fanon, F. (2008 [1952]) *Black Skin, White Masks*. New York: Grove Press.

Freud, S. (1955 [1919]) The 'uncanny'. In *Standard Edition of the Complete Psychological Works of Sigmund Freud* (vol. 17, pp. 217–256). Transl. J. Strachey *et al*. London: Hogarth Press.

Gillespie, A. (2007) Collapsing self/other positions: Identification through differentiation. *British Journal for Social Psychology* 46 (3), 579–595.

Hannerz, U. (1996) Cosmopolitans and locals in world culture. In *Transnational Connections: Culture People Places* (pp. 102–111). London: Routledge.

Hook, D. (2008) Postcolonial psychoanalysis. *Theory and Psychology* 18 (2), 269–283.

Hook, D. (2012) *A Critical Psychology of the Postcolonial: The Mind of Apartheid*. New York: Routledge.

Larsen, J. (2005) Families seen photographing: Performativity of tourist photography. *Space and Culture* 8, 416–434.

Larsen, J. (2010) Goffman and the tourist gaze: A performative perspective on tourism mobilities. In M.H. Jacobsen (ed.) *Contemporary Goffman* (pp. 313–332). London: Routledge.

Larsen, J. and Haldrup, M. (2010) *Tourism, Performance and the Everyday: Consuming the Orient* (Contemporary Geographies of Leisure, Tourism and Mobility). London: Routledge.

MacCannell, D. (1999 [1976]) Sightseeing and social structure. In *The Tourist: A New Theory of the Leisure Class* (pp. 39–56). Berkeley, CA: University of California Press.

McClintock, A. (1995) *Imperial Leather: Gender and Sexuality in the Colonial Context*. New York: Routledge.

Pratt, M-L. (1992) *Imperial Eyes: Travel Writing and Transculturation*. London: Routledge.

Salazar, N. (2012) Tourism imaginaries: A conceptual approach. *Annals of Tourism Research* 39 (2), 863–882.

Tomlin, L. (1999) Transgressing boundaries: Postmodern performance and the tourist trap. *Drama Review* 43 (2), 136–149.

Tucker, H. and Hall, M.C. (2008) *Tourism and Postcolonialism: Contested Discourses, Identities and Representations*. London: Routledge.

Wainaina, B. (2005) How to write about Africa. *Granta* 92: The View From Africa. See http://www.granta.com/Magazine/92/How-to-Write-about-Africa (accessed June 2011).

Wainaina, B. (2006) Ships in high transit. In N. Elam (ed.) *Discovering Home: Stories from the Caine Prize for African Writing 2002* (pp. 217–239). Bellevue: Jacana.

Zigon, J. (2009) Within a range of possibilities: Morality and ethics in social life. *Ethnos* 75 (2), 251–276.

Zizek, S. (1997) Desire: Drive = Truth: Knowledge. *Umbr(a)*, 147–152. See http://www.lacan.com/zizek-desire.htm (accessed February 2013).

10 Journeys to the Inner Self: Neo-Shamanism and the Search for Authenticity in Contemporary New Age Travel Practice

Christian Ghasarian

Introduction

The contemporary search for spiritual answers has led a growing number of Westerners to delve outside of the realms of the Christian religion. Coming from the United States, as well as from Western and Eastern Europe, the majority of people involved are educated and well-off, including a large proportion of women looking for different means of empowerment. For many of them, a spiritual investigation implies being in touch, through imagination or social interactions, with different people, situations and experiences. At first glance, this new attraction to other spiritualities may express another form of consumption of Otherness, through which practices borrowed from different cultures are appropriated and reformulated for one's own purposes. Indeed, a seduction of differences is clearly at work here through new spiritual models, symbols, artefacts, foods, involvements and so on. Yet, is it analytically relevant to consider this new dynamic as simply another form of tourism, or should we, rather, understand it as a real search for a better life by people not quite satisfied with what their culture of origin has to offer? I will try to answer this question here by exploring the circumstances and modalities of these immersions in alternative forms of spirituality through the example of contemporary neo-shamanism, a set of practices whose popularity has increased during the last two decades. My analysis is based on 15 years of multi-sited fieldwork in Europe and the United States, during which I met numerous people who had been exploring neo-shamanic practices.

Before presenting what people search for, and do, in these practices, especially when they take place abroad, I will briefly retrace the contemporary development of alternative spiritualities in the United States and in Europe, paying particular attention to the specific place neo-shamanism occupies in this new system of logic, as well as the main concepts at stake (healing, knowledge, experience, wisdom, etc.). These inherently imply the involvement of Others – different Others in different places – and a sometimes complex, though somewhat predictable, relationship to them. After addressing the consumption of models underlying these involvements and their consequences for the local populations, I will set these considerations in relation to individuals' desires to understand themselves.

Western Attractions to Alternative Spiritualities

During the last four decades in the United States and Europe, new forms of spirituality have appeared. These new spiritualities are considered by many people as capable of providing more appropriate answers to their quests for being than the traditional religious forms. A heterogeneous and complex dynamic labelled as 'New Age' thus developed on the two continents. This new system of meaning dissociates itself from Christian religion, its dogmas, rules and hierarchies, which are often perceived to be removed from an 'authentic spirituality'. The personal development or blossoming that New Age practitioners seek includes healing, and is a matter of personal responsibility and work on oneself. In some ways, the current spiritual quest can be seen in continuity with the mystical aspect of Christianity that praises a personal engagement with God and pilgrimages to sacred places. The Christian concept of a 'celestial authority'[1] indeed leaves room for the notion of the 'divine' and an individual search for well-being and desire to experience transcendence. This quest is also deeply rooted in the Socratic and Romantic philosophies, according to which the answers to the mysteries of life are within everyone. Some grand public interpretations associate New Age groups with 'cults' but this 'common sense' category cannot really satisfy anthropologists trying to understand the logics behind the activities undertaken by these groups.[2]

The people involved in these activities also express a growing interest in the ancient and the traditional (medicines, wisdoms, cultures, etc.), to which they attach such labels as 'authentic', 'depth' and a 'better connected to the natural world'. Nature is actually one of the main new themes of interest in the New Age system of meaning.[3] Intention and intelligence are attributed to nature that can, through animals, vegetables and minerals, therapeutically help humans in their life courses and in their attempt to understand the mysteries of the universe. A renewed relationship with nature (defined as 'Mother Earth', 'Mother Nature', 'Pangaïa', 'Pachamama', etc.) and its regenerating energy and power is thus constantly evoked, with the idea that each human consciousness comes from nature and therefore everybody can manifest this intelligence and beauty inside him/herself. The notion of 'deep ecology' is part of this logic, and includes animist conceptions that evoke a continuum between nature and culture, according to which animals, trees, plants, minerals and invisible entities need to be taken into account. In New Age models, a re-enchanted nature is a universe full of energy, spirits, guides and powerful totemic animals that one must discover and use for one's own benefit. It is thought that the same energy is present under different forms in the human body as in the universe.

The idea that Western cultures have 'forgotten' deep, holistic knowledge sustains these practices. In the context of increasing interest in the environment and the wish for another relationship to the world, indigenous populations and their knowledge are in themselves a source of legitimacy. This search for different existential answers, combined with the desire to undergo a quest for a non-dogmatic spirituality, explains the success of Carlos Castaneda's writings in Western popular culture and, as we shall specifically see in the present chapter, the symbolic position of shamanic practices, the shaman's wisdom and shamanic places of power in the New Age field of possibilities (Ghasarian, 2002). Considered as more appropriate for answering Westerners' emerging needs, these distinctive models involve the circulation of specific forms of ideas, objects and people. Significantly, the knowledge and wisdom attributed to these (selected) Others is considered as having a pan-cultural dimension, valid for all humanity.[4]

The valorisation of these alternative models of spirituality has taken the form of a social phenomenon in which the search for new therapeutic methods, rituals and experiences has led more and more people to engage in practices for which they have not been socialised. Starting with Indian yoga and meditation in the 1960s, and developing to include shamanic experiences from South America, a new consumption of signs and practices has taken place in the contemporary cultural moment. But the production of an ideal Otherness through its 'difference', 'authenticity' and 'wisdom' still underlies these implications. Yet, even if the current process involves a certain commodification of cultures, it does not prevent a person's sincere immersion in these practices. After having briefly retraced the main underlying models of this current spiritual dynamic in Western societies, I now address the types of involvements, encounters and experiences Westerners are looking for in their holistic search for authentic spirituality aimed at reconnecting oneself with nature and, through it, with the cosmos.

Neo-Shamanism as a New Form of Spirituality

The desire to maintain or recover one's health when conventional medical answers seem to be insufficient, on one side, and the hope for a better life, on the other side, have encouraged the provision of heterogeneous solutions (meditation, Ayurvedic medicine, Qigong, channelling, etc.). Alternative cultural models that are thought to be in close relationship with nature (a constant reference) are particularly valued in contemporary Western societies. In this logic, shamanism – precisely what it represents on the basis of what is known about it – occupies a major place in the new system of meaning, as its reformulated methods or techniques are highly individualised (even when referring to spirit helpers). Considered to be a 'direct road' to understanding oneself and the surrounding world of existence – yet a path at the margin of dominant religions – shamanism appears to be accessible to people searching for personal development who are open to other traditions.

In the postmodern context, this appropriation of shamanism is built on the reconsideration of practices previously denigrated by Christian authorities. Indeed, Western perceptions of tribal shamanism have progressively become highly valued, as cultures with oral traditions convey romantic images of ancient sacred knowledge and wisdom.[5] The writings of Carlos Castaneda (1972) and Mircea Eliade (1968) have in this respect contributed much to the revalorisation of shamanism among the Western public. Of course, many people refer to 'traditional' shamanism in very vague ways and, in the same manner as there is an alternative New Age spirituality, a reformulated shamanism, often called 'New Age shamanism' developed. I prefer to call it 'spiritualised shamanism', as spiritual involvements are at stake here. This shamanism makes reference to ancient or traditional cultures, and is reformulated as a holistic approach to the relationship between humans and nature – a nature conceived of as intrinsically spiritual. It also offers the possibility of experiencing transcendence for those who wish it.

This new Western interest slowly blurs the frontier between 'traditional' and 'adapted' shamanism, as shamans from shamanic cultures do sometimes come themselves to Western societies to organise ceremonies for interested people. Then, through a series of borrowings and multiple redefinitions, shamanisms that have for a long time operated at the margin of dominant (Christian and Islamic) models today slowly institutionalise themselves in societies where anthropologists did not look for them before (in places such as Portugal, Croatia and Switzerland). This again confirms the capacity for shamanic practices to adapt and persist whatever the surrounding social context. Yet some sharp differences can be found in the two forms of shamanism. For example, in 'traditional' shamanic conceptions, the spirit world is one of impersonal power with which the shaman interacts (and that he or she can control) for the well-being of the community. In Western shamanic reformulations, the relationship to spirits is also fundamental, but the dangers of the shamanic universe – described in anthropological reports as a world full of often malevolent spirits with whom the shaman often must fight to cure a patient (Chaumeil, 2003; Jakobsen, 1999) – are disregarded. Western participants learn to work with spirits of nature (animals, trees, minerals, etc.) but the power they are supposed to develop is seen as a mix of inner capacities and help from the spirits themselves, if they succeed in contacting them. A quest for wisdom is in this context more important than a pure search for power. My enquiries among Westerners involved in these practices in different countries led me to understand that the desires to be in better health, to be happier, to change one's life and to find new answers to the main existential problems are at the heart of such involvement. In line with Mircea Eliade's perspectives (according to which shamanism is a valuable 'archaic technique' to attain ecstasy), the approach of shamanism in non-shamanic societies is based on the idea that human nature possess a 'shamanic core', an idea that can be very useful for everybody's personal spiritual development.

Scholars argue that Western re-appropriations of shamanism, called 'neo-shamanism', mobilise exoticism, romanticism, ready-to-think ideas regarding indigenous knowledge, and control over mystical powers.[6] Yet even if, from an analytical perspective, these aspects are manifest, from the standpoint of practitioners, these new spiritual practices are considered to be transformative by imparting a sudden understanding of what happens in their body and their mind, and by placing them in what many consider a renewed relationship with the universe. However, in spite of this common goal, it should be emphasised that the activities, workshops and retreats aimed at personal development involve different kinds of reformulations of shamanism. Spiritualised shamanism is not a homogeneous movement but is, rather, characterised by a diversity of approaches. One could almost say that there are as many approaches as guides for them. Neo-shamanic retreats can thus combine meditations, chanting, breathing techniques, physical exercises, drumming, psychotropic plants and so on. These approaches often imply physical travelling and journeys to places associated with a 'true spirituality'.

Self-development practices specific to shamanism institutionalise themselves through what I call different 'epistemic sites', which, in the context of globalisation, are virtual, nomadic, temporary and durable: 'virtual sites' (very numerous on the internet) offer plenty of information on multiple shamanisms;[7] 'nomadic sites' (books and magazines,[8] as well as diverse shamanic artefacts such as drums, rattles, didgeridoos, quartz crystals, CDs, plants, etc.) can be found in specialised shops; 'temporary sites' are places invested and sometimes institutionalised by people for activities related to shamanism (such as conferences,[9] workshops, retreats, camps and cere-monies); 'durable sites' are institutional structures that support shamanic activities (such as the Foundation for Shamanic Studies, created by Michael Harner in California)[10] but also natural places that seem to lend themselves rediscovery and preservation, and where spiritual guides are sometimes invited to come to teach or organise ceremonies for Westerners.[11] These 'epistemic sites' (especially the 'virtual,' 'nomadic' and 'temporary' ones) can be created at home, in the country where Westerners live, but they also involve a journey abroad to the places where shamanism originally occurs (notably the 'durable sites').

Among the nomadic shamanic sites, Westerners are particularly attracted to those with psychotropic plants that produce visions after being consumed (usually drunk or smoked) (Baud & Ghasarian, 2010a, 2010b). The respect given to nature inscribes participants of 'traditional' shamanism in a humble and somewhat collaborative relationship with animals and plants – especially those that are considered as sacred medicine. If there are several means of attaining different states of consciousness in non-ordinary reality – such as the rhythmic repercussions of the drum or the rattle (Harner's method), singing, dancing, fasting, corporal austerities and special breathing techniques – several societies (notably Amazonian) believe psychotropic plants and specific mushrooms to be the fastest and easiest technique to change the perception of things (Schultes, 1976; Wasson, 1968). The use of these psychotropic agents to create particular states of consciousness and to access the invisible world is a very ancient practice that provides very strong psychical and physical experiences. Those who take these plants generally see them as plants of knowledge, plants of power or 'master plants', even if many consider that they reveal only that which is already in the person who consumes them. Besides mushrooms, notably used in Mexico and Siberia, the most popular shamanic plants are peyote (*Lophophora williamsii*), the San Pedro cactus (*Trichocereus pachanoi*) and ayahuasca (*Banisteriopsis caapi*), which are traditionally used in Mexico, Peru and Amazonia, respectively. Principally used to purify, cleanse and heal, these plants are considered in their shamanic re-appropriations a very important tool to produce altered states of consciousness that help people connect to themselves. Terms such as 'adaptogene', 'lucidogene' and 'en-theogens' (revelators of the divine inside), whose usage has lately become more popular than 'psychotropics' or 'hallucinogens' among the people who experience them, suggest how these plants are perceived. As experienced in 'traditional' societies, the states of consciousness acquired with the help of these plants are not considered by Western users as hallucinatory but visionary or intuitive (Gonzales, 2010).

The psychotropic plant that is most sought out today in spiritualised shamanism is ayahuasca. Used in Amazonia to know, to cleanse and to heal the body, this vine is also taken to enter altered states of consciousness to access information inscribed in the person (as the corporal matter is considered to carry memory cellules of humanity and the universe) but not easily accessible otherwise. The plant is thought to reveal the secrets of other plants to cure illness. The doses absorbed vary according to participants. Its action is considered to be totally unpredictable and to affect the individual on different levels (physical, mental and spiritual). Though it may be difficult to fully describe their inner experiences, the people who drink plant concoctions remain aware of what they live in the moment and keep a memory of what they have gone through; many refer to a feeling of hyperconsciousness. As many users represent it, beyond the active principal of the plant,[12] it is its spirit that is believed to be acting on them and helping them to face themselves in their totality. This is why ayahuasca is sacred and ritually treated with respect.[13] The plant's specific, curative teaching may be very difficult and painful, but my ethnographic research showed me that, afterwards, the participants practically always have a feeling of gratitude towards the plant – or more precisely the spirit of the plant – considered to have worked positively with them.[14] Today, ayahuasca has entered into the common sense of a growing number of Western people, even if what it is and what really happens after absorbing it is not very clear.

Physical and Psychical Delocalisation for Healing and Wisdom

The notions of adventure, experience, learning, healing, access to mysterious realities and power are fundamental in spiritualised shamanism. As mentioned earlier, for Westerners, the main objective of the shamanic experience is to enter into an altered state of consciousness and therefore to establish contact with a non-ordinary reality in which perceptions of time, space and objects are changed. There are no typical experiences, as each is considered unique. Everybody is supposed to reach by themselves their own conclusions regarding the nature and the limits of reality. Therefore, one can only speak about one's own experience, which cannot be a model for others. The absence of a common cultural context and cosmogony certainly favours that diversity of experiences among participants in these ceremonies.[15]

Neo-shamanic experiences may now occur in Europe and in the United States, with Western guides and teachers trained elsewhere, or with the intermediary of North, Central or South American shamans or African healers invited by associations, or directly in the places where these persons live, where journeys in shamanic lands (the 'durable epistemic sites') – with retreats and ceremonies based on plants (ayahuasca, San Pedro, peyote, iboga) – are organised. The important point is that the Western participants do not consider these new 'mediators' of experiences and knowledge to have a monopoly on wisdom.[16] The categories used to designate these mediators (which can be found in 'virtual' and 'nomadic sites') are, among others, native Amazonian shamans, master shamans, certified shamanic counsellors, recognised shaman, healer and ceremonial leader, guides and teachers. One of their characteristics is to welcome anybody interested in their practices and even to come themselves to places ('temporary sites') where they have been invited to work with Westerners. In South America or in Africa, in those societies where shamanic practices are still enacted and are even renewed or adapted for a Western public, foreign or local groups organise ceremonies based on the absorption of psychotropic plants (*ayahuasca* notably) for visitors. Today, South America (notably Brazil and Peru) particularly attracts people in search of spiritual answers with recognised or self-designated 'shamans' who adapt or create specific practices for them. Whether a long journey abroad or a simple one-hour drive (if the meeting takes place in one's own city) is required to meet these 'mediators of knowledge', the encounter is always a confrontation of different world-views (often leading to a selective adoption of views and practices by the practitioners). I focus here on the first form of neo-shamanic encounter, in which Westerners journey geographically and culturally often very far from where – and what – they live.

It is time to address in more detail what is at stake in these neo-shamanic experiences sought by Westerners. Spiritual development, preventive health and physical well-being are major motivations here. The holistic approach of shamanic activities gives a very important place to health and dealing with illness, with the idea that the potential for healing is inside the person, who has to establish the right connection to the universe, starting with the natural world. Spiritualised shamanism is thought of as re-sacralising the therapeutic act through sacred symbols and references to the divine, with the objective of reconnecting the person to the earth and the cosmos. The desire to (re)connect to nature follows from a certain detachment from biomedical standards. In the alternative medical logic, individuals are considered to be responsible of their health; pain and illness are signs sent by the body or the universe to help the person overcome a particular biographical moment.[17] The body is considered to intrinsically possess the potential to self-heal, and to be the first 'tool' of the spiritual work.[18] People thus speak about the 'wisdom of the body' and the importance of listening to it. A microcosm possessing in itself the macrocosm, the body is the container of the energies that, in the course of life, can stagnate and create diseases and psychical disharmony. Indeed, energy is constantly evoked as the most important component to increase in 'the spiritual work', as the healing process happens on a subtle plane of the body.[19]

Spiritual development and higher knowledge are not considered separate from the issue of health. As indicated above, body and consciousness are, in a holistic logic, related to, and feed off, each other.[20] Significantly, it is their own body that Westerners voluntarily expose when they take psychotropic plants that modify their state of consciousness. The work may thus take place in ceremonies during which people absorb ayahuasca to be receptive to themselves – facing the unknown – throughout an entire night. The experiences are diverse and can range from a (very) positive to a negative impact on the people involved (which is more unusual). There can also be a feeling that nothing happened. Incertitude is always present in the outcome of the experience. Some people have experienced difficulties, spending the night in convulsion, vomiting the drink they took, having frightening visions or physical pain, but the final interpretation of this physically and psychically demanding situation – notably when people have uncontrollable visions or extreme bodily reactions – is most of the time very positive, in terms of teaching, cleaning, purification and awareness. Being present to oneself and able to listen to the body's messages during these liminal moments can lead the participants to change their whole conception of life. I cannot describe here all of these experiences and, indeed, their consequences are always different from one person to another; however, I have observed their deep existential impact on the majority of people involved whom I have followed during many years of fieldwork (Ghasarian, 2006, 2009, 2010).

Consumption of Otherness and Quests for the Authentic

Whether they take place within an elaborated frame with a ritualistic dimension or in an informal setting, these spiritual experiences of inside and outside otherness involve a growing number of Westerners from diverse generations, genders and social classes. These practices are costly and now constitute an industry specialising in alternative spiritualities and therapies, which target a relatively well-off and well educated public. People buy books and DVDs, and participate in workshops, and the most motivated (who are not fully satisfied with only 'virtual' and 'nomadic' shamanic sites) who can afford it travel to where they can find specialists. A whole range of financial aspects is thus at stake as shamanic experiences are, in a way, another form of the Western consumption of Otherness (through the acquisition of diverse artefacts, decoctions of plants, songs, corporal techniques, clothes, etc.). Clearly, while it is inspired by 'traditional' representations and practices, a system of consumption of attractive alternative cultural models develops here.[21] Managed by locals or even Westerners, numerous centres ('temporary' or 'durable' epistemic sites) in which it is possible to engage in shamanic experiences in an adjusted ceremonial frame are being progressively created in South America. Sometimes paradoxical situations arise, such as shamanic workshops re-imported by Westerners into shamanic (or previously shamanic) societies themselves (Siberia, Amazonia, etc.).

This new context of practice invites local practitioners to try to answer Westerners' expectations – and, more precisely, the ideas they have of shamans and their knowledge. Significantly, Westerners' interest in shamanic practices mainly lies in the fact that some of their aspects (witchcraft, malevolent spirits, etc.) are neglected. For the adaptable local shamans, it is not a simple matter of negotiating with the spirits anymore, but rather they must also negotiate meaning with the Westerners in search of spiritual answers that make sense to them. Generally, during retreats and ceremonies, the (neo-)shamanism forms that are practised are simplified in order to be more compatible and digestible – if possible – by Western people who will at some point return home. Actually, Westerners who wish to be initiated most often do not really recognise the unique particularities of the culture in which they temporarily immerse themselves through a specific practice. For them, there is generally only 'one shamanism', beyond the specific forms it can take (through cultures and languages). Therefore, even in the deep rainforest, the teachings transmitted to foreigners can be impregnated with Asian philosophical and Western esoteric references (meditation, kundalini, chakra, self-realisation, etc.). Conversely, these new interests developed by foreigners create new business slots for some local 'shamans', who are sometimes self-designated and abusive. In this context, the sociological and economic impact of the organisation of these events aimed at Westerners' personal development on traditional cultures is not negligible. Since the journey and retreat, both in Amazonia and elsewhere, require shamans and other indigenous practitioners, who are paid more than usual to offer an original experience, it is appropriate to look at the local consequences of the search for mystical experiences, as well as at the nature of what is taught or 'provided' to the visitors.

Obviously, the search for spiritual and physical experiences is also a search for new sensations that can be analysed by referring to psychological and sociological predispositions. It is clear that at a macro or structural level, the 'interference' of Westerners with indigenous plants can be problematic, as it is related to economic transactions that have social consequences. Westerners' interest in the sacred plants of shamanic societies is not always animated by the best intentions, as the problems of bio-piracy or 'non-participative bioprospection' has made clear. These attempts to legally and economically exploit indigenous plants (notably ayahuasca) inevitably fuel the critiques of any external usage of 'traditional' cultural practices.

Related to a certain commodification of shamanism and shamanic cultures are some ethical problems posed by the Western re-appropriations of shamanic practices. Yet, what impacts do these re-appropriations really have on the cultures and societies from which such conceptions, practices and plants are exported? To associate these activities with a form of spiritual or mystical 'tourism' (Demenget, 2001), as often occurs, reveals an analytic emphasis on the material dimension of social and cultural facts. This cultural phenomenological approach, with all the imagery related to tourism, is relevant but it becomes insufficient if it is the only model of understanding the process at stake. Of course, there are problematic (and I may say) ridiculous cases of tourist groups visiting acting tribes, attending dances and sometimes taking ayahuasca – in a packaged, 2–3-hour consumption of otherness – but their motivations and experiences are not what I address here. Qualitative studies remain to be done on the local impacts of these new situations. Do they really transform a function (that of shamans) into a profession? Do they create a prejudicial homogenisation of indigenous rituals to answer expectations of Westerners looking for exoticism? If so, is 'indigenous' defined as somewhat static? Do these re-appropriations impoverish the cultures concerned, or are they a new means for their valorisation (Baud, 2006)? Finally, do they really concern tourists looking for 'mystical organised adventures'? In addition, should we not take into account the fact that cultures are by nature dynamic and subject to change, and that ayahuasqueros and mestizos who, for example, conduct ayahuasca ceremonies for foreigners can see no problem in sharing their knowledge and experiences of places with a counter-party who wishes it? In my opinion, the answers to these questions lie more in factual analysis (which ethnographic case studies can provide) than in hasty judgemental understandings of the situations.

Conclusion: Journeys in Quests for Meaning

With different personal involvements, a spiritual search for meaning characterises the present moment. Beginning in the 1960s, alternative spiritual discourses and practices have had a profound impact on Western societies, notably on certain groups of Western youths who were dissatisfied with their immediate social and cultural environment, and who were attracted by the possibility of engaging – in different places – in forms of initiation missing in their own society. The Western interest in natural or synthetic psychotropics relates in some ways to counter-cultural orientations, and neo-shamanic re-appropriations of shamanic plants can be understood from this perspective. Yet, based on the ethnographic data I have, the great majority of people involved are not, or have not previously been, attracted to what is normatively categorised as (mainstream) 'drugs'.

The emergence of a spiritualised shamanism enables multiple, and mostly negative, interpretative positions. Among the criticisms made of Westerners' involvement in shamanic practices abroad or at home is the denunciation of an irrational attitude (Vazeilles, 2003).[22] While admitting the possibility of some sort of 'experience' for practitioners, shamanism specialist Roberte Hamayon (2003) dismisses them as 'hypothetic states of consciousness'. Other anthropologists consider that Westerners' requests and false shamans who answer them denature shamanic practices.[23] Wolfgang Jilek explains, for instance, that altered states of consciousness 'are often accompanied with an altered perception of the time, an illusion of perception, an intense emotional experience to which special meanings are attached' but that would often be forgotten because of a 'non-organic amnesia' (Jilek, 2003: 219). These interpretations are interesting but they definitely do not say everything about the phenomenon that is taking place. Are neo-shamanic involvements the expression of a simple aestheticisation by an irrational imagination? One can wonder what relevance authoritarian external judgements of this kind have on these experiences.[24] My own participant observations of spiritualised shamanism allow me to affirm that those who have had experiences of altered states of consciousness do not forget them. On the contrary, these experiences remain in the mind, even if the people involved in spiritualised shamanism affirm that their 'transcendent experiences' cannot fully be translated into words.[25]

To conclude, I would say that in Western neo-shamanic re-appropriations there is, of course, a certain simplification of practices, since the symbolic cultural context is missing. In addition, these re-appropriations are without a doubt fed by an idealisation of 'traditional' indigenous rituals and societies that inscribes itself both in a search for meaning and in the modern production of particularity.[26] Yet, in my opinion, to criticise these adapted practices and to disqualify them as merely 'touristy' is problematic from an anthropological point of view, since it explicitly or implicitly refers to a 'true' (and also, therefore, a 'false') shamanism. If the general understanding of these practices and motivations by the broader public (and even sometimes by researchers) has a tendency to stigmatise the persons involved as merely naïve or even disturbed tourists, the fact is that the majority of those who are involved in these practices share an elaborately constructed, intersubjective universe that makes sense to them. Indeed, many of my informants have said that their life has changed (very often positively) after the experiences they had. They practise what they understand to be shamanism, without considering themselves to be 'shamans' or, even less, 'neo-shamans'.

On a material level, the logic of the market sustains – or is part of – such activities (shamanic retreats in Amazonia, Africa, Siberia, Alaska, Hawaii, etc.) and the financial cost for participants is palpable. Nevertheless, to understand these personal involvements only in terms of mass consumption is unsatisfactory, since therapeutic practices everywhere (in shamanic and non-shamanic cultures) involve forms of reciprocity through the circulation of money or other goods. Besides, the locals who organise workshops and ceremonies for foreigners evoke the idea that these activities can serve their own people.[27] The search for meaning in one's life through cultural borrowings (here shamanic practices based on the absorption of psychotropic plants) is the major motivation of Westerners involved in neo-shamanism. The recurrent notions that come out in practitioners' common sense – reflected in the use of terms such as 'serious work', 'courage', 'honesty', 'process', and 'intense experience' – are in this respect significant in revealing a general state of mind, although the path leading to the otherness that lies inside may necessitate a detour through the consumption of an otherness outside....

Notes

(1)   The idea that there is a supreme power above humans, who have to submit to it.

(2)   An author like Kocku Von Stuckrad sees in the New Age movement 'a challenge to both cultural anthropology and religious studies' (2003: 280; my translation).

(3)   This systematisation can be found in the following formulations, often used to value alternative products: natural source; nature's herbs; flower remedies; created in nature; organic, herbal source; no artificial fragrance, coloring, animal testing; all-natural medicine; organic food grown without the use of synthetics.

(4)   On one virtual shamanic site (http://www.shamanportal.org/display_details. php?id=685&country=north%20america&category=activities&sub_category= Workshops), one can read: 'The Huichol believe every human being can learn to walk the shamanic path'.

(5)   People thus often refer to: the personal development of one's inner potentiality; work with energies; harmonisation; and so on.

(6)   See notably Hamayon (2003), Von Stuckard (2003) and Vazeilles (2003).

(7)   Here is a very short indicative list:
www.cleargreen.com;
www.shamanism.org;

www.astro-therapie-chamanisme.com;
http://arutam.free.fr/Ayahuasca.html;
www.meditationfrance.com/chamanisme/degryse/index.htm.

(8) Among these: *Shaman's Drum: A Journal of Experiential Shamanism and Spiritual Healing* and *Sacred Hoop*.

(9) An increasing number of conferences focus on the topic of shamanism. One of them, called 'Ayahuasca: Shamanism, Science and Spirituality', in which international scientists, shamanistic explorers, consciousness researchers, indigenous healers and spiritual healers addressed the potential of transformation of the plant ayahuasca (also called the legendary Amazonian 'vine of the spirits'), took place in March 2000 at the California Institute of Integral Studies and gathered around 600 people. Such meetings – the list could be long – express a regained interest in both shamanism and psychotropic 'ancestral' plants in Western societies.

(10) The shamanic workshops this American anthropologist organises around the world are aimed at offering pan-cultural techniques (which he calls *core-shamanism*) specially created for Westerners (see his website www.shamanism.org). According to him, these techniques are 'simple', 'deep' and 'interchangeable' (Harner, 1980). The experiences he tries to promote (with his wife and a few instructors) are, in his words, a synthesis of very ancient shamanic methods that he himself learnt in North and South America. He notably proposes to attain what he calls the 'shamanic state of consciousness' (SSC) through the learning of the 'shamanic journey' to the lower and upper worlds, to 'consult spirit allies', to 'discover one's animal totem', to 'acquire power animals', and so on, with appropriate rhythmic percussion (with drums and rattles).

(11) References to 'places of power' favouring journeys and 'shamanic initiations' (Mount Shasta in California, Lake Titicaca in Peru, Himalayas, etc.) are common.

(12) Dimethyltryptamine is the main active agent of ayahuasca.

(13) 'Ayahuasca is an amazing plant, incredible, confusing, that defies Western logic.... This is the "Madre," the "Mother Plant" which ... opens doors previously closed. These doors are those of the experience and felt first through the body and sensorial system' (Delacroix, 2000: 22 and 24; my translation).

(14) '[The plant] gives me a lesson in letting go, without asking' (Delacroix, 2000: 63; my translation).

(15) A study by Claudio Naranjo (1973) on the psychological and cultural aspects related to taking ayahuasca indicates that the shamanic experience can have a transcultural dimension. The data match Michael Harner's idea that shamanism is not exclusively cultural, as everybody can 'shamanize', that is, get a spiritual experiences, through practices that can be learnt.

(16) My observations indicate that the people involved do not necessarily have an exclusive loyalty to a specific instructor. They actually tend to diversify the shamanic retreats in which they participate.

(17) This idea is clearly expressed in the following quote from a participant: 'I could see ... through visions during our work, when and why I set up this symptom....'

(18) In the cosmopolitan milieu of spiritualised shamanism, it is considered that the prenatal and postnatal genetic history of each person is inscribed in the body. These corporal inscriptions are supposed to determine each person's life.

(19) The healing is also that of the ego. That involves dealing with one's past (especially if it was difficult), avoiding bad thoughts and actions, changing one's life, one's work and one's friends if it can help spiritual development.

(20) Significantly, the main New Age slogan is 'body, mind and spirit'.

(21) Analysing the relationship between what she calls 'the traditional shamanism of Sioux Lakotas Indians', its renewal and some writings inside the 'New Age movement using shamanic beliefs and practices of Native North America', Danièle Vazeilles, in her article 'Chamanisme, néo-chamanisme et New Age' (in a section headed 'Dynamisme du "chamanisme" ou néo-colonialisme'), stigmatises what she defines as the 'somewhat consumerist and bulimic practices of mystical experiences' (Vazeilles, 2003: 239; my translation).

(22) Another author, Kocku Von Struckrad, considers that the 'irrational practices' of the modern West have been alimented by the Enlightenment and its 'fascination for the irrational' (2003: 296).

(23) Vazeilles, for instance, considers that what is given to outsiders relates to Western esoteric beliefs that have nothing to do with local traditions: 'After stealing their land, denying beliefs, the whites want to dispossess the Indians, a new perverse form of colonialism' (Vazeilles, 2003: 271; my translation).

(24) In a critical overview of psychiatric approaches of shamanism, Philippe Mitrani points out: 'the ethnological illusion ineluctably located between belief and knowledge, as it consists in pretending to know what other believe and to believe what they know' ('l'illusion ethnologique inéluctablement située entre la croyance et le savoir, puisqu'elle consiste à prétendre savoir ce que les autres croient et à croire ce qu'ils savent….') (Mitrani, 2003: 205; my translation).

(25) Bertrand Hell also states that 'The speech of the adherents themselves refers not to the acquisition of knowledge but first to an intimate and personal experience of the invisible' (Hell, 1999: 313; my translation).

(26) For Danièle Vazeilles, for instance, Michael Harner has satisfied 'the request of a Euro-American public eager for exoticism'. She thus sees in all the 'neo-shamanism/New Age' books an insulting simplification of rituals and beliefs of Amerindian populations (Vazeilles, 2003: 244; my translation). If there is certainly a market logic in spiritualised shamanism, the reference to an 'insulting simplification of rituals' reveals a localised understanding that is far removed from anthropological relativism.

(27) 'Don Jose … believed that the healing traditions are available for everyone who has an open heart. He also believed that when people learn about the inherent beauty and healing power found in the Huichol way of life, they would want to support the cultural and spiritual survival of the Huichol Indians' (see www.shamanism.com/about-us). From this perspective, the learning of ways of human beings is thought as potentially serving the Huichol cause.

References

Baud, S. (2006) Homogénéisation des pratiques dites chamaniques au Pérou. In J.P. Barbiche and S. Valter (eds) *Sociétés coloniales et sociétés modernes*. Paris: Le Manuscrit.

Baud, S. and Ghasarian, C. (eds) (2010a) *Des plantes psychotropes. Initations, therapies et quêtes de soi*. Paris: Imago.

Baud, S. and Ghasarian, C. (2010b) Retours sur les compréhensions et usages des substances psychotropes et leurs inductions. In S. Baud and C. Ghasarian (eds) *Des plantes psychotropes. Initations, therapies et quêtes de soi*. Paris: Imago.

Castaneda, C. (1972) *L'Herbe du diable et la petite fumée. Une voie yaqui de la connaissance*. Paris: Le soleil noir.

Chaumeil, J.P. (2003) Chamanismes à géométrie variable en Amazonie. *Revue Diogène. Chamanismes*, Coll. Quadrige. Paris: PUF.

Delacroix, J.M. (2000) *Ainsi parle l'esprit de la plante. Un psychothérapeute français à l'épreuve des thérapies ancestrales d'Amazonie*. Paris: Jouvence Editions.

Demenget, M. (2001) Reconstruction of the shamanic space and mystical tourism in the Mazatex region (Mexico). In H-P. Francfort and R. Hamayon (eds) *The Concept of Shamanism: Uses and Abuses*. Budapest: Akadémia Kiado.

Eliade, M. (1968) *Le Chamanisme et les techniques archaïques de l'extase*. Paris: Payot.

Ghasarian, C. (2002) Santé alternative et New Age à San Francisco. In R. Massé and J. Benoist (eds) *Convocations thérapeutiques du sacré*, col. Médecines du Monde. Paris: Karthala.

Ghasarian, C. (2006) Réflexions sur les rapports corps/conscience/esprit(s) dans les représentations et pratiques néo-shamaniques. In O. Schmitz (ed.) *Les médecines en parallèle: multiplicité des recours aux soins en Occident*. Paris: Karthala.

Ghasarian, C. (2009) Explorations néo-shamaniques en terra icognita de l'anthropologie. In S. Baud and N. Midol (eds) *La conscience dans tous ses états. Approches anthropologiques et psychiatriques: cultures et therapies*. Paris: Masson.

Ghasarian, C. (2010) Introspections néo-shamaniques au travers du San Pedro. In S. Baud and C. Ghasarian (eds) *Plantes psychotropes. Initations, therapies et quêtes de soi*. Paris: Imago.

Gonzales, J. (2010) Du concept 'hallucinogène' au concept 'lucidogène' (aller-retour). In S. Baud and C. Ghasarian (eds) *Plantes psychotropes. Initations, therapies et quêtes de soi*. Paris: Imago.

Hamayon, R. (2003) Introduction à chamanismes. Réalités autochtones, réinventions occidentales. *Revue Diogène 396, Chamanismes*. Coll. Quadrige. Paris: PUF.

Harner, M. (1980) *The Way of the Shaman: A Guide to Power and Healing*. San Francisco, CA: Harper and Row.

Hell, B. (1999) *Possession et chamanisme. Les maîtres du désordre*. Paris: Flammarion.

Jakobsen, M. (1999) *Shamanism: Traditional and Contemporary Approaches to the Mastery of Spirits and Healing*. Oxford: Berghahn Books.

Jilek, W. (2003) La métamorphose du chamane dans la perception occidentale. *Revue Diogène. Chamanismes*, Coll. Quadrige. Paris: PUF.

Mitrani, P. (2003) Aperçu critique des approches psychiatriques du chamanisme. *Revue Diogène. Chamanismes*, Coll. Quadrige. Paris: PUF.

Naranjo, C. (1973) Psychological aspects of the Yagé: Experience in an experimental setting. In M. Harner (ed.) *Hallucinogens and Shamanism*. New York: Oxford University Press.

Schultes, R. (1976) *Hallucinogenic Plants*. Houston, TX: Golden Press.

Vazeilles, D. (2003) Chamanisme, néo-chamanisme et New Age. *Revue Diogène. Chamanismes*, Coll. Quadrige. Paris: PUF.

Von Stuckrad, K. (2003) Le chamanisme occidental moderne et la dialectique de la science rationnelle. *Revue Diogène. Chamanismes*, Coll. Quadrige. Paris: PUF.

Wasson, R.G. (1968) *Soma: Divine Mushroom of Immortality*. New York: Harcourt Brace Jovanovich.

Index